GUIDE TO THE W

Four Counties
& the Welsh Canals

Nicholson

An imprint of HarperCollins*Publishers*

Also available:

Nicholson Guide to the Waterways

1. **London, Grand Union, Oxford & Lee**
2. **Severn, Avon & Birmingham**
3. **Birmingham & the Heart of England**
5. **North West & the Pennines**
6. **Nottingham, York & the North East**
7. **Thames, Wey, Kennet & Avon**

Nicholson Inland Waterways Map of Great Britain

Published by Nicholson
An imprint of HarperCollins*Publishers*
77-85 Fulham Palace Road
Hammersmith, London W6 8JB

www.**fire**and**water**.com
www.bartholomewmaps.com

First published by Nicholson and Ordnance Survey 1997
Reprinted 1998, 1999
New edition published by Nicholson 2000

The representation in this publication of a road, track or path is no evidence of the existence of a right of way.

Researched and written by David Perrott and Jonathan Mosse.
Design by Bob Vickers.

The publisher gratefully acknowledges the assistance given by British Waterways and its staff in the preparation of this guide.

Grateful thanks is also due to members of the Inland Waterways Association and CAMRA representatives and branch members.

Photographs reproduced by kind permission of the following picture libraries:
British Waterways Photo Library pages 16, 74, 90, 143;
Derek Pratt Photography pages 19, 51, 70, 78, 80, 98, 103, 120, 124, 127, 132, 146.

Printed in Italy.

ISBN 0 7028 4164 1
ME10290
97/2/34.5

The publisher welcomes comments from readers. Please address your letters to:
Nicholson Guides to the Waterways, HarperCollins Cartographic,
HarperCollins Publishers, Westerhill Road, Bishopbriggs, Glasgow, G64 2QT.

The canals and river navigations of Britain were built as a system of new trade routes, at a time when roads were virtually non-existent. After their desperately short boom period in the late 18th and early 19th centuries, they gracefully declined in the face of competition from the railways. A few canals disappeared completely, but thankfully most just decayed gently, carrying the odd working boat, and becoming havens for wildlife and the retreat of the waterways devotee.

It was two such enthusiasts, L.T.C. Rolt and Robert Aickman who, in 1946, formed the Inland Waterways Association, bringing together like-minded people from all walks of life to campaign for the preservation and restoration of the inland waterways. Their far-sightedness has at last seen its reward for, all over the country, an amazing transformation is taking place. British Waterways, the IWA, local councils, canal societies and volunteers have brought back to life great lengths of canal, and much of the dereliction which was once commonplace has been replaced with a network of 'linear parks'.

The canals provide something for everyone to enjoy: engineering feats such as aqueducts, tunnels and flights of locks; the brightly decorated narrow boats; a wealth of birds, animals and plants; the mellow unpretentious architecture of canalside buildings; friendly waterside pubs and the sheer beauty and quiet isolation that is a feature of so much of our inland waterways.

It is easy to enjoy this remarkable facet of our history, either on foot, often by bicycle, or on a boat. This book, with its splendid Ordnance Survey® mapping, is one of a series covering the waterways network, and gives you all the information you need.

▌ CONTENTS

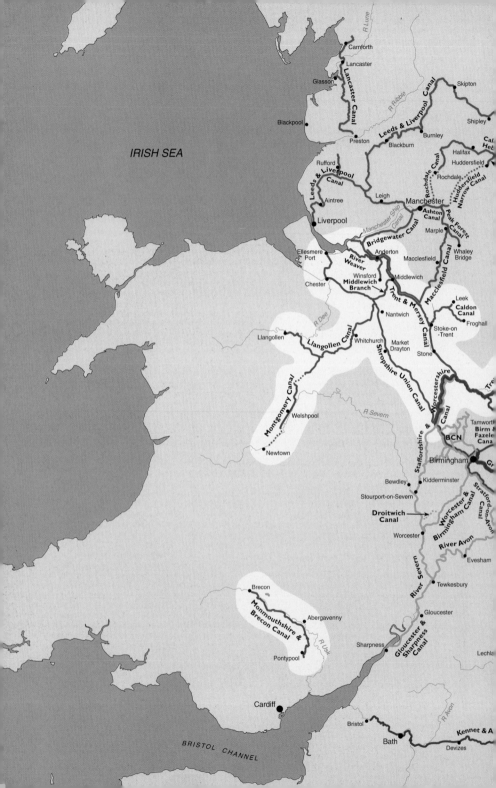

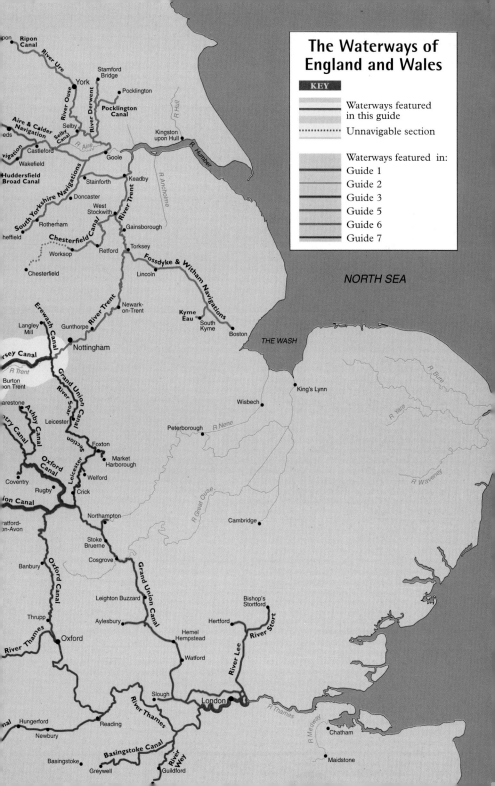

GENERAL INFORMATION FOR CANAL USERS

The slogan Waterways For All was coined to take account of the wide diversity of people using the inland waterways for recreation.

Today boaters, walkers, fishermen, cyclists and gongoozlers (on-lookers) throng our canals and rivers, to share in the enjoyment of our quite amazing waterway heritage. British Waterways (BW), along with other navigation authorities, is empowered to develop, maintain and control this resource in order to maximise its potential: namely our enjoyment. It is to this end that a series of guides, codes, and regulations have come into existence over the years, evolving to match a burgeoning – and occasionally conflicting – demand. Set out below are the key points as they relate to everyone wishing to enjoy the waterways.

LICENSING – BOATS

The majority of the navigations covered in this book are controlled by BW and are managed on a day-to-day basis by local waterway offices. Waterway Managers are detailed in the introduction to each waterway. All craft using BW waterways must be licenced and charges are based on the length of the craft. This licence covers all navigable waterways under BW's control and in a few cases includes reciprocal agreements with other waterway authorities (as indicated in the text). As this edition goes to print, BW and the Environment Agency are preparing to go to consultation on an optional joint licence to cover both authorities' waterways. Permits for permanent mooring on the canals are also issued by BW. For further information contact BW Customer Services (see inside front cover). You can download licence fees and charges and an application form from the BW website (see inside front cover).

Since 1 January 1997, BW and the Environment Agency have introduced the Boat Safety Scheme, setting technical requirements for good and safe boat-building practice. A Boat Safety Certificate or, for new boats, a Declaration of Conformity, is necessary to obtain a craft licence. For powered boats proof of insurance for Third Party Liability for a minimum of £1,000,000 is also required. Further details from BW Customer Services. Other navigational authorities relevant to this book are mentioned where appropriate.

LICENSING – CYCLISTS

Not all towpaths are open to cyclists. This is because many stretches are too rough or narrow, or because cyclists cause too great a risk to other users. The maps on the BW website show which stretches of towpaths are open to cyclists. This information is also available from your local waterway office, which you should contact in any case to obtain the necessary permit to cycle on the towpath and a copy of the Waterways Code. When using the towpaths for cycling, you will encounter other towpath users, such as fishermen, walkers and boaters. The Waterways Code gives advice on taking care and staying safe, considering others and helping to look after the waterways. A complete list of towpaths available for cycling is available in a National Cycle Pack, price £5.00 from BW Customer Services.

TOWPATHS

Few, if any, artificial cuts or canals in this country are without an intact towpath accessible to the walker at least. However, on river navigations towpaths have on occasion fallen into disuse or, sometimes, been lost to erosion. In today's leisure climate considerable efforts are being made to provide access to all towpaths with some available to the disabled. Notes on individual waterways in this book detail the supposed status of the path, but the indication of a towpath does not necessarily imply a public right of way or mean that a right to cycle along it exists. Maps on the BW website show all towpaths on the BW network, and whether they are open to cyclists. Motorcycling and horse riding are forbidden on all towpaths.

INDIVIDUAL WATERWAY GUIDES

No national guide can cover the minutiae of individual waterways and some Waterway Managers produce guides to specific navigations under their charge. Copies of individual guides (where they are available) can be obtained from the Waterway Office detailed in the introduction. Please note that times – such as operating times of bridges and locks – do change year by year and from winter to summer.

STOPPAGES

BW works hard to programme its major engineering works into the winter period when demand for cruising is low. It publishes a National Stoppage Programme and Winter Opening Hours leaflet which is sent out to all licence holders, boatyards and hire companies. Inevitably, emergencies occur necessitating the unexpected closure of a waterway, perhaps during the peak season. You can check for stoppages on individual waterways between specific dates on the BW website. Details are also announced on lockside noticeboards and on Canalphone (see inside front cover).

STARTING OUT

Extensive information and advice on booking a boating holiday is available on the BW website. Please book a waterway holiday from a licenced operator – only in this way can you be sure that you have proper insurance cover, service and support during your holiday. It is illegal for private boat owners to hire out their craft. If in doubt, please contact BW Customer Services. If you are hiring a canal boat for the first time, the boatyard will brief you thoroughly. Take notes, follow their instructions and *don't be afraid to ask* if there is anything you do not understand. BW have produced a short video giving basic information on using a boat safely. Copies of the video, and the Waterways Code for Boaters, are available free of charge from BW Customer Services.

GENERAL CRUISING NOTES

Most canals are saucer-shaped in section so are deepest at the middle. Few have more than 3–4ft of water and many have much less. Keep to the centre of the channel except on bends, where the deepest water is on the outside of the bend. When you meet another boat, keep to the right, slow down and aim to miss the approaching craft by a couple of yards: do not steer right over to the bank or you are likely to run aground. If you meet a loaded commercial boat keep right out of the way and be prepared to follow his instructions. Do not assume that you should pass on the right. If you meet a boat being towed from the bank, pass it on the inside. When overtaking, keep the other boat on your right side.

A large number of BW facilities in their north-east region – pump-outs, showers, electrical hook-ups and so on – are currently operated by smart cards, obtainable from BW Regional Office, Neptune Street, Leeds (0113 281 6800); local waterways offices (see introductions to individual navigations); lock keepers and some boatyards within the region. At the time of printing, a £6 card will purchase one pump-out, about 12 showers and electricity pro rata. Please note that if you are a week-end visitor, you should purchase cards *in advance*.

Speed

There is a general speed limit of 4 mph on most BW canals. This is not just an arbitrary limit: there is no need to go any faster and in many cases it is impossible to cruise even at this speed: if the wash is breaking against the bank or causing large waves, slow down.

Slow down also when passing moored craft, engineering works and anglers; when there is a lot of floating rubbish on the water (and try to drift over obvious obstructions in neutral); when approaching blind corners, narrow bridges and junctions.

Mooring

Generally speaking you may moor where you wish on BW property, as long as there is sufficient depth of water, and you are *not causing an obstruction*. Your boat should carry metal mooring stakes, and these should be driven firmly into the ground with a mallet if there are no mooring rings. Do not stretch mooring lines across the towpath. Always consider the security of your boat when there is no one aboard. On tideways and commercial waterways it is advisable to moor only at recognised sites, and allow for any rise or fall of the tide.

Bridges

On narrow canals slow down and aim to miss one side (usually the towpath side) by about 9 inches. *Keep everyone inboard when passing under bridges*, and take special care with moveable structures – the crew member operating the bridge should hold it steady as the boat passes through.

Tunnels

Make sure the tunnel is clear before you enter, and use your headlight. Follow any instructions given on notice boards by the entrance.

Fuel

Hire craft usually carry fuel sufficient for the rental period.

Water

It is advisable to top up every day.

Lavatories

Hire craft usually have pump-out toilets. Have these emptied *before* things become critical. Keep the receipt and your boatyard will usually reimburse you for this expense.

Boatyards

Hire fleets are usually turned around on a Saturday, making this a bad time to call in for services. Remember that moorings at popular destinations fill quickly during the summer months, so do not assume there will be room for your boat. Always ask.

LOCKS AND THEIR USE

A lock is a simple and ingenious device for transporting your craft from one water level to another.

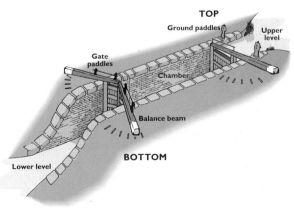

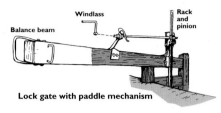

Lock gate with paddle mechanism

When both sets of gates are closed it may be filled or emptied using gate or ground paddles at the top or bottom of the lock. These are operated with a windlass.

General tips
- Make safety your prime concern. *Keep a close eye on young children.*
- Always take your time, and do not leap about.
- Never open the paddles at one end without ensuring those at the other are closed.
- Never drop the paddles – always wind them down.
- Keep to the landward side of the balance beam when opening and closing gates.
- Never leave your windlass slotted onto the paddle spindle – it will be dangerous should anything slip.
- Keep your boat away from the top and bottom gates to prevent it getting caught on the gate or the lock cill.
- Be wary of fierce *top gate* paddles, especially in wide locks. Operate them slowly, and close them if there is *any* adverse effect.
- Always follow the navigation authority's instructions, where these are given on notices or by their staff.

PLANNING A CRUISE

Many a canal holiday has been spoiled by trying to go too far too fast. Go slowly, don't be too ambitious, and enjoy the experience. Note that mileages indicated on the maps are for guidance only.

A *rough* calculation of time taken to cover the ground is the lock-miles system:

Add the number of *miles* to the number of *locks* on your proposed journey, and divide the resulting figure by three. This will give you a guide to the number of *hours* it will take. But don't forget your service stops (water, shopping, pump-out), and allow plenty of time to visit that special pub!

TIDAL WATERWAYS

The typical steel narrow boat found on the inland waterways system has the sea-going characteristics of a bathtub, which renders it totally unsuitable for all-weather cruising on tidal estuaries. However, the more adventurous will inevitably wish to add additional ring cruises to the more predictable circuits within the calm havens of inland Britain. Passage is possible in most estuaries if careful consideration is given to the key factors of weather

conditions, crew experience, the condition of the boat and its equipment and, perhaps of overriding importance, the need to take expert advice. In many cases it will be prudent to employ the skilled services of a local pilot. Within the text, where inland navigations connect with a tidal waterway, details are given of sources of both advice and pilotage. This guide is to the inland waterways of Britain and therefore recognizes that tideways – and especially estuaries – require a different skill and approach. We therefore do not hesitate to draw the boater's attention to the appropriate source material.

GENERAL

Most inland navigations are managed by BW or the Environment Agency, but there are several other navigation authorities responsible for smaller stretches of canals and rivers. For details of these, contact the Association of Inland Navigation Authorities at www.cam.net.uk/home/aina or BW Customer Services. The boater, conditioned perhaps by the uniformity of our national road network, should be sensitive to the need to observe different codes and operating practices. Similarly it is important to be aware that some waterways are only available for navigation today solely because of the care and dedication of a particular restoration body, often using volunteer labour and usually taking several decades to complete the project. This is the reason that, in cruising the national waterways network, additional licence charges are sometimes incurred. The introduction to each waterway gives its background history, details of recent restoration (where relevant) and also lists the operating authority.

BW is a public corporation, responsible to the Department of the Environment, Transport and the Regions and, as subscribers to the Citizen's Charter, they are linked with an ombudsman. BW has a comprehensive complaints procedure and a free explanatory leaflet is available from Customer Services. Problems and complaints should be addressed to the local Waterway Manager in the first instance – the telephone number is listed in the introduction to individual waterways.

The Inland Waterways Association campaigns for the 'conservation, use, maintenance, restoration and development of the inland waterways', through branches all over the country. For more information contact them at PO Box 114, Rickmansworth, WD3 1ZY, telephone 01923 711114, fax 01923 897000, email iwa@waterways.org.uk or visit their website at www.waterways.org.uk/index.htm.

FREEPHONE CANALS

Emergency help is available from BW outside normal office hours on weekdays and throughout weekends via Freephone Canals (see inside front cover). You should give details of the problem and your location.

CALDON CANAL

MAXIMUM DIMENSIONS	MILEAGE
to Consall Forge	*ETRURIA TOP LOCK*
Length: 72'	(Trent & Mersey Canal) to
Beam: 7'	Hanley: 2 miles
Headroom: 6' 6"	Foxley: 4½ miles
	Stockton Brook Summit: 7 miles
through Froghall Tunnel	Hazelhurst Junction (Leek Branch): 9½ miles
Length: 72'	*LEEK TERMINUS:* 12¼ miles
Beam: 6' 6"	Cheddleton Flint Mill: 11½ miles
Headroom: 4' 9"	*FROGHALL TERMINUS:* 17 miles
MANAGER	Locks: 17
0161 427 1079	

The Caldon Canal – or, more correctly, the Caldon Branch of the Trent & Mersey Canal – was designed as an outlet on to the canal system for the Caldon limestone quarries near Froghall. It was opened as a single branch to Froghall in 1779, tramways being constructed to bring the vast quantities of limestone down from Caldon Low quarries a couple of miles to the east. Froghall soon became a very busy terminus. Eighteen years later the Caldon's owners, the Trent & Mersey Canal Company, decided to build a secondary branch from the Caldon Canal to Leek, the main purpose of the extension being to use the line as a feeder from their new reservoir at Rudyard. The fact that the feeders from Rudyard had to enter the summit level of the canal, and the later advent of the railway, brought about significant changes in the layout of the canal between Endon and Hazelhurst, and resulted in the fascinating cross-over junction that exists at Denford today. In 1811 yet another branch was completed from Froghall down the Churnet Valley for 13 miles to Uttoxeter. This branch was short-lived, however. In 1845 a railway line was built, much of the track using the canal bed.

The limestone from Froghall remained the chief commodity carried on the Caldon Canal for years. With its 17 locks and roundabout route the Caldon must have been an obvious target for railway competitors. However, the canal, with the rest of the Trent & Mersey, was owned by the North Staffordshire Railway from the 1840s onward, so presumably the NSR saw no point in competing against itself. But at the beginning of the 20thC a new railway line was eventually opened and inevitably canal traffic slumped badly. The canal then gradually deteriorated until it became more or less unnavigable in the early 1960s.

The Caldon Canal Society led the struggle to re-open the route; public interest grew and local authorities recognised the great recreational potential of this beautiful waterway for the thousands of people living in the nearby Potteries. Much was achieved in the way of essential works by the British Waterways Board (now BW) and volunteer efforts. The canal was finally fully reopened to navigation in 1974, representing a splendid addition to the cruising network, and a much-needed linear park for the Potteries.

Hanley

The Caldon Branch of the Trent & Mersey Canal leaves the main line at Etruria Top Lock, and soon passes a statue of James Brindley, builder of the Trent & Mersey, erected here in 1989. The first two locks up are combined in a staircase – the only one in north Staffordshire. Planet Lock is soon reached, with shops and pubs close by: this is followed by Hanley Park, where there are good moorings. Ivy House lift bridge, once notoriously stiff, is now operated by push buttons. At Foxley the navigation turns sharp right, and Engine Lock follows. This is so called because a huge beam engine used to be housed nearby to pump water from mine workings. At the next lift bridge the unnavigable feeder from Knypersley Reservoir joins the canal. Five locks at Stockton Brook raise the canal up to the summit level 484ft above the sea.

● **Hanley**
   Staffs. All services (laundrette 1/4 mile N of bridge 4). Hanley is one of the six towns that were amalgamated in 1910 to form the present Stoke-on-Trent. Stoke City Museum and Art Gallery is in Bethesda Street, Hanley.
   Bridgewater Factory Shop Lichfield Street (01782 201328). Just north of bridge 8. Earthenware, textiles and gifts. *Open Mon-Sat 09.30-16.30.*
   Jesse Shirley's Etruscan Bone & Flint Mill Lower Bedford Street, Etruria (01782 287557). At the junction with the Trent & Mersey. This is a Victorian steam-powered potter's miller's works, built in 1857 and which ground bone, flint and stone for the pottery industry, until closure in 1972. It has now been restored as part of an industrial complex incorporating a blacksmith's shop with working steam-powered machinery. Originally the raw materials and ground products were transported by canal, and present-day canal travellers will find plenty of moorings available. *Open for guided tours Wed–Sun 10.00-16.00, closed Mon & Tue.* Also operate special steam days

The towpath
This is generally in good condition throughout.

NAVIGATIONAL NOTES

1 Some of the bridges on this section are very low.
2 Your BW key will be required for Ivy House Lift Bridge, 11.
3 You will need a windlass and a BW key to operate bridge 21, and a windlass for bridge 23.

first weekend each month Apr-Dec. Charge. Tea room & shop.
Tourist Information Centre Potteries Shopping Centre, Quadrant Road, Hanley (01782 236000).
● **Knypersley Reservoir**
3½ miles north of Milton. This feeds water to the Trent & Mersey summit level via the Caldon Canal. Surrounded by woodland, the reservoir is a delightful setting for picnicking and rambling. Fishing rights are exercised by an angling club.

● **Milton**
Staffs. PO, tel, stores, fish & chips. A little village on the side of a hill, forming an agreeable background to the canal.
● **Stockton Brook**
Staffs. PO, tel, stores. A pleasant and useful place. The five locks have a charming position, with views back down the headwaters of the River Trent. There is a splendid Victorian waterworks at the bottom of the flight, and pubs and shops near the middle.

Boatyards

Ⓑ **BW Etruria Yard** at junction with Trent & Mersey Canal (01782 215597). 🗑 🚽 ⚓ Toilet.

Pubs and Restaurants

🍺 **Bird in Hand** Etruria Vale Road, Etruria (01782 205048). A canal enthusiasts' pub serving Banks's and Marston's real ale. Modest bar meals and snacks are served. Children welcome.
🍺 **Duke of Bridgewater** Rectory Street, off Etruria Vale Road, Shelton (01782 219097). Comfortable refurbished pub with satellite TV, serving Bass real ale. Food is served *lunchtimes and evenings,* and children are welcome if you are eating.
🍺 **Old Corner Cupboard** Caldon Road, opposite Hanley Park, Shelton (01782 418911). Bass real ale and bar meals are available *luchtimes and evenings, except Sun evenings.* Children welcome *at meal times.*
🍺 **Sneyd Arms** (01782 268317). North of bridge 3. A friendly and welcoming pub which serves real ale. Food is available *lunchtimes and evenings, but not Sun evening.* Children are welcome.
🍺 **Norfolk** Norfolk Street, overlooking Planet Lock, Shelton (01782 281967). Marston's real ale in a recently refurbished pub. Meals available *lunchtimes and evenings,* with a limited vegetarian choice. Children welcome while eating. Regular entertainment. Mooring above and below the lock.
🍺 **Duke of Wellington** Lichfield Street, Joiners Square, Hanley (01782 271424). Bass real ale in a comfortable lounge. Bar meals and snacks *regularly available.* Entertainment.
🍺 **Miners Arms** Millrise Road, Milton (01782

545510). By bridge 18. Real ales include Bass, Marston's, Webster's and a guest. Children welcome *until 20.00.* Garden.
🍺 **Millrace** Maunders Road, Milton (01782 543338). By bridge 18. A handsome refurbished pub with coal fires and a traditional bar area. Burtonwood real ale. Children welcome and there is outside seating. *Shops nearby.*
🍺 **Foaming Quart** Frobisher Street, Norton Green (01782 538231). Burtonwood real ale and bar snacks. Regular entertainment.
🍺 **Foxley** Foxley Lane (01782 545525). Canalside at the junction with the former Foxley Arm, this is a traditional red-brick pub. Bar meals served *lunchtimes and evenings every day,* with a vegetarian menu. Children welcome. Garden. Bingo played some nights.
🍺 ✗ **Holly Bush** Stanley Road, Stockton Brook (01782 502116). Bass real ale and restaurant and bar meals available *lunchtimes and evenings every day,* with vegetarian options. Family room, and the garden sports a bowling green. *Mon* is quiz night.
🍺 **Rose & Crown** Stanley Road, Stockton Brook (01782 503893). Marston's real ale and food *lunchtimes and evenings (not Mon).* Children are welcome at mealtimes. Garden.
🍺 **Sportsman** New Leek Road, Stockton Brook (01782 504536). Close to Railway Lock. Marston's real ale in a cosy, traditional pub. Snacks and skittles.

Hazelhurst Locks

The canal passes to the east of Endon and approaches Hazelhurst, where it divides. The main line falls through three locks before turning east and then south to accompany the River Churnet, while the Leek Branch bears right along the hillside, then crosses the main line on a large aqueduct. The railway and Endon Brook are also traversed by aqueducts and eventually the Leek Branch reaches the north side of this narrow valley. Just north of bridge 6 there is a tiny post office/store. A large lagoon provides an opportunity to wind just before the 130yd Leek Tunnel. Beyond the tunnel, only a short stretch of canal remains, ending on a fine stone aqueduct over the River Churnet. The last half-mile beyond the Churnet and straight along to Leek Basin has been filled in. However, there is a pleasant walk westwards, following the feeder that brings water down from Rudyard Lake into the navigation.

The main line to Froghall drops through three attractive and isolated locks and passes under the Leek Branch. The canal and the River Churnet now run side by side for the next 7 miles. Cheddleton Flint Mill makes a fascinating stop.

● **Stanley**
Staffs. PO, tel, stores. A stiff climb southwards from bridge 28 leads to this brown-stone hill village. Fine views across the valley to Endon.

● **Endon**
Staffs. Tel, stores, garage, bank. The real village is up the hill just north of the main road and is attractive, especially during its traditional well-dressing ceremony. Endon Basin, built in 1917, and once a canal/railway interchange basin, is now used as the Stoke-on-Trent Boat Club's base.

● **Leek**
Staffs. MD Wed. All services. A silk town, which also gained a reputation for for its dyeing and embroidery: the Leek School of Embroidery was founded here in the 1870s by Lady Wardle, and it was about this time that William Morris, founder of the Arts & Crafts Movement, worked here. James

Brindley, the canal engineer, started in business as a millwright in Leek. The parish church of St Edward is 14th-C, but was restored in 1856, and the chancel rebuilt in 1867.

Brindley Mill Macclesfield Road, Leek (01538 384195). Turn right along the A53 from the canal feeder, and then follow signs to Macclesfield. The mill will be seen about 2 miles from the canal terminus, by the A523. It is a working corn mill built in 1752 by James Brindley, the canal engineer, when he worked as a millwright in Leek. Milling display, Brindley's notebook and theodolite. *Open Easter–Sep, weekends and B. Hols, also Mon, Tue and Wed in late Jul & Aug 14.00–17.00 only.* Modest charge.

Tourist Information Centre 1 Market Place, Leek (01538 483741).

● **Cheddleton**

Staffs. PO, tel, stores, garage nearby. A main road rumbles through the village, but away from this is the charming Flint Mill, by the canal. The village is grouped around the ancient stone church of St Edward the Confessor. Little of the original building remains, but some 14th-C work is worth a look.

Cheddleton Flint Mill A superbly restored mill where you can watch two water wheels driving the flint grinding pans, in a charming and picturesque setting. Machinery collection includes a 100hp Robey steam engine and a 1770 haystack boiler. For group visits please *write* to: Eddie Royal, 5 Caroline Crescent, Brown Edge, Stoke-on-Trent (01782 502907). *Open Sat & Sun afternoons and most weekdays.* Free. The beautifully restored narrow boat *Vienna* is usually moored at the wharf.

Pubs and Restaurants

Travellers Rest Tompkin Road, Stanley (01782 502580). A choice of Marston's and Morland real ale, with bar meals served *lunchtimes and evenings every day.* There is a vegetarian menu. Children welcome. Outside seating.

Black Horse Inn Leek Road, Endon (01782 502239). Recently refurbished pub serving Bass real ale and meals *lunchtimes and evenings.* Outside seating.

Toby Carvery Endon Leek Road, Endon (01782 502115). A refurbished Toby Inn serving Bass and Stones real ale, along with meals *lunchtimes and evenings every day*, including vegetarian dishes. Children welcome.

Holly Bush Denford (01538 371819). Near bridge 38. Traditional 17th-C canalside pub with an open fire set in 3 acres of grounds, with a children's play area. There is a choice of eight real ales, including Morland's, Eldridge Pope and Theakstons, and food is served *lunchtimes and evenings every day.* Family room. Mooring on the main (lower) line, although access from the Leek Branch is easy enough. B & B.

Red Lion 37 Cheadle Road, Cheddleton (01538 360935). Near bridge 43. Bass and Worthington real ale. Bar meals available *lunchtimes and evenings (not Tue)* with vegetarian options. Children welcome, and garden with play equipment.

Wheel Inn Leek Road, Longsdon (01538 385012). Tetley's, Bass and guest real ales and bar meals and snacks available *lunchtimes and evenings every day,* with vegetarian options and traditional *Sunday lunch.* Children welcome. Garden.

New Inn Leek Road, Longsdon (01538 385356). About 300 yards from Denford Locks, this country local has two open fires, and serves Marston's and Banks's real ales. *Lunchtime* bar meals plus a full *evening* menu *every day.* Children welcome. Garden.

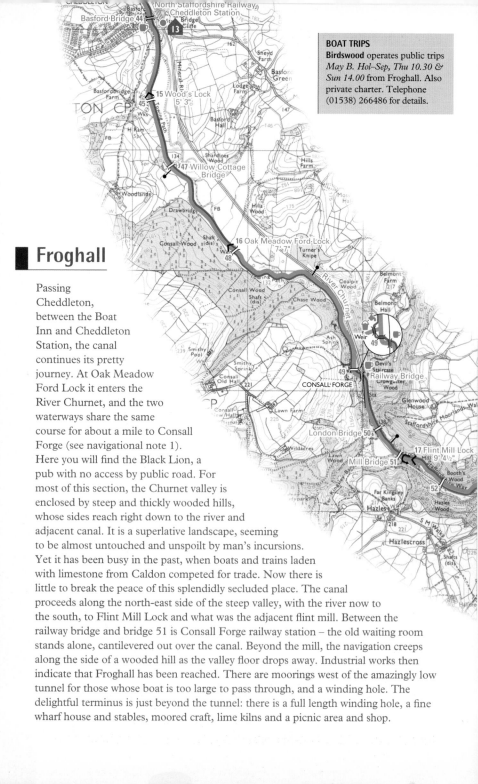

Froghall

Passing Cheddleton, between the Boat Inn and Cheddleton Station, the canal continues its pretty journey. At Oak Meadow Ford Lock it enters the River Churnet, and the two waterways share the same course for about a mile to Consall Forge (see navigational note 1). Here you will find the Black Lion, a pub with no access by public road. For most of this section, the Churnet valley is enclosed by steep and thickly wooded hills, whose sides reach right down to the river and adjacent canal. It is a superlative landscape, seeming to be almost untouched and unspoilt by man's incursions. Yet it has been busy in the past, when boats and trains laden with limestone from Caldon competed for trade. Now there is little to break the peace of this splendidly secluded place. The canal proceeds along the north-east side of the steep valley, with the river now to the south, to Flint Mill Lock and what was the adjacent flint mill. Between the railway bridge and bridge 51 is Consall Forge railway station – the old waiting room stands alone, cantilevered out over the canal. Beyond the mill, the navigation creeps along the side of a wooded hill as the valley floor drops away. Industrial works then indicate that Froghall has been reached. There are moorings west of the amazingly low tunnel for those whose boat is too large to pass through, and a winding hole. The delightful terminus is just beyond the tunnel: there is a full length winding hole, a fine wharf house and stables, moored craft, lime kilns and a picnic area and shop.

NAVIGATIONAL NOTES

1 The canal and river share a common course between Oak Meadow Ford Lock and Consall Forge, and care should be exercised along here.
2 Boats which cannot pass through Froghall Tunnel can wind just before it.
3 The last mile or so of canal is very narrow – in places two boats cannot pass.

Churnett Valley Railway Cheddleton Station (01538 360522). Near bridge 44. Opened by the North Staffordshire Railway in 1849 between North Rode and Macclesfield, the last stretch of this line closed in 1988. Purchased by enthusiasts, a steam operated passenger train first ran again in August 1996. The line is presently open between Consall and Leekbrook Junction, soon extending to Kingsley & Froghall. *Steam trains Easter-Sep every Sun; Aug every Wed and all B.Hol Mons. Diesels Jul-Aug every Sat. Plus other special events.*

● **Froghall**
Staffs. PO, tel. Tucked away in the heart of unspoilt Staffordshire, Froghall has been an outpost of industry ever since the advent of the canal fostered the growth of the Caldon lime quarries a few miles east. The limestone was carted down the hills by a plate tramway, built originally in 1758 and the first to use iron rails. This was re-aligned in 1785, and finally re-built in 1800. A cable railway replaced the whole lot in 1849. The limestone was transhipped into waiting canal boats at Froghall Basin, serviced by the locomotives *Frog, Toad* and *Bobs*. Production ceased in 1920, with much of the trade being lost to the railways. Just west of the final bridge by the basin was the junction with the old canal arm to Uttoxeter (explaining the distances on the milestones): this locked down to the Churnet valley. The branch was closed in 1847 and the railway now occupies most of the canal's course, although much of the canal bed can still be traced. Froghall these days comprises almost entirely of factories and dwellings associated with Thomas Bolton's copper works.

Pubs and Restaurants

🍺 **The Boat Inn** Basford Bridge Lane, Cheddleton (01538 360683). Canalside at bridge 44. A handsome stone-built pub, with a long low-ceilinged bar decorated with plates and jugs. Marston's real ale is served here and bar meals are available *lunchtimes and evenings every day (less often in winter)*, with a vegetarian menu. Children welcome. Outside seating. Regular entertainment. There is an old bridge across the River Churnet nearby.

🍺 **Black Lion** Hollow Lane, Cheddleton (01538 361647). Up the hill by the church south of Bridge 42. Fine traditional and welcoming old country pub, with log fires, serving Marston's real ale. Families are made very welcome.

✗🍽 **Flint Lock** Canalside at Cheddleton Lock. Recently rennovated bistro, serving meals *L & D*. Beneath lie flint mines some 350 years old.

🍺 **Black Lion** Consall Forge (01782 550294). A splendid canalside pub of outstanding isolation, in a beautiful setting and with a fine garden. Although the interior is quite straightforward, there is an open fire, and Marston's and guest real ales to enjoy, along with *lunchtime and evening* bar meals and snacks, with vegetarian options. A popular place in summer, when it is busy with boaters, back packers and families. B & B.

🍺 **Railway Hotel** Bank View, Froghall (01538 754782). Handy for the steam railway, the real ales served here include Marston's, Morland's, Banks's and Tetley's. Bar meals *lunchtimes and evenings,* with vegetarian choices. Garden. Traditional pub games nights. B & B.

Pontcysyllte Aqueduct, Llangollen Canal (see page 30)

■ LLANGOLLEN CANAL

Llangollen Canal Introduction

MAXIMUM DIMENSIONS

Length: 72'
Beam: 6' 10"
Headroom: 7'
Draught:
Hurleston to Pontcysyllte: 2' 3"
Pontcysyllte to Llangollen: 2'

MANAGER
01244 390372

MILEAGE

Hurleston Junction (Shropshire Union) to
Frankton Junction: 29 miles
Pontcysyllte Aqueduct: 40 miles
Llangollen: 44½ miles
Llantysilio: 46 miles

Locks: 21

In 1791 a plan was published for a canal from the Mersey to the Severn, to pass through Chester, and the iron and coal fields around Ruabon, Ellesmere and Shrewsbury. There were to be branches to the limestone quarries at Llanymynech, and to the Chester Canal via Whitchurch. The new terminus on the Mersey was to be at the little fishing village of Netherpool, known after 1796 as Ellesmere Port. After extensive arguments about routes, the company received its Act in 1793. William Jessop was appointed engineer, and work began. By 1796 the Wirral line from Chester to Ellesmere Port was open, and was immediately successful, carrying goods and passengers (in express flyboats) to Liverpool. The same year, the Llanymynech Branch was completed. The company continued to expand and build inwards, but failed to make the vital connections with the Dee and the Severn; the line south to Shrewsbury never got further than Weston, and the line northwards to Chester stopped at Pontcysyllte. By 1806 the Ellesmere company had opened 68 miles of canal, which included lines from Hurleston on the Chester Canal to Plas Kynaston via Frankton, and from Chester to Ellesmere Port; there were branches to Llanymynech, Whitchurch, Prees and Ellesmere, and a navigable feeder to Llangollen; the two great aqueducts at Chirk and Pontcysyllte were complete. However, it was a totally self-contained system, its only outlet being via the old Chester Canal at Hurleston. Despite this, the Ellesmere Canal was profitable; it serviced a widespread local network, and gave an outlet to Liverpool (via the River Mersey) for the iron works and the coalfields that were grouped at the centre of the system. This profitability was dependent upon good relations with the Chester Canal Company. An attempted take over in 1804 failed, but in 1813 the inevitable merger took place, and the Ellesmere & Chester Canal Company was formed. Today the Llangollen Canal is quite justly one of the most popular canals in the country, with fascinating architecture, spectacular aqueducts and splendid scenery. As a result it can get very crowded during the summer months. Those who cruise out of the peak season, or avoid the mid-week rush to Llangollen, will have a more relaxing time. And of course now you can always divert for a short way along the Montgomery Canal from Frankton Junction.

84 HURLESTON RESERVOIR

Pipe Bridge

Hurleston Junction

Oaktree Farm

Hurleston Bridge 1

Hurleston Locks 34 3°

Shropshire Union Canal

Bache House Farm

96 Cornes Bridge

Cornes Bridge

Poole Hills Farm

Bachehouse Bridge 2

Bachehouse Pool

48 Poolehill

Martin's Bridge 3

Park Farm

New Farm

HURLESTON CP

Lee's Bridge 4

Henhullbridge Farm

95 Henhull Bridge

BURFORD

Bluestone

Police Dog Scho

Burland Hall Farm

Burland Upper Green

Brindley

Platt's Bridge 5

Bank Farm

Cuckoo Lane

Acton Grange

Acton Bridge

93 Acton Bridge

Welshmen Green

Wrexham Road

Wrexham Bridge 6

HENH

BURLAND

Acton

Monks Lane

Windmill

Chester Road

83

Nant

BURLAND CP

Pipe Bridge

Swanley Lane

Cottage Plantation

Swanley No. 2 Lock 6' 3"

Swanley Bridge 8

Madam's Farm

Dorfold Hall

Springs Lane

Bridge Farm

SWANLEY

Haybays

Aque

Springelane

Butcher's Bridge 9

Ravens Lane

Swanley No. 1 Lock 6' 7"

Admiral's Plantation

Pear Tree Farm

Stoneley Green 10 Bridge

Stoneley Green

Baddiley Farm

Pipe Bridge

Bethills Bridge 11

Tally-ho Covert

Baddiley Gorse

Baddiley Corner

Halls Lane Bridge 12

RAVENSMOOR

Sound Lane

Greenfield Bridge 13

Crabmill Farm

Old House Farm

Baddiley Hall

Baddiley Lane

BADDILEY CP

Baddiley No. 3 Lock 6' 1"

Clays Farm

Villa Farm

Norton House Farm

Baddiley No. 2 Lock 6' 10"

Oaklands

Baddiley Hulse

Baddiley Bridge 14

21

Sound Oak

Baddiley No. 1 Lock 6' 9"

Starkeys Farm

Hurleston Junction

The Llangollen rapidly establishes its character as a generally remote and pretty canal. Considering the spectacular scenery further west, it is not surprising that this is also one of the most popular cruising water-ways in the country. Leaving Hurleston Junction, the canal immediately climbs the four tidy Hurleston Locks before running through a very shallow valley past the hamlet of Burland, where there is a general store, to reach Swanley Locks. A few houses, some with attractive canalside gardens, are passed before the canal once again enters the flat, rich farmland. Those who do not mind a moderate ten minute walk can venture east from bridge 12, and turn left at the main road, to find the excellent general store at Ravensmoor (*open every day*). The next three locks encountered are at Baddiley (note the unusual paddle gear at lock no 2); the tall Georgian house surrounded by trees to the west of the bottom lock is Baddiley Hall.

NAVIGATIONAL NOTES

The Llangollen Canal is fed directly by the River Dee at Llantysilio, and there is a noticeable flow of water from the west to east. Navigators should allow more time for journeys to Llangollen – *against the flow*. The flow can be particularly strong at the tails of locks where bypass weirs discharge – and can sometimes make the approach to the locks from below rather difficult unless the resulting cross-current is taken into consideration.

● **Hurleston Reservoir**
With a capacity of 85,000,000 gallons, Hurleston Reservoir receives its supply, via the Llangollen Canal, from the River Dee at Llantysilio. It is used both as drinking water, and as a supply for the Shropshire Union Canal.

● **Burland**
Ches. Tel, stores, garage. A straggling settlement by the canal, useful as a supply centre; the general store here is *open 08.00–18.30 daily (early closing Tue & Sat)*. Daily papers and gas.

Pubs and Restaurants

● ✕ **Farmers Arms** Ravensmoor (01270 623522). A welcoming creeper-clad inn serving Greenalls real ale and bar and restaurant meals *lunchtimes and evenings, every day,* with a vegetarian choice. Children welcome. Garden. Best access is probably from bridge 12 – the store is a short walk north of here.

The towpath
This is in reasonable condition *for walkers* throughout most of its length, although there is a difficult stretch between bridges 43 & 45. Cyclists will not find it easy.

Traditional canal boat decoration

Wrenbury

The canal passes Wrenbury Hall, north west of bridge 17, formerly the home of Sir John Stapleton Cotton, one of Wellington's generals, on its way towards Wrenbury, where the first of many delightful lift bridges is encountered. Their scale seems entirely sympathetic with that of the canal, and, whilst most are generally left open, those that require operation provide added interest. Wrenbury Wharf is a splendid place where there is a fine restored warehouse converted into a pub, a former mill now occupied by a boatyard, and another pub, all grouped around the push-button lift bridge. Beyond the wharf, the soft green Cheshire countryside leads to Marbury Lock: the village is a short walk to the south, along School Lane, and is well worth visiting. The tall obelisk visible to the south east is in distant Combermere Park. Leaving Marbury the waterway again enters remote and peaceful countryside before reaching Quoisley Lock, where the road briefly intrudes, and then continues towards Willeymoor Lock.

NAVIGATIONAL NOTES

A BW key is required for the lift bridge at Wrenbury.

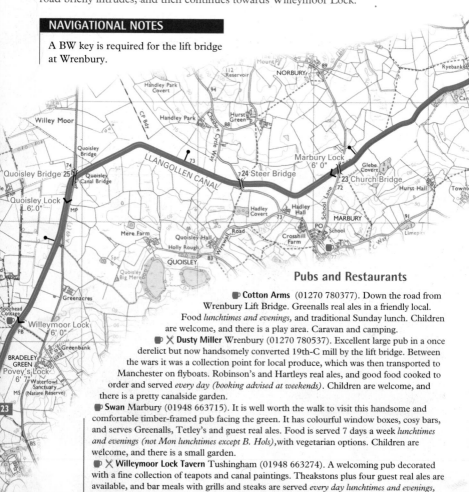

Pubs and Restaurants

Cotton Arms (01270 780377). Down the road from Wrenbury Lift Bridge. Greenalls real ales in a friendly local. Food *lunchtimes and evenings,* and traditional Sunday lunch. Children are welcome, and there is a play area. Caravan and camping.

✗ **Dusty Miller** Wrenbury (01270 780537). Excellent large pub in a once derelict but now handsomely converted 19th-C mill by the lift bridge. Between the wars it was a collection point for local produce, which was then transported to Manchester on flyboats. Robinson's and Hartleys real ales, and good food cooked to order and served *every day (booking advised at weekends)*. Children are welcome, and there is a pretty canalside garden.

Swan Marbury (01948 663715). It is well worth the walk to visit this handsome and comfortable timber-framed pub facing the green. It has colourful window boxes, cosy bars, and serves Greenalls, Tetley's and guest real ales. Food is served 7 days a week *lunchtimes and evenings (not Mon lunchtimes except B. Hols),*with vegetarian options. Children are welcome, and there is a small garden.

✗ **Willeymoor Lock Tavern** Tushingham (01948 663274). A welcoming pub decorated with a fine collection of teapots and canal paintings. Theakstons plus four guest real ales are available, and bar meals with grills and steaks are served *every day lunchtimes and evenings,* with vegetarian options. Children welcome. Lockside garden.

Boatyards

Ⓑ **Alvechurch Boat Centre** Wrenbury, in the old mill by bridge 20 (01270 780544). 📞 ⛽ 🔧 D Pump-out, gas, narrow boat hire, day hire craft, overnight mooring, crane, boat sales, boat & engine repairs, toilets, showers, gifts, public telephone nearby.

[Map of the Llangollen Canal around Wrenbury, showing Baddiley No 2 Lock 6' 10", Baddiley Hulse, Baddiley Bridge 14, Baddiley No 1 Lock 6' 9", Starkeys Farm, Wrenbury Heath 15 Bridge, Wrenbury Hall Farm, Woodcott House, Wrenbury Bridge 16, Wrenbury Heath, Summerfield House, Wrenbury Hall, 19 Wrenbury Church Lift Bridge, Wrenbury Hall 17 Bridge, Ryton House Farm, Wrenbury 20 Lift Bridge, Porter's Hill, 18 Starkey's Bridge, Wrenbury House, Woodcotthill Farm, WRENBURY, The Woodlands, Cheshire Cycle Way, 21 Wrenbury Frith Lift Bridge, Oaklands, School, Field Farm, 22 Thomason's Bridge, Sandfield House, Smeaton Hall, South Cheshire Way, Marbury Heyes]

● **Wrenbury**
Ches. Tel, garage, station.
1/4 mile from the wharf – access can be made from the footpath by bridge 19. A quiet and suitably ancient village, recorded in the Domesday Book as Warenberie. Two miles to the southeast are the remains of Combermere Abbey, established by Cistercian monks in 1133 who, in 1180, took the village church as a daughter chapel. By the church gates is the schoolmaster's cottage: this stood next door to one of the earliest parish schools in Cheshire, founded in 1605. There are some thatched magpie cottages around the green, and, remarkably, the railway station still operates, and is to be found a further 1/4 mile to the south east. The line goes from Crewe to Shrewsbury.

St Margaret's Church Overlooking Wrenbury village green, this large, battlemented 14th-C church is built from red Cheshire sandstone, with a late 15th-C west tower and an early 17th-C chancel and pulpit. The interior is very light and airy and contains a number of fine monuments. You will also notice the visible manifestation of an enduring dispute between two important local families: the Cottons of Combermere Abbey, and the Starkeys of Wrenbury Hall. They challenged each other's ownership of land and rights to church pews for over 400 years, to such an extent that an arbitrator, in 1748, allocated the south side of the church to the Cottons and the north to the Starkeys, in an effort to resolve matters. Next to the door is 'the dog-whippers pew'. The job of the dog-whipper, later known as Beadle, was to throw out unruly dogs, and to keep dozing parishioners awake during particularly tedious sermons. The last holder of this esteemed position, Thomas Vaughan, died in 1879 and is buried by the door. Have a look in the churchyard for the most unusual cast iron grave plaques, dating from the early 1800s. These were an expression, in their time, of the very latest technology.

● **Marbury**
Ches. Tel. An enchanting village 1/2 mile south of Marbury Lock. Centred on an ancient farm, the village boasts several other old and timbered buildings.

St Michael's Church This is a gem, and its setting is unrivalled: it stands on top of a little hill that overlooks the beautiful Little Mere. The church was first mentioned in 1299; as it remains today it is wholly Perpendicular in style, dating from the 15thC. When you walk around the building look out for the many gargoyles carved by the medieval masons: it seems they must have enlivened their days fashioning monkeys and grotesque faces expressing both pleasure and pain. The pulpit is the second oldest in Cheshire and, dating from the 15thC, is in excellent condition. The grounds contain not just a graveyard but a charming garden: from here you will be able to see that the tower is succumbing to subsidence, and has developed an alarming tilt. The sympathetically restored rectory stands next door.

Grindley Brook

The canal continues to rise through a series of isolated locks as the sides of the valley begin to close in. At the end of a straight stretch a massive railway embankment precedes a sharp bend to the bottom of the six locks at Grindley Brook; care should be exercised on the approach to these locks, and any boats stopping to visit the garage or pub nearby should remain below the railway embankment. The first three locks are followed at the A41 bridge by three staircase locks. Anyone requiring assistance or advice should look for the lock keeper, whose handsome house is at the top lock, where fresh vegetables, windlasses and mooring spikes can be purchased. The garage is by bridge 28 and sells provisions *every day 08.00–21.00*. The canal now swerves around the side of a hill near Whitchurch: the first of a spattering of lift bridges marks the entrance to the Whitchurch Arm, where you can moor to take the 1/2 mile walk to visit the town centre. After passing under the busy road bridge, and by the boatyard, the canal once again enters typically quiet and pretty countryside.

● **Whitchurch**
Shropshire. MD Fri. PO, tel, stores, garage, bank, station, laundrette, swimming pool. A fine town with some beautiful old houses of all periods in the centre. The streets are narrow and there is much to discover. It has its origins in Roman times as Mediolanum, 'the place in the middle of the plain', a stop on the route from Chester to Wroxeter. It was recorded in the Domesday Book as Westune, but was later to become White Church, or Whitchurch, for obvious reasons. There are plenty of splendid pubs in the town, but unfortunately none near the canal. If you visit on *Friday*, look out for farmhouse Cheshire cheese in the market.
St Alkmund's Church This striking church on the hill was built in 1713 by William and Richard Smith as the replacement for a late 14th-C building which 'fell ye 31 of July 1711'. This in turn had been built to succeed the Norman White Church which was attributed to William de

Warren, one of William the Conqueror's lieutenants who died in 1089. In 1862 the old pews were removed, and many human bones were found beneath them. These were re-buried and a new floor was laid. The pews, remodelled to make them more comfortable, were then replaced. Under the porch is buried the heart of John Talbot, who was killed in 1453 at the Battle of Castille, the last of the Hundred Years Wars. He was Earl of Shrewsbury and a principal character in Shakespeare's *Henry VI*. The rector here in 1779 was Francis Henry Egerton, 8th and last Earl of Bridgewater and a successor to the third Duke, who built the Bridgewater Canal. Those who know the Oxford Canal will recognise the present church's similarity to the magnificent church of the same vintage at Banbury. It has very big windows: indeed the whole church is on a grand scale and is well worth a visit.
Tourist Information Centre Civic Centre, High Street, Whitchurch (01948 664577).

Pubs and Restaurants

🍺 **Horse and Jockey** Grindley Brook, near the bottom lock (01948 662723). A large, friendly, family-run pub with a cosy woodburing stove in the lounge, and a resident ghost. Banks's plus a wide range of guest real ales. Grills and bar meals are available *lunchtimes and evenings every day*. Play area and garden. Moorings nearby.
🍺 **Old Town Hall Vaults** St Mary's Street, Whitchurch (01948 662251). Marston's real ale in the birthplace of Sir Edward German (1862–1936), composer of *Merrie England* and *Tom Jones*. Bar meals available *lunchtimes (not Wed or Sun evenings)*, with vegetarian options. Children welcome. Outside seating.

🍺 **White Bear** High Street, Whitchurch (01948 662638). An attractive former coaching inn with a pretty courtyard. John Smith's and Theakstons real ale and food at *lunchtimes (not Tue)*, with vegetarian options. Children welcome.
🍺 **Black Bear** High Street, Whitchurch (01948 663624). Popular and friendly black and white timbered pub in a Grade II listed building, serving guest real ales. Garden, and a very nice cat.
🍺 **The Greyhound** Whitchurch (01948 663269). A recently refurbished 15th-C inn, with a resident ghost. Vaux real ale and food *lunchtimes and evenings (not lunchtime Tue & Sun)*. Patio.

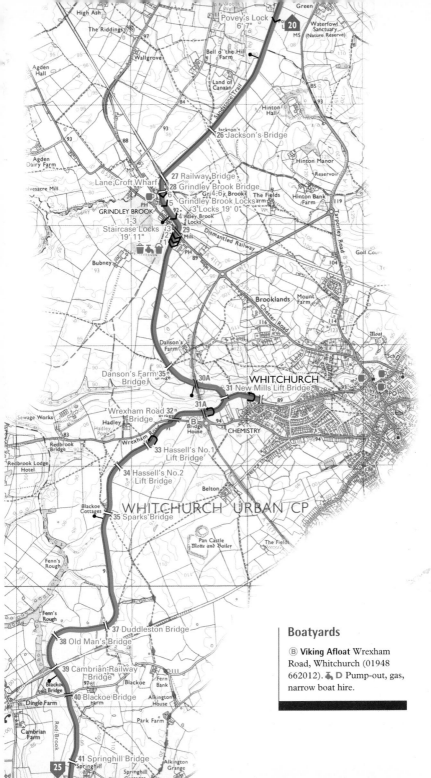

Grindley Brook

Boatyards

Ⓑ **Viking Afloat** Wrexham
Road, Whitchurch (01948
662012). ⚓ **D** Pump-out, gas,
narrow boat hire.

Whixall Moss

The canal now begins to traverse a very remote and underpopulated area, passing no villages for miles. At Platt Lane the navigation straightens out and is carried on an embankment across the strange area of Whixall Moss. Between bridges 43 and 44 is the Shop in the Garden, a convenient store selling milk, fruit and vegetables, groceries and daily papers. A solitary lift bridge interrupts the long straight, then there is a junction with the Prees Branch, which leads to a marina and a nature reserve. The main line veers off to the north west along another straight embankment, this time accompanied by woodlands, crossing the border between England and Wales. Leaving Whixall Moss, the canal passes Bettisfield and begins to wind this way and that, passing into Wales and then out again.

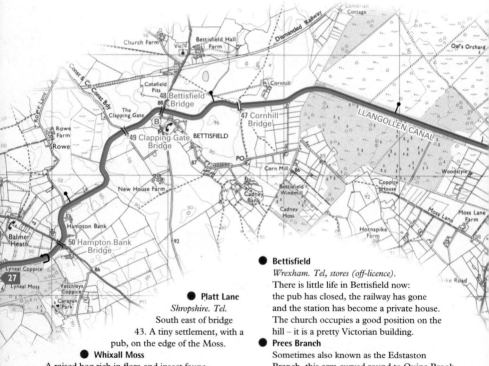

● **Platt Lane**
Shropshire. Tel.
South east of bridge 43. A tiny settlement, with a pub, on the edge of the Moss.

● **Whixall Moss**
A raised bog rich in flora and insect fauna – including mosquitoes! Like other meres and bogs in the area, Whixall Moss came into existence at the end of the Ice Age, as huge blocks of ice were left behind when the remainder of the ice cap melted and drained off into what is now the Severn valley. The peat surface remains, in spite of the past cutting of the peat for garden use, and is now a SSSI, and an important site for rare insect and plant life which survive on this delicate habitat. Access is restricted, for safety reasons, to annual permits obtainable from: the Site Manager, English Nature, Manor House, Moss Lane, Whixall, Shropshire SY13 2PD (01948 880362).

● **Bettisfield**
Wrexham. Tel, stores (off-licence).
There is little life in Bettisfield now: the pub has closed, the railway has gone and the station has become a private house. The church occupies a good position on the hill – it is a pretty Victorian building.

● **Prees Branch**
Sometimes also known as the Edstaston Branch, this arm curved round to Quina Brook – it never did reach Prees. Its principal value in recent years lay in the clay pits just over a mile from the junction: the clay from here was used until a few years ago for repairing the 'puddle' in local canals. The arm had been disused for some years, but now the first 1/2 mile gives access to a marina constructed in the old pit. It is all very pleasant, and the canal arm has two splendid old lift bridges – one of which is a rare skewed bridge. Naturalists may find interesting plant communities along the unrestored section of the branch: enquiries may be made to English Nature at the number given above.

Pubs and Restaurants

🍺 ✕ **Waggoners** Platt Lane, Whixall (01948 880259). Bass and guest real ales in a popular and welcoming local. Reasonably priced food available in the bar or restaurant *lunchtimes and evenings every day*, with vegetarian options and children's menu. Garden with children's play area. Caravan site.

Boatyards

Ⓑ **Whixall Marine** At the end of the Prees Branch (01948 880540). 🏠 ⚓ **D** Pump-out, gas, long-term mooring, slipway, boat sales, boat and engine repairs, public telephone, toilets, chandlery, gifts, grocery, off-licence.

Ⓑ **Bettisfield Boats** Bridge House, Canalside, Bettisfield, Whitchurch (01948 710465). ⚓ **D** Pump-out, long-term mooring, boat sales, boat building, boat and engine repairs.

Ellesmere

Soon the open countryside gives way to the hilly wooded landscape that lies to the east of Ellesmere and contains several beautiful meres. The canal first skirts Cole Mere, which is below and mostly hidden from it by tall trees; there is a delightful timbered cottage at the west end. Then the navigation runs right beside Blake Mere: this is a charming little lake, surrounded by steep and thickly wooded hills. The canal then plunges immediately into the 87yd Ellesmere Tunnel and then out into the open parkland beyond. You will notice many oak trees alongside the canal around here – this is said to be the legacy of the Shropshire Union's policy of planting oak and elm to provide the raw materials to replace their carrying fleet. The elms succumbed to Dutch Elm Disease. Leaving Blake Mere and the tunnel, Ellesmere is soon reached, and access is via a short arm. Fine old warehouses and a small canalside crane testify to the canal trading that used to be carried on from here. The main line of the canal to Llangollen bears round sharply to the south-west at the junction: the fine old buildings here house a BW office and maintenance yard, with facilities for pleasure boats.

Within the yard is 'Beech House', once the canal company's office. Beyond the yard, the country once again becomes quiet and entirely rural, while the canal's course becomes very winding. At Frankton Junction the Montgomery Canal branches south towards Newtown: it is currently navigable a short way beyond Queens Head (you can wind), and further restoration is under way.

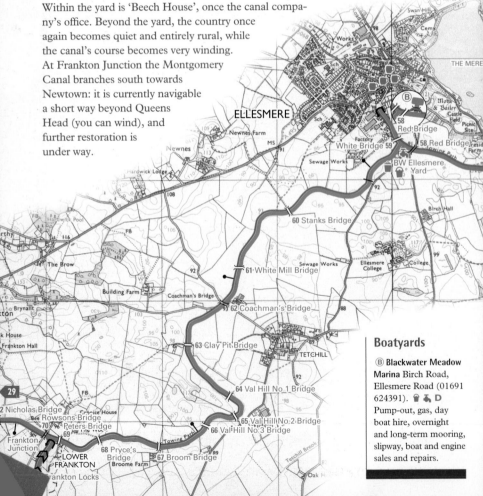

Boatyards

Ⓑ **Blackwater Meadow Marina** Birch Road, Ellesmere Road (01691 624391). ⛽ 🛁 **D** Pump-out, gas, day boat hire, overnight and long-term mooring, slipway, boat and engine sales and repairs.

● **Welshampton**
Shropshire. Tel, stores, garage. 1 mile west of bridge 50, the village contains the only pub since Platt Lane.

● **Tetchill**
Shropshire. A small farming village, quiet and unpretentious.

● **Ellesmere**
Shropshire. PO, tel, stores (excellent greengrocer with local produce), garage, laundrette, bank. This handsome and busy 18thC market town, with its narrow winding streets, is an attractive place to visit. There are many tall red brick houses and several terraces of old cottages. It takes its name from the large and beautiful mere beside it. The Meres Visitor Centre, next to the Mere, has well presented information and organised activities. *Open Easter–Oct (01692 622981).*

St Mary's Church Standing on a hill overlooking the mere, the general appearance of this large red-stone church is Victorian, belying its medieval origins. It contains a medieval chest hewn out of a solid block of oak, many fine effigies and a beautiful 15thC font.

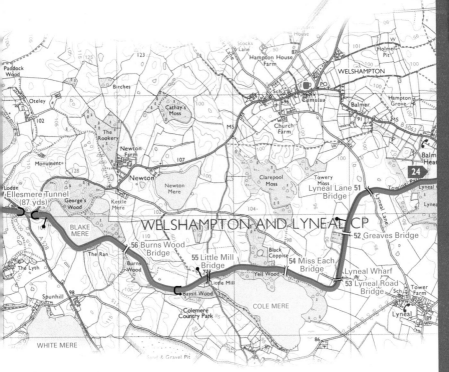

Pubs and Restaurants

🍺 **Sun** Welshampton (01948 710637). A quiet local serving Tetley's real ale. Bar meals available *lunchtimes and evenings, 7 days a week.* Garden and children's play area. Caravan site.

🍺 **White Hart** Birch Road, Ellesmere (01691 622333). Marston's real ale in a grade III-listed building. Meals, with vegetarian options, *lunchtimes and evenings every day.* Children are welcome.

✗ 🍷 **Boathouse** Ellesmere (01691 623828). North of Ellesmere Tunnel, 500yds along the A528. Coffee shop and restaurant with an alcohol licence, serving from *09.00–17.00 daily,* with traditional *Sun lunch* (book) and vegetarian options. Children welcome. Garden overlooking the heronry.

The **Black Lion** and the **Ellesmere**, both in Ellesmere, are also worth a visit.

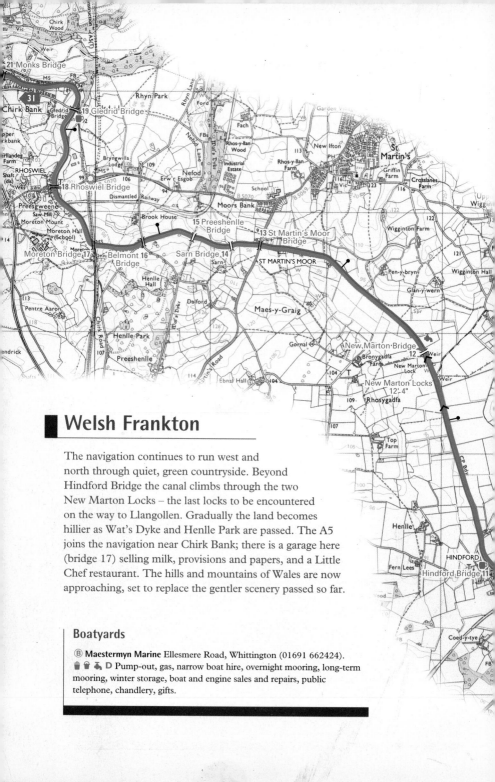

Welsh Frankton

The navigation continues to run west and
north through quiet, green countryside. Beyond
Hindford Bridge the canal climbs through the two
New Marton Locks – the last locks to be encountered
on the way to Llangollen. Gradually the land becomes
hillier as Wat's Dyke and Henlle Park are passed. The A5
joins the navigation near Chirk Bank; there is a garage here
(bridge 17) selling milk, provisions and papers, and a Little
Chef restaurant. The hills and mountains of Wales are now
approaching, set to replace the gentler scenery passed so far.

Boatyards

Ⓑ **Maestermyn Marine** Ellesmere Road, Whittington (01691 662424).
🚮 🛢 ⚓ D Pump-out, gas, narrow boat hire, overnight mooring, long-term
mooring, winter storage, boat and engine sales and repairs, public
telephone, chandlery, gifts.

● **Rhoswiel**
Shropshire. Tel, stores. A tiny village on the Welsh border; the canal runs through it in a slight cutting.

Pubs and Restaurants

🍺 **Narrowboat Inn** Maestermyn Marine, Ellesmere Road, Whittington (01691 661051). A friendly pub with a nautical theme, serving a choice of three real ales. Bar and restaurant meals are available *lunchtimes and evenings every day*, with vegetarian options and a children's menu. Garden with a summer bar, and moorings.

🍺 ✕ **Jack Mytton Inn and Restaurant** Hindford (01691 679861). A fine pub in an attractive hamlet with a wide range of food available *lunchtimes and evenings every day*, including a vegetarian menu. Children welcome. There is a garden, and moorings.

🍺 **Poachers Pocket** Gledrid, Chirk (01691 773250). Popular and friendly pub serving Banks's real ale. Good value, home-cooked bar meals *lunchtimes and evenings and all day Sun*, with vegetarian and children's menu. Outside seating, and you can go and pat the artificial horse.

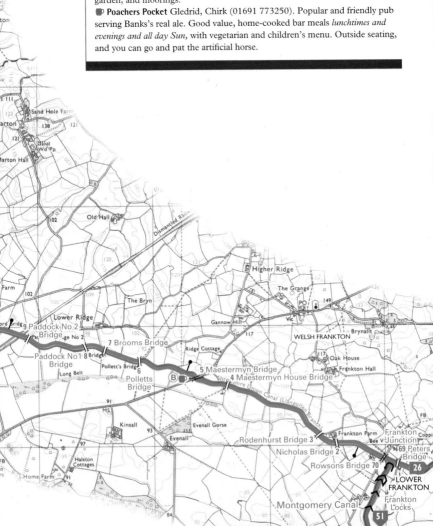

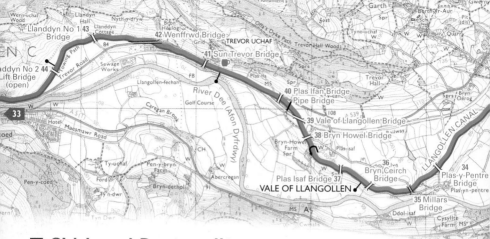

Chirk and Pontcysyllte

As Chirk Bank is reached, the approach of the Welsh mountains drives the navigation into a side cutting half-way up the side of a hill. The canal then rounds a corner and suddenly Chirk Aqueduct appears – an impressive structure by any canal enthusiast's standards, and accompanied by a very fine railway viaduct alongside. At the end of the aqueduct the canal immediately enters a tunnel, with Chirk Station nearby. A long wooded cutting follows, and then the railway reappears alongside. Another, shorter, tunnel at Whitehouses is negotiated before the canal meets the valley of the River Dee. Here the railway charges off to the north on a magnificent viaduct, while the canal clings to the hillside. Now the scenery really is superb and the views over and along the valley of the River Dee are excellent. Passing the village of Froncysyllte, the canal launches out into this deep valley on a massive embankment, then crosses the River Dee on the breathtaking Pontcysyllte Aqueduct. At the north end of the aqueduct there is a short arm with a boatyard straight ahead, but to continue to Llangollen it is necessary to make a tricky 90-degree turn. The short arm towards Ruabon was originally projected as the canal's main line towards Chester and the Mersey, and the dry dock at Trevor Junction dates from this time. The line from Trevor to Llantysilio was envisaged purely as a navigable feeder. However the idea of a direct line to Chester was soon dropped and a connection made instead with the Chester Canal at Hurleston Junction. There are good moorings at the north end of Chirk Tunnel, and moorings and a turning place in the restored basins beyond the Anglo-Welsh boatyard. The canal, now generally quite narrow, continues in a westerly direction towards Llangollen, clinging spectacularly to the side of the valley above the Dee. In places the mountain-side is very steep, making the canal so narrow that only one boat can negotiate the channel at a time. The scene of several major breaches between 1982–5, repairs have cost a breathtaking £5 million over the 10-mile stretch between Chirk and Llangollen.

NAVIGATIONAL NOTES

1 Do not enter the Pontcysyllte Aqueduct if a boat is approaching from the opposite direction. Wait until it is clear.
2 From Trevor to Llangollen the canal is very shallow, accentuating the flow downstream. It is not recommended for boats drawing more than 21 inches. It is also, in places, very narrow. Just go slowly, keep a sharp watch for approaching boats, and enjoy the superb scenery.

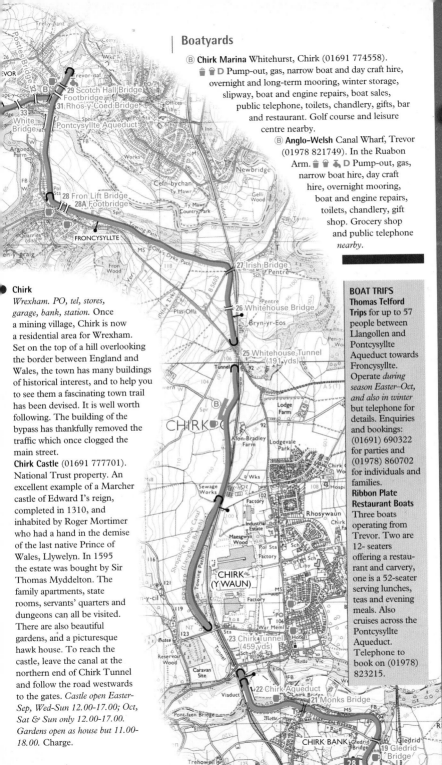

Boatyards

Ⓑ **Chirk Marina** Whitehurst, Chirk (01691 774558). D Pump-out, gas, narrow boat and day craft hire, overnight and long-term mooring, winter storage, slipway, boat and engine repairs, boat sales, public telephone, toilets, chandlery, gifts, bar and restaurant. Golf course and leisure centre nearby.

Ⓑ **Anglo-Welsh** Canal Wharf, Trevor (01978 821749). In the Ruabon Arm. D Pump-out, gas, narrow boat hire, day craft hire, overnight mooring, boat and engine repairs, toilets, chandlery, gift shop. Grocery shop and public telephone *nearby*.

Chirk

Wrexham. PO, tel, stores, garage, bank, station. Once a mining village, Chirk is now a residential area for Wrexham. Set on the top of a hill overlooking the border between England and Wales, the town has many buildings of historical interest, and to help you to see them a fascinating town trail has been devised. It is well worth following. The building of the bypass has thankfully removed the traffic which once clogged the main street.

Chirk Castle (01691 777701). National Trust property. An excellent example of a Marcher castle of Edward I's reign, completed in 1310, and inhabited by Roger Mortimer who had a hand in the demise of the last native Prince of Wales, Llywelyn. In 1595 the estate was bought by Sir Thomas Myddelton. The family apartments, state rooms, servants' quarters and dungeons can all be visited. There are also beautiful gardens, and a picturesque hawk house. To reach the castle, leave the canal at the northern end of Chirk Tunnel and follow the road westwards to the gates. *Castle open Easter-Sep, Wed-Sun 12.00-17.00; Oct, Sat & Sun only 12.00-17.00. Gardens open as house but 11.00-18.00.* Charge.

BOAT TRIPS
Thomas Telford Trips for up to 57 people between Llangollen and Pontcysyllte Aqueduct towards Froncysyllte. Operate *during season Easter–Oct, and also in winter* but telephone for details. Enquiries and bookings: (01691) 690322 for parties and (01978) 860702 for individuals and families.
Ribbon Plate Restaurant Boats Three boats operating from Trevor. Two are 12- seaters offering a restaurant and carvery, one is a 52-seater serving lunches, teas and evening meals. Also cruises across the Pontcysyllte Aqueduct. Telephone to book on (01978) 823215.

Chirk and Whitehouses Tunnels Neither of these tunnels is wide enough for two boats to pass, although each tunnel has a towpath running through it. Chirk Tunnel is 459yds long. Whitehouses Tunnel is 191yds long.

● **Chirk Aqueduct**
Opened in 1801, this is a splendidly massive brick and stone aqueduct carrying the canal in a narrow cast iron trough from England into Wales. The River Ceiriog flows 70ft below, and the great railway viaduct is beside and a little higher than the aqueduct.

● **Froncysyllte**
Wrexham. PO, tel, stores. A village distinguished by its superb position on the side of the valley, with a friendly gift shop.

● **Pontcysyllte Aqueduct**
Easily the most famous and most spectacular feature on the whole canal system, this aqueduct cannot fail to astonish visitors. Apart from its great height of 126ft above the River Dee and its length of 1007ft, the excitement to be derived from crossing this structure by boat is partly due to the fact that, while the towpath side is safely fenced off with iron railings, the offside is completely unprotected from about 12in above the water level *so the safest way for children to enjoy the great aqueduct is from inside the boat.* It is generally considered to have been built by

Thomas Telford, and if so is reckoned to be one of his most brilliant and successful works. The concept of laying a cast iron trough along the top of a row of stone piers was entirely new, and entirely Telford's: he realised that such a high crossing of the Dee valley was inevitable if time- and water-wasting locks were to be avoided, and it was obvious to the canal company that a conventional brick or stone aqueduct would be quite unsuitable. His plan for the aqueduct was greeted at first with derision; but the work went ahead, was completed in ten years and opened in 1805 at an estimated cost of £47,018. One can hardly imagine the utter amazement felt by people of that time as they witnessed boats moving easily across this tall, beautiful and unique structure. Today, the aqueduct remains as built, apart from renewals of balustrading and the towpath structure. The masonry is apparently in prime condition (note the very thin masonry joints, which were bonded by a mortar made from a mixture of lime and ox blood), and the dovetailed joints in the iron trough, sealed with a combination of Welsh flannel and lead dipped in boiling sugar, hardly leak at all. The cast-iron side plates of the trough are all wedge shaped, like the stones in a masonry arch. It is, without doubt, a master-piece.

Pubs and Restaurants

🍺 **Poachers Pocket** Gledrid, Chirk (01691 773250). Popular and friendly pub serving Banks's real ale. Good value, home-cooked bar meals *lunchtimes and evenings and all day Sun,* with vegetarian and children's menu. Outside seating.

🍺 **Bridge** Chirk Bank (01691 773213). The 'last pub in England', on the old A5 downhill from bridge 21. A cosy bar, with Banks's real ale and bar meals and snacks *lunchtimes and evenings every day,* with a vegetarian menu. Garden. Children welcome. B & B.

🍺 ✕ **Hand Hotel** Church Street, Chirk (01691 773472). Smart residential hotel with a fine collection of tobaccanalia, serving Tetley's real ale. Food available in the buttery bar, regency and steak restaurant *lunchtimes and evenings daily,* with a vegetarian menu. Garden with children's play area. Function suite with cabaret at weekends. Leisure suite. B & B.

🍺 ✕ **Watering Hole** Chirk Marina. Canalside pub with moorings. Real ale and reasonably priced bar meals. Separate restaurant with à la carte menu. Children welcome.

🍺 ✕ **Britannia** Holyhead Road, Froncysyllte (01691 774635). On the hillside above bridge 28. Banks's real ale and bar and restaurant meals

(vegetarian menu available) *7 days a week, lunchtimes and evenings, and take-away food (fish & chips).* Children welcome. Large garden.

🍺 **Aqueduct** Holyhead Road, Froncysyllte (01691 772481). Perched high above the aqueduct at bridge 28, and serving Marston's and a guest real ale. Bar meals *lunchtimes and evenings every day,* with vegetarian options available. Children welcome, and there is a patio and garden. Traditional pub games.

🍺 ✕ **Telford Inn** Scotch Hall, Trevor, next to Anglo-Welsh (01978 820469). Tetley's real ale in a busy pub with canalside seating. Food, including vegetarian dishes, available *lunchtimes and evenings 7 days a week.* Children welcome, and there is a play area.

🍺 ✕ **Sun Trevor** Sun Bank (01978 860651). Above bridge 41. A beautifully situated pub with exceptional views of the valley, river and canal. Brasses, beams and a fine inglenook with a cosy curved settle are there to enjoy in a building which has its origins in the 14thC. Courage, John Smith's, and guest real ales in summer. Bar and restaurant meals available *lunchtimes and evenings,* with vegetarian and children's menu. Garden. Occasional entertainment. Moorings.

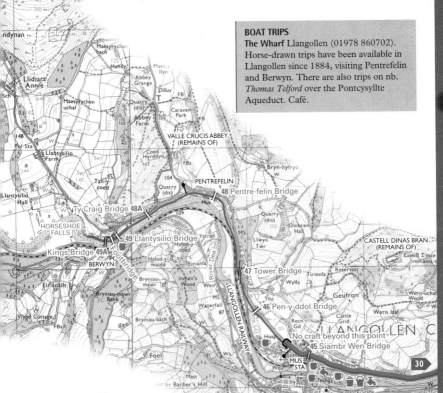

Llangollen

This is another stretch of very
great beauty, as the waterway's
route through Llangollen is made on
the side of tree-covered mountains, with views
down into the Vale of Llangollen. The canal passes
high above the town, but it doesn't stop there: the tiny channel
continues as a feeder to weave up the valley to Llantysilio. At Horseshoe Falls a
large semi circular weir built by Telford across the Dee provides the water which
is constantly passed from the river through a sluice and meter into the canal.
Then it flows past Llangollen and the aqueducts, right back down to Hurleston
reservoir – to the tune of twelve million gallons a day.

NAVIGATIONAL NOTES

1 There is **no** turning point west of the winding hole at Llangollen, so boats
   longer than about 10' must not venture up the feeder. However, the towpath is
   in excellent shape and makes a very enjoyable walk.

2 Moorings are restricted in Llangollen. *Between 18.45–09.45 you may moor only
   between bridges 45 and the winding hole; there is a 48 hour restriction below
   bridge 45. No mooring beyond the winding hole.*

Llangollen

Denbighshire. MD Tue. PO, tel, stores, garage, bank. Renowned for its International Musical Eisteddfod *every July.* It is a great centre for pony trekking and other outdoor pursuits, especially climbing and walking. The parish church of St Collen in Church Street is a fine 13th-C building, enlarged in 1865 and containing a superb carved oak ceiling.

The Llangollen Railway Llangollen Station (01978 860979 for enquiries, or 01978 860951 for a talking timetable). Operates steam and heritage diesel trains to Carrog on over 8 miles of track in the direction of Corwen. Beautifully restored stations. They also operate a canal/rail service, special dining trains and a vintage bus service (*Sat & Sun in summer*).

International Musical Eisteddfod Eisteddfod Office, Llangollen (01978 860236). For a *week every July* the town becomes a lively cultural centre, attracting singers, dancers and musicians from all over the world who perform both in organised concerts, and impromptu street events.

Tourist Information Centre Parade Street, Llangollen (01978 860828).

Plas Newydd (01978 861314). On the southern outskirts of town. From 1779–1831 it was the home of the eccentric Lady Eleanor Butler and Miss Sarah Ponsonby. Their visitors, who included Browning, Tennyson, Walter Scott and Wordsworth, presented them with antique curios, which are now on display in the elaborately panelled rooms. Part of the 12-acre grounds is a public park. *House open daily Apr–Oct,*

10.00–17.00. Charge. Entry to the grounds is free, and these are *open all year round.*

The Motor Museum Pentrefelin, Llangollen (01978 8690324). Over 30 vehicles from the 1920s to the 1970s, plus models and automobilia. Also a canal exhibition. *Open Apr–Oct, Tue–Sun 10.00–17.00; Nov–Dec & Feb–Mar, Wed–Sun 11.00–16.00.* Charge.

Castell Dinas Bran 1/2 mile north of canal. The ruins of the castle built for Eliseg, Prince of Powys, can be seen from the waterway while approaching the town, and stand on a 1100ft mountain accessible to energetic walkers from various points along the canal, including bridge 45.

Eliseg's Pillar 1/4 mile north of the abbey. Erected in the 18thC to commemorate Eliseg, who built the fortress on the top of Dinas Bran.

Llantysilio

Denbighshire. Overlooking Horseshoe Falls. Parts of the interior of the Victorian church are taken from the nearby Valle Crucis Abbey, and the south window still contains 16th-C glass.

Valle Crucis Abbey (01222 500200). 1 1/2 miles north west of the town. Finely preserved ruins of the Cistercian abbey founded in 1201 by Madoc, Prince of Powys, and rebuilt in more lavish style after a fire in 1250. The abbey fell into neglect following the dissolution of the monasteries in 1539. Its finest feature is the vaulted chapter house and screened library cupboard. There is also the only surviving monastic fish pond to be seen in Wales. Occasional theatrical and musical events are held in the grounds. *Open Apr–Sep, daily 10.00–17.00; Oct–Mar, daily 09.30–16.00.* Charge.

Pubs and Restaurants

There are a variety of friendly pubs and restaurants in Llangollen, including;

The Sarah Ponsonby Mill Street (01978 861119). On the A539 east of bridge 45. Theakston's real ale in a pub overlooking the River Dee, handy for the Llangollen moorings. No pool, darts or machines, but a good choice of music, and plenty of board games. Bar meals and large à la carte menus served *lunchtimes and evenings every day,* with vegetarian menu. Children's play area in garden. Regular entertainment.

Bridge End Hotel (01978 860634) Below bridge 45. Large and comfortable pub serving Robinson's real ale. Bar meals *lunchtimes and evenings every day,* with vegetarian options. Music *Tue and Sun.* Children welcome. Outside seating. B & B.

The Wharf Llangollen (01978 860702). Friendly restaurant right by original town wharf, complete with a crane, *open daytime only.* Fine views.

Royal Hotel (01978 860202). Smart residential hotel with a restaurant. Marston's

and Courage real ales in the small bar, and bar meals *lunchtimes and evenings every day* with vegetarian menu. Restaurant open *D only.* Children welcome.

Gales Bridge Street (01978 860089). Wine bar in an 18th-C building, with an exciting menu including vegetarian dishes. *Open L & D (closed Sun).* Children welcome. Outside seating. Wine-tasting evenings *every first Mon of the month in winter.* B & B.

Jenny Jones Hotel Abbey Road, 300yds west of bridge 45 (01978 860653). Jenny Jones, Tetley's and guest real ales. Bar meals served *lunchtimes and evenings every day.* Restaurant open *D only and Sun L, closed Mon,* includes vegetarian menu. Children welcome until *21.30.* Country and Western music on *Wed* and traditional and dixieland jazz on *Thus & Sat.*

Chain Bridge Hotel Llantysilio (01978 860215). In a splendid position overlooking the river, this hotel serves meals *lunchtimes and evenings every day,* with a vegetarian menu, in the attractive bar. Restaurant meals should be booked. Children welcome. Garden.

MONMOUTHSHIRE & BRECON CANAL

MAXIMUM DIMENSIONS	MILEAGE
Length: 44' 3"	*CWMBRAN Five Locks to*
Beam: 8' 6"	Pontymoile Bridge: 2¹/₂ miles
Headroom: 5' 6"	Goytre Wharf: 8¹/₂ miles
Draught: 2' 6"	Llanfoist: 14 miles
	Gilwern: 17 miles
MANAGER	Llangattock Bridge: 20¹/₂ miles
01873 830328	Talybont: 29 miles
	BRECON: 35³/₄ miles
	Locks: 6

In 1792 the Act of Authorisation for the Monmouthshire Canal was passed. This gave permission for a canal to be cut from the estuary of the River Usk at Newport to Pontnewydd, north of Pontypool. In addition to this 11-mile main line, there was to be an 11-mile branch from Malpas to Crumlin. The canal was designed to connect with a large network of tramways that were to be built to serve the iron ore, limestone and coal mines of the area. Thomas Dadford was appointed engineer, and the canal was opened in 1796. The close relationship between canal and tramway from the start of the scheme was a feature of South Wales. When the Act for the Brecknock & Abergavenny Canal was passed in 1793, the canal was planned to connect Brecon with the River Usk at Caerleon, to serve as a link between the various tramways and the Usk Navigation. The directors of the Monmouthshire Canal persuaded the promoters of this rival venture to alter their plans to include a junction with their own canal. And so the Brecknock & Abergavenny Canal, with Thomas Dadford again as engineer, was cut from Brecon to Pontymoile Basin, where it joined the Monmouth-shire Canal. Construction was begun in 1797 and the Brecknock & Abergavenny Canal was opened throughout in 1812. For a while the two canals were profitable, because the iron and coal cargoes justified the use of both canal and tramway. However, the greater speed and efficiency of the railways soon became apparent, and by the 1850s there were many schemes to give up the canals and rely entirely on the rail system. In 1865 the Monmouthshire and the Brecknock & Abergavenny Canal Companies amalgamated, becoming the Monmouthshire & Brecon Canal Company; but already it was too late for the merger to be effective. Later the whole system was bought by the Great Western Railway. Bit by bit the original Monmouthshire Canal was closed, but the Brecon line was kept open as a water channel. In 1962 the network was formally abandoned, and parts were filled in. However, with the development of the Brecon Beacons National Park, the amenity potential of the Brecon line was realised. In 1964 the slow task of restoration was begun by BWB, with the help of Brecon and Monmouth County Councils. The locks were restored, and boats were once more able to cruise from Pontymoile to Talybont. In 1970 the low fixed bridge at Talybont was replaced with a new lifting bridge, and navigation was open all along the old Brecknock & Abergavenny Canal. April 1995 saw the official opening of the canal as far as Crown Bridge, Sebastopol, thanks to the efforts of Torfaen Borough Council and grants from local companies. In May 1996 the navigable waterway crept further south as far as Five Locks, which is at present the limit of the navigation.

Pontypool

The first section of the navigation as far as Sebastopol is under the care of Torfaen Borough Council. Overnight moorings are available at Cross Keys Bridge. Heading north towards Pontypool the canal enters the short Cwmbran Tunnel, constructed to cope with the watershed from the adjacent mountains. One of the old Monmouthshire Canal Company mileposts stands beside the towpath, a memory of when the navigation extended its full course. Emerging from the tunnel, the land designated as Five Locks Nature Reserve is on the west bank. At Crown Bridge fish & chips are available opposite the pub and there is a telephone and PO to the east of the bridge. At Pontymoile, formerly the limit of the navigation, the town centre is about one mile to the north west, through the lovely Pontypool park. The old toll cottage at Pontymoile Basin, now available for rent as a holiday cottage, marks the junction of the Brecknock & Abergavenny Canal with the Monmouthshire Canal. The cottage, built in 1874, gauged boats which were moving from one canal to the other by measuring the height of the hull above the water.

● **Pontypool**
Torfaen. MD Wed, Fri, Sat. Pontypool has been an industrial town since Roman times, concentrating on the production of iron. In 1720 tinplate was produced here for the first time in Britain and in the 19thC the town was a centre for japanning – the coating of objects with an extract of oils from coal, so producing a black varnish similar to Japanese lacquer. Japan ware remained popular well into the 19thC. Despite its industrial heritage, Pontypool has always remained a farming centre and so the hard industrial elements are softened by the traditions of a rural market town.
Pontypool Park Originally the seat of the Hanburys, the famous iron and steel family, this Georgian mansion is now a school. The park is open to the public.

Torfaen Museum Trust (01495 752036). Situated in the stable block of Pontypool Park House. Tells the story of the Torfaen valley and its people. *Open daily Mon–Sat 10.00–17.00; Sun 14.00–17.00. Closed Xmas.* Charge.
The Shell Grotto Pontypool Park (01495 762200). Built by Capel Hanbury Leigh in the 1830s with internal decorations of shell, animal bones and crystals. *Open May–Sep, Sat, Sun and B. Hols 14.00–17.00.* Free.
The Folly Tower Pontypool Park. Commanding views over Gwent. The tower was demolished in 1940 by order of the Ministry of Defence as there were fears that it might guide the Luftwaffe bombers to the Royal Ordnance factory at Glascoed. Rebuilt in 1992. Opening details as for the Shell Grotto (above).

Pubs and Restaurants

🍺 **Cross Keys Inn** Five Locks, Cwmbran (01633 861545). Canalside at bridge 45. Hancock's real ale and bar meals *Tue–Sat evenings and Sun lunchtimes.*
🍺 **The Crown** Sebastopol (01495 764197). Canalside at bridge 48. Town local serving Hancock's, Worthington and Tetley's real ales. Family room. Canalside patio.
🍺 ✕ **Open Hearth** Sebastopol (01495 763752). Canalside, between bridges 48 and 49, south of Pontymoile Basin. A fine collection of at least nine real ales including Hancock's, Archers, Buckley's, Greene King and Boddingtons await you at this friendly pub. An extensive collection of bottled beers decorates the lounge bar. An imaginative choice of food, including vegetarian, is available *lunchtimes and evenings.* Garden. Children welcome. Mooring. *Open all day Sat.*
🍺 **Masons Arms** Griffithstown, Pontypool

(01495 763819). South of bridge 50. Up to six rotating guest ales are served in this friendly, canalside pub together with a range of home-cooked food. Children welcome and vegetarians catered for. Mooring and outside seating.
✕ **Marina Tearooms** The Canal Basin, Pontymoile, Pontypool (0800 5422663). Tea, coffee, ice-creams and light snacks. Moorings and slipway adjacent. Self-catering holiday cottage available in the unusual and attractive toll house. *Open weekends and lunchtimes throughout the year and all day during the summer holidays.*
🍺 ✕ **Horse & Jockey** Pontymoile (01495 762721). On the A472, 100yds east of bridge 55. A picturesque, thatched pub with a warm welcome serving Hancock's and a guest real ale. Reasonably priced bar food with daily specials on offer *lunchtimes and evenings, 7 days a week.* Children welcome. Garden and children's play area.

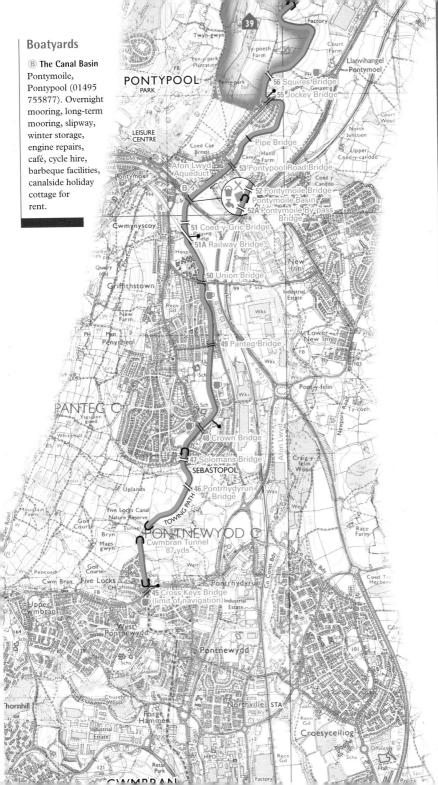

Boatyards

Ⓑ **The Canal Basin**
Pontymoile,
Pontypool (01495
755877). Overnight
mooring, long-term
mooring, slipway,
winter storage,
engine repairs,
café, cycle hire,
barbeque facilities,
canalside holiday
cottage for
rent.

Map labels:

PONTYPOOL
PARK

LEISURE
CENTRE

56 Squires Bridge
55 Jockey Bridge

Pipe Bridge

Afon Lwyd
Aqueduct

53 Pontypool Road Bridge

Ⓑ

52 Pontymoile Bridge
Pontymoile Basin
52A Pontymoile By-pass
Bridge

51 Coed-y-Gric Bridge
51A Railway Bridge

50 Union Bridge

Cwmynyscoy

Griffithstown

49 Panteg Bridge

PANTEG C

48 Crown Bridge

47 Solomans Bridge

SEBASTOPOL

46 Pontrhydyrun
Bridge

PONTNEWYOD C

TOWING PATH

Five Locks Canal
Nature Reserve

Cwmbran Tunnel
87 yds

Five Locks

West
Pontnewydd

45 Cross Keys Bridge
(limit of navigation)

Pontrhydyrun

PONTNEWYDD

Croesyceiliog

Goytre Wharf

As the canal leaves Pontypool it twists and turns, clinging to the hillside on the west, while to the east wide views open up across the rolling pastures and woods of the Usk valley. The winding course and the frequent stone bridges make the canal interesting, for every bend offers a different view of the steep hills to the west and the valley to the east, while the canal itself remains entirely quiet, rural and isolated. Navigators should look out for the cast-iron mileposts which survive irregularly along the length of the canal. There are no villages by the canal in this section, but services and pubs are never more than a short walk away at Mamhilad and at Penperlleni where the stores are open every day. Provisions are available at Ty-bach, west of bridge 62, and also at Pen-croes-oped, 300 yards west of bridge 76. Main roads keep their distance, although they are generally clearly visible in the valley below the canal. After passing the long tunnel-like Saron's bridge, the seclusion is interrupted by long lines of moored boats, which are the prelude to Goytre Wharf. Just beyond the wharf the canal passes through a thick, wooded cutting before continuing its winding course with the open valley to the east.

Goytre Wharf Heritage, Activity & Study Centre
Goytre Wharf, Llanover, Nr Abergavenny (01873 881069). Steeped in over 200 years of industrial history Goytre Wharf occupies an 8-acre site and offers the visitor a rich diversity of walks, wildlife and the chance to absorb the feats of a bygone industrial era. There is a coffee shop, also selling crafts and souvenirs, canoe hire (01873 880661), exhibitions and sales of stained glass (01873 880131) and a natural amphitheatre; together with a children's play area and picnic area. Visitor moorings.

● **Mamhilad**
Torfaen. Tel. A little hillside hamlet scattered around the church of St Illtyd. The pleasantly-kept churchyard is overshadowed by massive yew trees, the largest of which reaches some 38 feet in circumference. This suggests that the tree could well be between two to three thousand years old and would have therefore been standing when missionaries from the monastery of St Illtyd at Llantwit Major first visited in the 6thC.

● **Penperlleni**
Monmouth. PO, tel, stores (open 7 days), garage. Main road village useful for supplies. The estate here was bought in 1794 by Colonel Henry Bird who is depicted on the pub sign.

Boatyards

Ⓑ **Red Line Boats** Goytre Wharf, Llanover, Abergavenny, Monmouth (01873 880516). 🚻 🛢 🛠 D Pump-out, gas, narrow boat hire, day hirecraft, overnight mooring, long-term mooring, winter storage, slipway, dry dock, wet dock, boat sales, engine sales and repairs (including outboards), telephone, toilets, showers, café, chandlery, books and maps, gifts. Emergency call-out.

Pubs and Restaurants

🍺 ✗ **Goytre Arms** Penperlleni (01873 880376). ¼ mile east of bridge 72. The unusual inn sign depicts Colonel Henry Bird returning from the American War in 1794 with his new Indian wife. Whitbread real ales plus a guest ale are served in the bar which once specialised in the making of coffins! Food, including vegetarian and children's menu, is served *lunchtimes and evenings*. Children welcome. Garden.

🍺 ✗ **Horseshoe Inn** Goetre Fawr (01873 880542). ¼ mile north of bridge 65. It is worth the short walk uphill to this pleasant little pub. A sign outside, referring to the view, reads, 'Relax, take in the view. God made this place when he finished his apprenticeship.' Bass real ale plus a guest ale are available in the unusual bar where optics are suspended from an old wheel. A well-priced menu, including a good selection of fish, game and vegetarian dishes, is served *lunchtimes and evenings*. Outside seating. Children welcome.

🍺 **Star** Mamhilad (01495 785319). 200yds east of bridge 62. A choice of four real ales including Hancock's and Bass are served in this cosy little pub. Food, including vegetarian, is available *lunchtimes and evenings (not Mon)*. Children welcome. Garden. *Closed Mon lunchtime.*

BOAT TRIPS
Lord William de Braose (01873 881069). Restaurant boat operating from Goytre Wharf.

80 Mount Pleasant Upper Bridge

79 Mount Pleasant Lower Bridge

78 Mill Turn Bridge

77 Preacher's Bridge

76 Lapstone Bridge

75 Jenkin Rosser's Bridge

GOYTRE WHARF

74 Saron's Bridge

73 Penroel Bridge

72 Park-y-Brain Upper Bridge

Park-y-Brain Lower Bridge 71

PENPERLLENI

Birdspool Bridge 70

69 High House Bridge

Mortimers Bridge 65

Skinners Bridge 64

66 Brook Farm Bridge

68 Croes-y-Pant Bridge

Mamhilad Bridge 63

Pentre Bridge 67

TY-BACH

High Bridge 62

MAMHILAD

61 Troed-y-Rhiw Bridge

60 Govera Bridge

59 Keepers Bridge

58 Upper-Wern Bridge

57 Lower Wern

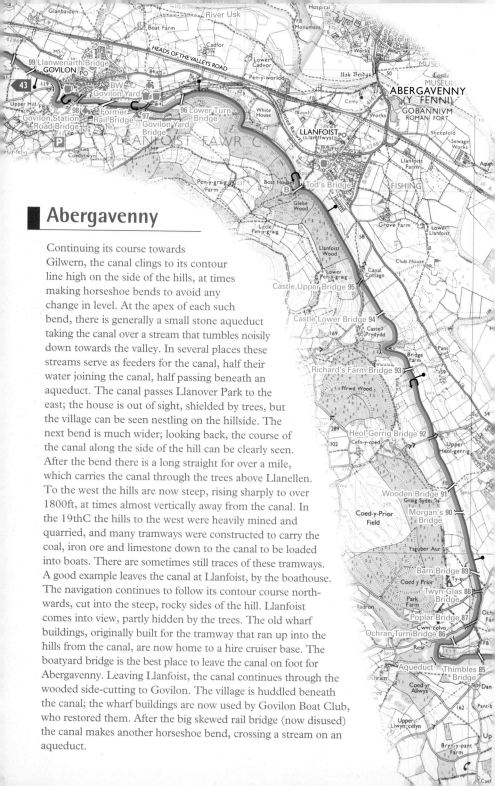

Abergavenny

Continuing its course towards
Gilwern, the canal clings to its contour
line high on the side of the hills, at times
making horseshoe bends to avoid any
change in level. At the apex of each such
bend, there is generally a small stone aqueduct
taking the canal over a stream that tumbles noisily
down towards the valley. In several places these
streams serve as feeders for the canal, half their
water joining the canal, half passing beneath an
aqueduct. The canal passes Llanover Park to the
east; the house is out of sight, shielded by trees, but
the village can be seen nestling on the hillside. The
next bend is much wider; looking back, the course of
the canal along the side of the hill can be clearly seen.
After the bend there is a long straight for over a mile,
which carries the canal through the trees above Llanellen.
To the west the hills are now steep, rising sharply to over
1800ft, at times almost vertically away from the canal. In
the 19thC the hills to the west were heavily mined and
quarried, and many tramways were constructed to carry the
coal, iron ore and limestone down to the canal to be loaded
into boats. There are sometimes still traces of these tramways.
A good example leaves the canal at Llanfoist, by the boathouse.
The navigation continues to follow its contour course northwards, cut into the steep, rocky sides of the hill. Llanfoist
comes into view, partly hidden by the trees. The old wharf
buildings, originally built for the tramway that ran up into the
hills from the canal, are now home to a hire cruiser base. The
boatyard bridge is the best place to leave the canal on foot for
Abergavenny. Leaving Llanfoist, the canal continues through the
wooded side-cutting to Govilon. The village is huddled beneath
the canal; the wharf buildings are now used by Govilon Boat Club,
who restored them. After the big skewed rail bridge (now disused)
the canal makes another horseshoe bend, crossing a stream on an
aqueduct.

Pubs and Restaurants

🍺 **Bridge Inn** Llanfoist (01873 853045). Bass, Flowers and Brains real ales are served at this popular pub. Bar food is available *lunchtimes and evenings, all day Sat, Sun & Tue.* Barbeques are held in the beer garden *Sun only in summer.*

🍺 **Llanfoist Inn** Llanfoist (01873 852754). Courage real ale and food served *lunchtimes and evenings, all day in summer.*

🍺 **Bridge End** Govilon (01873 830177). Below the aqueduct. A cosy, well-kept pub where you can enjoy Bass, Boddingtons and Worthington real ales. Food available *lunchtimes and evenings, not Mon.* Patio, children welcome. Boules court.

There are many pubs and restaurants in Abergavenny.

● **Llanover**
Monmouth. PO, tel, garage. The famous bell Big Ben in Westminster was named after the politician Benjamin Hall (Lord Llanover) who was responsible for the construction of the tower whilst Chief Commissioner of Works. He also initiated the tramway from Buckland House Wharf to Rhymney Ironworks, east of Talybont reservoir.

● **Llanellen**
Monmouth. PO, tel, stores. Although modern housing has greatly extended Llanellen into a suburb of Abergavenny, it is still an attractive village.

● **Llanfoist**
Monmouth. PO, tel, stores. The boatyard, housed in the old stone wharf buildings, has given this area of the waterway a new lease of life. There is a good walk from the boathouse into the mountains, following the course of the old tramway.

● **Abergavenny**
Monmouth. MD Tue. All services. Abergavenny lies beside the fast flowing River Usk, surrounded on all sides by mountains and hills; the Sugar Loaf, Blorenge and the Skirrids overlook the town. There is an annual event held at the end of March which involves the ascent of three peaks in one day.
Abergavenny Tourist Information Centre The Bus Station, Swan Meadow, Monmouth Road (01873 857588). *Open Apr–Oct, daily 10.00–18.00; Nov–Mar, 09.30-16.30.*
Abergavenny Museum and Castle Castle Street, Abergavenny (01873 854282). The mound of the castle dominates the town. Built in the 11thC, the castle now houses the museum which presents the story of the market town from prehistoric times to the present day. *Open Mar–Apr, Mon–Sat 11.00–13.00 and 14.00–17.00, Sun 14.00–17.00; Nov–Feb, closed at 16.00 and all day Sun.* Charge. Children free when accompanied by an adult.
St Mary's Church Originally the chapel of the Benedictine priory, the church was extensively rebuilt in the 14thC. It contains a fine carving of Jesse, hewn from a single oak trunk.
Abergavenny Leisure Centre Old Hereford Road (01873 857444).
Sugar Loaf A conspicuous landmark 2 miles north west of Abergavenny, so named because of its shape. The National Trust owns 2130 acres, including the 1955ft summit.

● **Govilon**
Monmouth. PO, tel, stores, garage. Beside the aqueduct are steps leading down to Govilon, little of which can be seen from the canal.

Boatyards

Ⓑ **Beacon Park Boats** The Boathouse, Llanfoist, Abergavenny (01873 858277). Narrow boat hire, day hire craft.

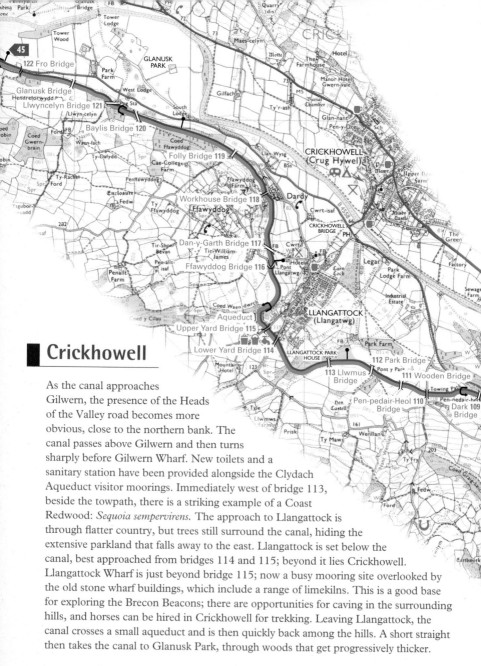

Crickhowell

As the canal approaches
Gilwern, the presence of the Heads
of the Valley road becomes more
obvious, close to the northern bank. The
canal passes above Gilwern and then turns
sharply before Gilwern Wharf. New toilets and a
sanitary station have been provided alongside the Clydach
Aqueduct visitor moorings. Immediately west of bridge 113,
beside the towpath, there is a striking example of a Coast
Redwood: *Sequoia sempervirens*. The approach to Llangattock is
through flatter country, but trees still surround the canal, hiding the
extensive parkland that falls away to the east. Llangattock is set below the
canal, best approached from bridges 114 and 115; beyond it lies Crickhowell.
Llangattock Wharf is just beyond bridge 115; now a busy mooring site overlooked by
the old stone wharf buildings, which include a range of limekilns. This is a good base
for exploring the Brecon Beacons; there are opportunities for caving in the surrounding
hills, and horses can be hired in Crickhowell for trekking. Leaving Llangattock, the
canal crosses a small aqueduct and is then quickly back among the hills. A short straight
then takes the canal to Glanusk Park, through woods that get progressively thicker.

Boatyards

Ⓑ **Castle Narrowboats** Church Road Wharf,
Gilwern (01873 830001). 🛁 🪣 Pump-out,
narrow boat hire, books, maps and gifts.
Ⓑ **Road House Narrowboats** 50 Main Road,

Gilwern (01873 830240). Pump-out, gas,
narrow boat hire, engine and boat repairs, boat
fitting-out, chandlery, books, maps, gifts. *24
hour* emergency call-out.

● **Gilwern**
Monmouth. PO, tel, stores. The village is built along one main street which falls steeply away from the canal. There is a useful, well stocked, gift shop across the road at bridge 103.

● **Llangattock**
Powys. PO, tel, stores. This little village, just down the lane from bridge 116, was once famous for its weaving and its limekilns. It also has a 12th-C church, founded in the 6thC. The hills behind the village are riddled with limestone caves and quarries.

● **Crickhowell**
Powys. MD Thu. PO, tel, stores, butcher, garage, bank, fish & chips. The road down through Llangattock leads to the 13-arch medieval

stone bridge over the Usk. In the centre of the town are the scant remains of the Norman castle. Apart from hill walking, there are opportunities for fishing and pony trekking.

Tourist Information Centre Beaufort Chambers, Crickhowell (01873 812105). *Open Apr-Oct, 09.00-17.00.*

Tretower Court and Castle (01874 730279). Three miles north west of Crickhowell on A479. Ruins of a late 15th-C fortified manor house, which was built to replace a Norman castle whose remains still exist nearby. An ornamental garden was created in 1991. *Open Mar-Oct, daily at 10.00. Closing time varies between 16.00 & 18.00.* Charge.

Pubs and Restaurants

⬤ **Beaufort Arms** Gilwern (01873 832235). Downhill from bridge 103. Flowers and Marston's real ale and food *lunchtimes and evenings.*

⬤ **Bridgend** Gilwern (01873 830939). Canalside at bridge 103. Felinfoel, Wadworth and Young's real ales. Food *lunchtimes and evenings in season.* Garden, children welcome.

⬤ **Corn Exchange** Gilwern (01873 830337). Worthington, Bass and guest real ales. Food *lunchtimes and evenings.* Outside seating, children welcome.

⬤ **Navigation** Gilwern (01873 830213). Canalside at bridge 103. A fine canalside beer garden and children's play area make this a good place to stop. Brains and Morland real ales. Food *lunchtimes and evenings.*

⬤ ✕ **Bridgend Inn** Crickhowell (01873 810338). Well worth the one mile walk from either bridge 114 or 116. Bass and Hancock's real ales and good food *lunchtimes and evenings.* Riverside garden. B & B.

⬤ **Old Rectory Hotel** Llangattock, Crickhowell (01873 810373). ¼ mile east of either bridges 116 or 117. *Open 7 days a week* for breakfast, lunch and evening meals; teas and coffees. Showers by negotiation.

⬤ ✕ **Bear Hotel** Crickhowell (01873 810408). The Bear has won many awards for its excellent food. Bass, Ruddles and John Smith's real ales. Food in the bar and restaurant *lunchtimes and evenings. Restaurant closed Sun.* Children's room, outside seating and B & B.

⬤ **White Hart Inn** Brecon Road, Crickhowell (01873 810473). Bass, Brains, Hancock's and guest real ales served in this friendly roadside local, once a toll house. Good food (including local dishes) available *lunchtimes and evenings.* Outside seating and pub games. Camping. *Open all day Sat.*

⬤ **Horse Shoe** Llangattock (01873 810393). 200yds from bridge 114 or 115. Bass real ale. Food *lunchtimes and evenings in season.*

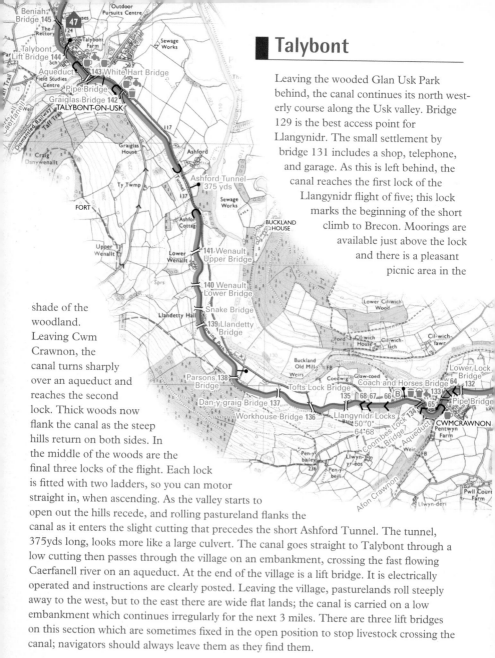

Talybont

Leaving the wooded Glan Usk Park behind, the canal continues its north westerly course along the Usk valley. Bridge 129 is the best access point for Llangynidr. The small settlement by bridge 131 includes a shop, telephone, and garage. As this is left behind, the canal reaches the first lock of the Llangynidr flight of five; this lock marks the beginning of the short climb to Brecon. Moorings are available just above the lock and there is a pleasant picnic area in the shade of the woodland. Leaving Cwm Crawnon, the canal turns sharply over an aqueduct and reaches the second lock. Thick woods now flank the canal as the steep hills return on both sides. In the middle of the woods are the final three locks of the flight. Each lock is fitted with two ladders, so you can motor straight in, when ascending. As the valley starts to open out the hills recede, and rolling pastureland flanks the canal as it enters the slight cutting that precedes the short Ashford Tunnel. The tunnel, 375yds long, looks more like a large culvert. The canal goes straight to Talybont through a low cutting then passes through the village on an embankment, crossing the fast flowing Caerfanell river on an aqueduct. At the end of the village is a lift bridge. It is electrically operated and instructions are clearly posted. Leaving the village, pasturelands roll steeply away to the west, but to the east there are wide flat lands; the canal is carried on a low embankment which continues irregularly for the next 3 miles. There are three lift bridges on this section which are sometimes fixed in the open position to stop livestock crossing the canal; navigators should always leave them as they find them.

Boatyards

Ⓑ **Country Craft Narrowboat Holidays** Cwm Crawnon Warehouse, Llangynidr (01874 730850). Weekly narrow boat hire and short breaks.

Ⓑ **Brecon Boats** Travellers' Rest, Talybont-on-Usk (01874 676401). Day boats with cabins seating up to five. Booking advised.

NAVIGATIONAL NOTES

Llangynidr locks should be left empty with the bottom gates open.

- **Llangynidr**
  Powys. PO, tel, stores (open every day). New housing now sprawls up the hillside, linking the upper and lower parts of the village. There is a splendid stone bridge c.1600 which spans the Usk and a pretty 19th-C church.
- **Cwm Crawnon**
  Powys. Clustered round the canal as it climbs the Llangynidr locks, this hamlet is famous for the Coach & Horses, an attractive pub and restaurant.
- **Talybont-on-Usk**
  Powys. PO, tel, stores (open 08.00–13.00 & 14.00–17.30, Sun 08.00–13.00). When the railway and canal were both operating commercially, Talybont must have been a busy village. Today it is a quiet holiday centre with facilities

for fishing, pony trekking, mountain biking and hill walking, details of which can be obtained at the Talybont Venture Centre in the village. There is a useful stores and PO at bridge 144, selling groceries and gas, which also serves as an off-licence. The village also has an impressive line-up of three pubs. The leat to the old mill brought water from Afon Caerfanell which falls rapidly from Talybont reservoir in the hills to the south to join the Usk. The large wharf overlooks the village, which is clustered round the Caerfanell Aqueduct.
Talybont Venture Centre The Old Shop, Talybont-on-Usk (01874 676458). Mountain bikes, caving, abseiling, canoeing, group activities. Shop *open summer 09.30–17.30 (closed all day Tue and Wed am); winter open weekends only.* Activities may be booked by telephone.

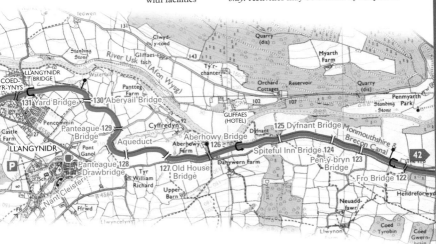

Pubs and Restaurants

🍴✕ **Red Lion** Llangynidr (01874 730223). Hancock's, Felinfoel, John Smith's and Worthington real ales. Food *lunchtimes and evenings (not Mon & Tue lunchtimes).* Garden. B & B.

🍴✕ **Coach & Horses** Cwm Crawnon. Llangynidr (01874 730245). Canalside at bridge 133. Morland, Bass and Hancock's real ales. Interesting and well-priced menu, available *all day.* Garden.

🍴 **Travellers Rest** Talybont (01874 676233). Canalside pub at bridge 142 offering five real ales and a good choice of bar food *lunchtimes and evenings. Restaurant open every evening and Sat & Sun lunchtimes.* Vegetarians and vegans

catered for. Children welcome. Garden. Camping and B & B.

🍴 **White Hart** Talybont (01874 676227). Canalside at bridge 143. Banks's, Camerons, Marston's, Morrells and two guest real ales and food, including vegetarian, are served in the bar and dining room *lunchtimes and evenings.* Children welcome. Garden. B & B. Take-away food.

🍴 **Star Inn** Talybont (01874 676635). Canalside by the aqueduct. A pub for real ale enthusiasts. Now recovered from disastrous flooding in 1994, this pub offers 12 real ales and good pub food *lunchtimes and evenings, all day Sat.* Live music *Wed.* Garden. Children welcome. B & B. Camping. *Open all day Sat.*

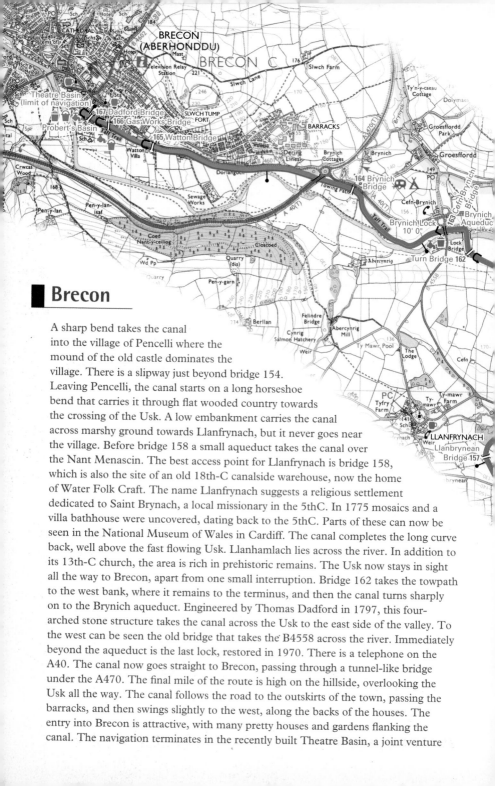

Brecon

A sharp bend takes the canal into the village of Pencelli where the mound of the old castle dominates the village. There is a slipway just beyond bridge 154. Leaving Pencelli, the canal starts on a long horseshoe bend that carries it through flat wooded country towards the crossing of the Usk. A low embankment carries the canal across marshy ground towards Llanfrynach, but it never goes near the village. Before bridge 158 a small aqueduct takes the canal over the Nant Menascin. The best access point for Llanfrynach is bridge 158, which is also the site of an old 18th-C canalside warehouse, now the home of Water Folk Craft. The name Llanfrynach suggests a religious settlement dedicated to Saint Brynach, a local missionary in the 5thC. In 1775 mosaics and a villa bathhouse were uncovered, dating back to the 5thC. Parts of these can now be seen in the National Museum of Wales in Cardiff. The canal completes the long curve back, well above the fast flowing Usk. Llanhamlach lies across the river. In addition to its 13th-C church, the area is rich in prehistoric remains. The Usk now stays in sight all the way to Brecon, apart from one small interruption. Bridge 162 takes the towpath to the west bank, where it remains to the terminus, and then the canal turns sharply on to the Brynich aqueduct. Engineered by Thomas Dadford in 1797, this four-arched stone structure takes the canal across the Usk to the east side of the valley. To the west can be seen the old bridge that takes the B4558 across the river. Immediately beyond the aqueduct is the last lock, restored in 1970. There is a telephone on the A40. The canal now goes straight to Brecon, passing through a tunnel-like bridge under the A470. The final mile of the route is high on the hillside, overlooking the Usk all the way. The canal follows the road to the outskirts of the town, passing the barracks, and then swings slightly to the west, along the backs of the houses. The entry into Brecon is attractive, with many pretty houses and gardens flanking the canal. The navigation terminates in the recently built Theatre Basin, a joint venture by local bodies which has resulted in attracting grants worth £6 million from the Welsh Office and Welsh Arts Council and a further £2.5 million from the private sector. The first phase of the development has seen the partial rebuilding of the Brecknock Boat Company Wharf, filled in in 1881. A new canal bridge named after Thomas Dadford has also been constructed, giving access to the Theatre Basin. The basin provides mooring for 40 boats as well as a welcome turning area.

Pubs and Restaurants

🍺 **White Swan**, Llanfrynach (01874 665276). A well-kept pub dating back some 300 years. Brains and Flowers real ales are served along with well-priced, imaginative food *lunchtimes and evenings. Pub closed Mon except for B. Hols.*

🍺 **Royal Oak** Pencelli (01874 665396). Canalside at bridge 153. Hancock's, Flowers and guest real ales served in this traditional village local. Home-cooked food available *lunchtimes and evenings during the summer*

There are many pubs and restaurants in Brecon, including:

🍺 **George Hotel** George Street, Brecon (01874 623421). A popular establishment serving Greene King, Burton, Morland and Tetley real ales from its 17th-C bars. Appetising bar food available *lunchtimes and evenings. Open all day.* B&B.

🍺 **Old Boar's Head** 14 Ship Street, Brecon (01874 622856). Everards, Fuller's, Thwaites and guest real ales are available in this friendly, old pub overlooking the river. Bar food *lunchtimes only.* Outside seating and pub games. *Open all day Fri & Sat.*

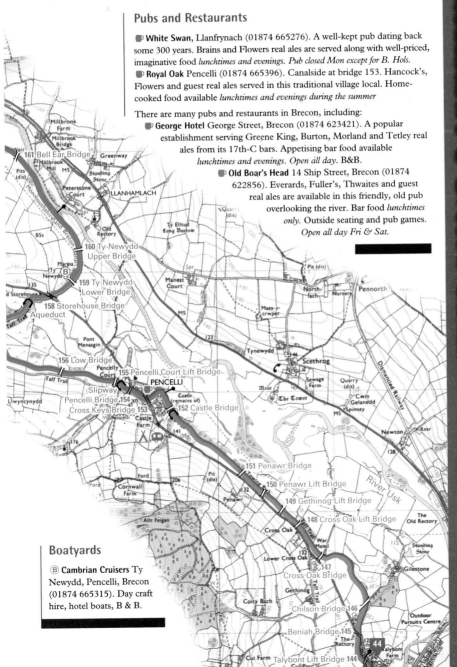

Boatyards

Ⓑ **Cambrian Cruisers** Ty Newydd, Pencelli, Brecon (01874 665315). Day craft hire, hotel boats, B & B.

Pencelli

Powys. This little village was at one time the head of a medieval lordship: but the only indication of this today is the castle mound. The castle farm occupies the site of the old castle which can now only be recognised by the footings of some of the walls laid down in the 13thC. The castle is not open to the public.

Llanfrynach

Powys. An attractive village built in a square round the pretty church. Nearby is the site of a Roman bathhouse.

Water Folk Canal Centre Old Storehouse, Llanfrynach (01874 665382). Horse-drawn boat trips (see below). Canal museum and craft shop, tea room and garden. *Open daily 10.00–17.30 (closed Fri).* Charge.

Brecon

Powys. MD Tue Fri. PO, tel, stores, garage, bank, cinema, swimming pool. Built at the confluence of the Usk and Honddu rivers, Brecon has long been the administrative centre and market town for the Breconshire uplands. It dates back to the Roman period, and although little remains, the narrow streets that surround the castle give an idea of medieval Brecon. Today the town is famous as a touring centre and for its annual Jazz Festival which takes the town by storm every August. The cathedral and generous 18th-C architecture make it seem more English than Welsh. The Usk waterfront is especially attractive, dominated by the old stone bridge. Sarah Siddons and her brother Charles Kemble lived in the High Street.

Brecon Cathedral Originally the Priory Church of St John, founded by Bernard Newmarch, it was given cathedral status in 1923. Most of the building is 13th-C, although the nave is a century later. There is some fine glass, and side chapels dedicated to various medieval guilds.

Brecon Cathedral New Heritage Centre (01874 625222). Situated in the beautiful Cathedral Close the centre houses an exhibition on cathedral life alongside a restored 16th-C tithe barn. Restaurant, morning coffees, afternoon teas. *Open Easter–mid Dec, daily except Sun.* Lunch served *12.30–14.00.* Charge.

Brecon Castle Most of the remains of the 11th-C castle now stand in the grounds of the Brecon Hotel and permission to view must be obtained from the hotel. A large motte and bailey, parts of the walls and two towers survive. The destruction of the castle during the Civil War was hastened by the inhabitants of Brecon, who did not want either side to occupy it.

Brecknock Museum Glamorgan Street, Brecon (01874 624121). The collections include local history, natural history and a large archaeology section, from pre-Roman to medieval times. The museum also houses a fine collection of Welsh lovespoons. *Open Apr–Sep, Mon–Fri 10.00–17.00, Sat 10.00–13.00 & 14.00–17.00, Sun 12.00–17.00.* Free.

Museum of the South Wales Borderers and the Monmouthshire Regiment The Barracks, Brecon (01874 613310). History of two famous regiments over 280 years. *Open Apr–Sep, daily 09.00–17.00 & Oct–Mar, Mon–Fri. Last admission 16.15.*

Theatre Brycheiniog Theatre Basin, Brecon (01874 611622). A newly constructed theatre, host to a rich diversity of touring drama and music, overlooking the canal terminus. Also café, bar and ice-creams.

Tourist Information Centre Market Car Park, Brecon (01874 622485). *Open summer 10.00–18.00; winter 09.00–17.00.*

National Parks Information Market Car Park, Brecon (01874 623156). *Open Apr–Oct, 09.30–17.30.*

BOAT TRIPS

Water Folk Canal Centre Old Storehouse, Llanfrynach (01874 665382 & 01874 611722). Horse-drawn boat trips *Easter–Oct, Wed, Sat & Sun 12.00 & 15.00; also every day during August.*

Dragonfly Cruises, Canal Wharf, Brecon (07831 685222). 2½ hour canal boat trip including a lock and an aqueduct. *Easter–Oct, Sat, Sun & Wed; Jul, Thu; Aug, Tue, Thu & Fri. Telephone for times.*

BRECON BEACONS NATIONAL PARK

The park covers 519 square miles of mountain and hill country, embracing parts of the old counties of Herefordshire, Monmouthshire, Breconshire and Carmarthenshire. The Park includes three nature reserves, a forest reserve, opportunities for fishing, caving, pony trekking, sailing and boating, and several towns of interest to tourists, notably Brecon, Crickhowell, Talgarth and Hay-on-Wye. Virtually all the canal is within the park – a factor that greatly strengthened the case for its restoration and reopening. The canal is an excellent introduction to the park, crossing it roughly from south east to north west; in several places there are foot and bridle paths leading away into the mountains from the towpath. A good place to start any exploration is the Mountain Centre, 1000ft up on Mynydd Illtud, above the village of Libanus, 5 miles south west of Brecon. There are rest and refreshment rooms, car parks and picnic sites overlooking the Brecon Beacons.

MONTGOMERY CANAL

MAXIMUM DIMENSIONS

Length: 72'
Beam: 6' 10"
Headroom: 7'
Draught: 2'

MANAGER
01244 390372

MILEAGE

FRANKTON JUNCTION to
Carreghofa: 11 1/2 miles
Welshpool: 21 1/2 miles
Garthmyl: 27 3/4 miles
ABERBECHAN: 32 1/2 miles

Locks: 25 (to Freestone Lock)

RESTORATION

The future of the Montgomery Canal as a navigable waterway now seems secure. A snapshot of the restoration programme, as we go to press, is as follows:
From Frankton through Queens Head and as far as Parkmill Bridge: should be open;
Parkmill Bridge to Gronwyn Bridge: end of 2000;
Short section at Maesbury: open;
Burgedin to Berriew, including Welshpool: open;
Remaining section: under discussion.
If you are planning to navigate this beautiful canal, telephone British Waterways to check the current situation.

The Montgomery Canal has much to offer walkers and boaters alike, with its characteristic rurality and peacefulness. It is both rich in wildlife and in reminders of its industrial past. The villages dotted along the canal are mostly quiet and picturesque self-contained communities with pleasant country pubs, in which boaters and walkers can relax and explore. Welshpool is a good shopping centre and, of course, the impressive Powis Castle is well worth visiting.

The initial development of this canal was sparked by the publication of the plans for the Ellesmere Canal, which inspired a separate company to plan a canal from Newtown northwards to join the Llanymynech branch of the Ellesmere Canal at Carreghofa. The canal was authorised in 1793, and by 1797 the line was open from Carreghofa to Garthmyl. The Montgomery Canal was mainly agricultural; apart from the limestone, it existed to serve the farms and villages through which it passed, and so was never really profitable. The lack of capital and income greatly delayed the completion of the western extension to Newtown, which was not finally opened until 1821, having been financed by a separate company. So what eventually became known as the Montgomery Canal was in fact built by three separate companies over a period of 30 years. The downfall of the canal became inevitable with the 1914–18 war when a pattern of regular and heavy losses started, from which the company was never able to recover. In 1921 the company gave up canal carrying and sold most of its boats to private operators. Locks began to close at weekends and standards of maintenance began to slip. From 1922 onwards many changes in the company ownership of the Shropshire Union Canal system began and, although the network remained open despite these changes, trade declined rapidly. Many traders were driven away by the lack of maintenance, which meant that most boats could only operate half full. In 1936 the breach of the Montgomery Canal at the Perry Aqueduct, just one mile south of Frankton Junction, precipitated the eventual closure of the line. Although the company set out to repair the damage they changed their minds, and with trade at a standstill there were no complaints. In 1944 an Act was passed making the closure official. The situation remained this way for many years, and with many road bridges lowered, it was thought that the waterway would fade away gracefully. But today the canal is dotted with restoration works, and considerable lengths are once again open to navigation. The distinctive paddle gear found on most locks was fitted by George Buck.

Frankton Junction

At Welsh Frankton, what was the original main line of the canal heads south towards Newtown, while the Llangollen Canal continues to the west (see page 26). Leaving the junction at Lower Frankton, the canal descends the four Frankton Locks – a staircase of two, and then two singles. At Lockgate bridge (71) there is a parking area encouraging walkers to visit the area, and moorings and a sanitary station are provided in a short remnant of the Weston Branch – the remainder is now a linear nature reserve. The canal then falls through the new Graham Palmer Lock and curves through open fields to Perry Aqueduct. During February 1936, a 40 yard breach occurred in the east bank, north of the aqueduct. This was the major factor in the closure of the canal and its eventual demise in 1944. The canal then passes the unnavigable Rednal Basin and Heath Houses, where there is a fine restored warehouse by the canal. Open arable farmland and woods then surround the navigation as it approaches Queen's Head, where there is a winding hole, moorings and a welcoming pub. The three Aston Locks, adjacent to Aston Nature Reserve, lower the canal as it approaches Llanymynech.

● Heath Houses

Shropshire. A few cottages surround the turn-over bridge, which takes the towpath to the east bank where it remains until Newtown. To the north a short unnavigable arm leads towards Rednal Basin. On 7 June 1865 a railway disaster occurred 600yds north of the canal on the Great Western line, which crossed over just east of bridge 74. A way gang were lifting the line and, as a warning to any oncoming trains, placed a green flag on top of a pole. A large excursion train consisting of thirty-two coaches and two brake vans hauled by two engines, failed to see this crude warning. The train speeded on until the working men were seen, but by this time it was too late to shut off steam. Four coaches were destroyed, eleven damaged and twelve people were killed.

● Queen's Head

Shropshire. Tel. A canalside settlement intersected by the old main road and the busy A5. The pub is a focal point for canal visitors, with the village spreading south eastwards from the bridge.

The towpath

Although the canal is not yet fully open to navigation, the towpath makes a fascinating walk. You will, however, have to cross main roads here and there, and make one or two short diversions, until the waterway is completely restored.

Pubs and Restaurants

● ✕ **Queen's Head** (01691 610255). A smart canalside pub with conservatory eating area, popular with motorists. Serves Theakston's and a guest real ale, and home-cooked bar and restaurant meals *lunchtimes & evenings every day*, with a vegetarian option. There is a garden, and children are welcome.

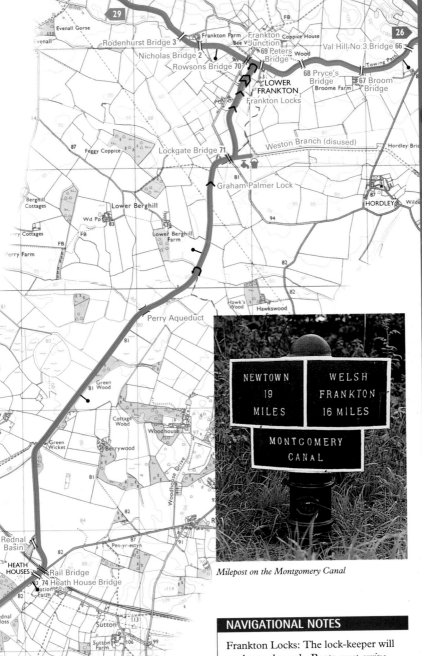

Milepost on the Montgomery Canal

Map labels:

29

Evenall Gorse
Evenall
Rodenhurst Bridge 3
Nicholas Bridge 2
Rowsons Bridge 70
FB
Frankton Farm
Frankton
Bee V'y
Coppice House
Junction
69 Peters
Bridge
Wood
Val Hill No.3 Bridge 66
Towing Path
LOWER
FRANKTON
Frankton Locks
68 Pryce's
Bridge
Broome Farm
67 Broom
Bridge
26

Feggy Coppice
Lockgate Bridge 71
Weston Branch (disused)
Hordley Bridge

81
Graham Palmer Lock

Berghill
Cottages
Lower Berghill
Wd Pp 83
87
HORDLEY
Wilde
erry Cottages
FB
FB
Lower Berghill
Farm
94
Perry Farm

82
Hawk's
Wood
Hawkswood
82

Perry Aqueduct
80
81

81
Green
Bl Wood

NEWTOWN
19
MILES

WELSH
FRANKTON
16 MILES

MONTGOMERY
CANAL

Decoy
Farm
86
Green
Wicket
Cottage
Wood
Woodhouse
97

81
Berrywood

82
84

Rednal
Basin
82
Pen-yr-estyn
91

HEATH
HOUSES
Rail Bridge
74 Heath House Bridge
Farm
82
113
Sutton
Sutton
Farm
106
99

Rednal
Moss

WEST FELTON CP
114
105

Twyford
90

NAVIGATIONAL NOTES

Frankton Locks: The lock-keeper will
see boats through. Boats *must arrive*
during the following times: *Mon-Fri
09.30-10.30 & 14.30-15.30, Sat
10.00-12.00, Sun 14.00-16.00. Do not
arrive late! During the winter stoppage
period please book with the Waterway
Office on 01691 622549.*

Llanymynech

The canal continues southwards – after Aston Locks the level remains constant for a while, the canal crossing fields on low embankments or through shallow cuttings. At Maesbury Marsh a fine crane, built by Ormerod & Crierson of Manchester and thought to be the only surviving example of a 15 cwt crane, stands opposite the pub and marks the wharf, carefully restored and used as a small cruiser base. Beyond here, at Gronwyn Bridge, the remains of the old tramway from Morda can be seen. Note the fine lime kilns by bridge 91, and the prominent chimney to the north, as the canal approaches Llanymynech. This marks the remains of a Warner Kiln, built in 1890 and which finally brought a virtual end to canal traffic. The waterway begins to meander as it approaches Pant.

Boatyards

Ⓑ **Maesbury Wharf Cruisers**
Maesbury Marsh, by bridge 79 (01691 670826 or 670849). Narrow boat hire or trips on two small canal boats. Picnic area, tea, coffee, souvenirs.

● **West Felton**
Shropshire. PO, tel, stores. A pleasant rural village which can be reached from Aston Locks.

● **Woolston**
Shropshire. A tiny collection of houses by St Winifred's Well.
St Winifred's Well A 7th-C princess, St Winifred was brought back to life by St Bueno after being decapitated by an angry suitor at Holywell in Flintshire. In the 12thC her body was brought to Shrewsbury from its grave in Denbighshire, and this well is said to mark a resting place on that journey, and where a spring miraculously appeared. It has been visited by pilgrims for centuries. The pretty timbered building has been restored by the Landmark Trust for holiday lets (01628 825925) so, when you visit, please *respect the privacy* of any visitors who may be staying in the cottage.

● **Maesbury Marsh**
Shropshire. PO, tel, stores, garage. A superb canal village clustered around the wharf and

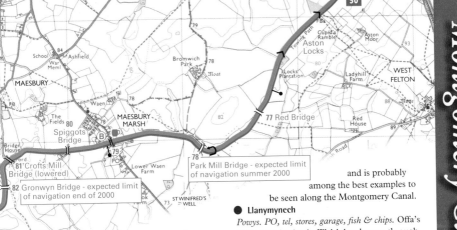

78 Park Mill Bridge - expected limit of navigation summer 2000

82 Gronwyn Bridge - expected limit of navigation end of 2000

and is probably among the best examples to be seen along the Montgomery Canal.

pub. The church is a curious white corrugated iron structure which appears to be well used.

● Llynclys

Shropshire. Tel. This village is drowned out by traffic on the A5, but the pub is just about close enough for those who leave the canal at Crickheath Wharf (bridge 85) and follow the footpath to the north west across farmland.

● Pant

Shropshire. PO, tel, stores, garage. The Pant grew up around the limestone quarries, one of the main reasons for the existence of the canal. The lime-kiln bank on the offside of the canal before bridge 91 has been excellently restored

● Llanymynech

Powys. PO, tel, stores, garage, fish & chips. Offa's Dyke and the Anglo-Welsh border run through the village, their line actually passing through the bar of the Lion Hotel; it is possible to drink with one foot in each country. The church, St Agatha's, is very interesting, a 19th-C French style Norman building with a lateral bell tower and huge clock face. Such Norman revival buildings were rare in the 19thC.

Llanymynech Heritage Area A short walk from the village along the towpath, this intriguing area is reached giving an insight to the industrial history and significance of Llanymynech in the production of limestone. There are some fine old kilns to be explored here.

Llanymynech Rocks Nature Reserve The limestone cliffs reach 500ft and the abandoned limestone quarry is now part of the nature reserve.

Pubs and Restaurants

The Punch Bowl Inn West Felton (01691 610201). A brisk walk from the towpath along the footpath which leaves Aston Locks to the south east. Banks's and other real ales, and there is a garden with a play area. Children welcome.

The Navigation Inn Maesbury Marsh (01691 672958). A warm and friendly pub in a listed canal warehouse, dating from 1796, and serving Flowers and Wadworth's real ale. The restored towpath bar features prints and photographs of canal life 1800-1976. Meals *lunchtimes Wed-Sat & evenings Tue-Sat,* with a vegetarian choice. Children welcome. Moorings.

White Lion Llynclys (01691 830357). Situated at the A438/B4396 crossroads. Meals are served *all day every day,* with a vegetarian option. Children are welcome. garden.

Cross Guns Inn Pant (01691 830821). At the northern end of the village. Marston's and Banks's real ale and bar meals, with a

vegetarian choice *lunchtimes & evenings every day.* Garden. Children welcome.

Dolphin Inn Llanymynech (01691 831078). Reached by crossing the stile past bridge 92 and walking through the car park to the street. Friendly and sociable pub serving Boddingtons real ale. Meals *lunchtimes & evenings every day,* with a vegetarian choice. Children welcome, garden. B & B.

The Bradford Arms Llanymynech (01691 830582). One regularly changing guest real ale, plus excellent food, including vegetarian, served at the bar, in the restaurant and in the conservatory *lunchtimes & evenings Tue–Sun.* Children are welcome. *Closed Mon.*

Lion Hotel Llanymynech (01691 830234). At the far end of the village, half in England, half in Wales. Bass real ale. Bar meals *lunchtimes & evenings every day (please book evening meals)* with a vegetarian option. Children are welcome. B & B.

Ardd-lin

The two locks at Carreghofa, in a beautiful setting, continue the descent, while the line of the old Tanat feeder can still be seen to the west of the road bridge which used to join the canal between the locks. The lock cottage here is inhabited. The toll house, built in 1825, has also been restored by volunteers and this makes a good resting place for walkers of the towpath and of Offa's Dyke, which follows the canal to the east here, after crossing at Llanymynech. South of the Vyrnwy Aqueduct a wooden crane stands beside a sturdy stone wharf building: the canal follows the course of the hills to the west, often running through woods in an embanked sidecutting. The canal continues south through rolling countryside, dominated by hills to the west, its position on the western side of the Severn. Before the two pretty Burgedin Locks further lower the canal, the disused Guilsfield Arm can be seen running away to the west. From the locks there are superb views of the Breiddan Hills to the east, and the Long Mountain, which reaches a height of 1338ft. Henry Tudor camped here in 1485, gathering strength for his battle against Richard III at Bosworth, in which Henry was victorious and took the English throne.

● **Vyrnwy Aqueduct**
Opened in 1796, the stone aqueduct across the river Vyrnwy is one of the canal's original features. Its building was fraught with problems; one arch collapsed during construction, and after completion subsidence distorted the whole structure, necessitating the addition of iron braces in 1823. The distortion also caused continual leakage problems; in 1971 repairs were undertaken to try yet again to stop the leaks, and further restoration has subsequently been carried out. To the north a long embankment precedes the aqueduct, partly of earth and partly of brick arches, which makes it altogether a much longer structure than it appears at first sight.

● **Offa's Dyke**
Offa's Dyke, which runs from Chepstow to Prestatyn, passes near the canal at several points in the area. Although the dyke is at times only fragmentary, its 168-mile course has been designated a long-distance public footpath. The dyke was constructed by Offa, King of Mercia, between 750 and 800AD to mark the boundary of Wales. The impressive structure consisted of a long mound of earth with a ditch on one side, though in parts it is hardly recognisable as such.

● **Four Crosses**
Powys. PO, tel, stores, garage. Main road village comprising old and new housing built around Offa's Dyke.

● **Guilsfield Arm**
This two-mile arm runs close to the village of Guilsfield and is reached by crossing the road just before bridge 104. It is now a nature reserve, providing a haven for wildlife.

● **Ardd-lin**
Powys. PO. A small settlement to the west of the canal.

Pubs and Restaurants

🍺 **Horseshoe Inn** Ardd-lin (01938 590318). Small and friendly village pub offering Bass, Wadworth's and Worthington real ale, along with bar meals *lunchtimes and evenings every day*, all prepared with fresh vegetables. Children are welcome, and there is a large secure play area with swings.

🍺 **Four Crosses Inn** Four Crosses (01691 830184). 400yds east of Clafton Bridge on the A483. A small village pub offering real ale, along with bar meals. Children are welcome, and there is a small garden with a secure children's play area.

🍺 **Golden Lion Hotel** Four Crosses (01691 830295). A short walk from the Four Crosses Inn. Banks's, Worthington and a guest real ale are available here, along with bar meals *lunchtimes & evenings every day.* Vegetarians are catered for, children are welcomed and there is a garden. B & B.

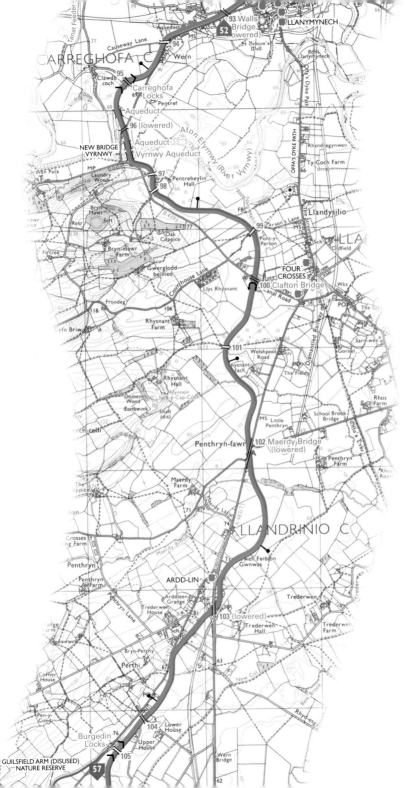

Pool Quay

Continuing south the canal clings to the steep hills to the west of the Severn Valley, often in a wooded side cutting. Four locks around the Pool Quay area and one in the centre of Welshpool begin the canal's rise towards Newtown. The stretch of canal between Pool Quay and Welshpool is known as the Prince of Wales length, restored by the Prince of Wales Trust and the Shropshire Union Canal Society. There are many reminders of the industrial history of the canal along here, especially at Pool Quay, once the highest navigable point on the Severn, and later a transhipment point between river and canal. The Wern corn mill remains, and the clay pit is now a nature reserve. Information boards interpret the former uses of the site. Between the lock south of bridge 111 and Abbey Bridge (112) Offa's Dyke long distance footpath follows the towpath. There is a cast-iron milepost halfway along this stretch, similar to the one south of bridge 110. These were placed by the Montgomery Waterway Restoration Trust in 1983 and 1984 respectively. Before Welshpool there are two draw bridges, Abbey Bridge (112) and Moors Farm Bridge (114). Immediately south of bridge 114 is the Moors Bird Collection.

The Wern

At the Red Bridge (106) there is parking and a picnic site with circular walks around the nature reserve, which was created in 1987. The water from the lock overflow and bypass weir once powered the corn mill here, an ingenious use of the otherwise wasted 25,000 gallons of water released each time the lock operated. The sump level (or bottom level) of the canal is at the Wern, and this meant that the water-powered mill was in an excellent position for receiving the surplus water. Only the foundations of the mill remain with a small pool and sluice visible. The information boards here show what the mill would have looked like. Today the overflow weir provides water for the small but pleasant nature reserve created on the site of the Wern clay pits. This was the major source of puddling clay used to line the canal.

Pool Quay

Powys. Tel. This was a former river port at the limit of viable merchant transport up the River Severn from Bristol. Travelling northwards toward Welshpool the white-washed lock keepers house, dating from 1820, is one of several interesting buildings here. Further along are the relics of buildings serving the grinding mills and maltings that were based in the village. The Powis Arms pub is well worth visiting – the beam in the bar was marked by navigators stranded here when the River Severn was in drought. An 18th-C red-brick warehouse stands nearby. Across the road is a now overgrown area beside the river, once known as Swan Wharf. This was a transhipment point where, amongst many other goods, fine oaks, which the area was once famous for, were stored prior to being loaded for carriage downstream to the naval dockyards at Bristol.

The Moors Bird Collection Moors Farm, Welshpool (01938 553395). Over 140 varieties of poultry, waterfowl, pheasants, sheep, goats and horses, including rare breeds such as pigmy goats, unusual waterfowl and parakeets. There is a pets corner, play area, picnic area and putting green. Access from bridge 114. *Open Easter–Oct, 10.30–17.30; closed Tue and Wed except in July & Aug.* Charge. No dogs.

Buttington

Powys. 1/2 mile east of bridge 115. The church is a medieval building, restored in 1876. The village has twice suffered from attempted invasions – in 894 by the Danish army which was evicted from here by King Alfred the Great, and in 1916 by a presumptuous German Zeppelin, whose crew mistakenly believed that the Welsh would offer less resistance than the English. Today the only air traffic floating overhead are the hot air balloons that regularly pass this area at sunset from Oswestry.

Buttington Wharf Just to the north of Buttington Bridge (115). A former kiln-bank, now a picnic site. The charging holes of the three kilns are still visible. The moorings here are good.

Breidden Hills

East of Buttington are the three impressive peaks of the Breidden Hills which dominate the flat landscape of the Shropshire Plain. The Breidden Crag (1324ft), increasingly defaced by quarrying, is best climbed from Criggion. An 18th-C pillar on the summit commemorates Admiral Rodney, who defeated a French fleet off Cape St Vincent, Dominica, in 1782. The excellent view from the summit across the Shropshire Plain highlights the meandering nature of the River Severn, particularly around the village of Melverley, which is constantly under threat of flood waters.

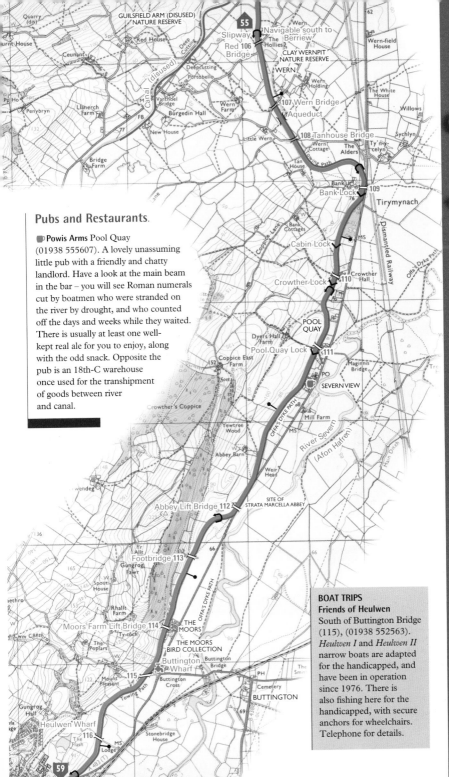

Pubs and Restaurants.

Powis Arms Pool Quay
(01938 555607). A lovely unassuming
little pub with a friendly and chatty
landlord. Have a look at the main beam
in the bar – you will see Roman numerals
cut by boatmen who were stranded on
the river by drought, and who counted
off the days and weeks while they waited.
There is usually at least one well-
kept real ale for you to enjoy, along
with the odd snack. Opposite the
pub is an 18th-C warehouse
once used for the transhipment
of goods between river
and canal.

BOAT TRIPS
Friends of Heulwen
South of Buttington Bridge
(115), (01938 552563).
Heulwen I and *Heulwen II*
narrow boats are adapted
for the handicapped, and
have been in operation
since 1976. There is
also fishing here for the
handicapped, with secure
anchors for wheelchairs.
Telephone for details.

Welshpool

As you enter Welshpool, there are few remains which give a hint of the importance of the canal to the town, for there were once lime kilns, dry docks and wharfs, a gas works and factories. Note the old Canal Agent's office by the museum. The town is a useful stop for boaters, with moorings and typical town centre facilities. The canal runs at the foot of the landscaped grounds of Powis Castle, flanked by the A483, and then dives under the new Whitehouse Bridge, edging away from the River Severn for a few miles. Four locks continue the rise towards Newtown, with two at Belan, recently restored, and then two singles north of Berriew. The stretch towards Brithdir is an excellent area for bird watchers, with sightings of a broad range of species from kingfishers to herons and, high in the sky, buzzards, which can be seen circling the hilltops. At Brithdir there is a nature reserve adjacent to the lock. Beyond this, the antiquated Luggy Aqueduct carries the canal towards Berriew.

● **Welshpool**

Powys. MD Mon. PO, tel, stores, garage, bank, station, cinema. The canal runs through the east of the town, passing attractive gardens and a traditional wharf and warehouse c.1880, now housing a museum (see below). The work of the Shropshire Union Canal Society and the Waterways Recovery Group contributed greatly to the improvement of this stretch of waterway and to the success of the reopening of part of the Montgomery Canal. There are excellent moorings here with three jetties and a slipway, south of bridge 118.

Powysland Museum and Montgomery Canal Centre Salop Road (01938 554656). Illustrates the archaeology, history and literature of the local area, and includes a canal exhibition. *Open summer, Mon-Tue & Thu-Fri 11.00-13.00 & 14.00-17.00, Sat & Sun 10.00-13.00 & 14.00-17.00; winter, Mon-Tue & Thu-Fri 11.00-13.00 & 14.00-17.00, Sat 14.00-17.00.* Free.

Powis Castle *NT property.* Access from High Street, Welshpool (information line – 01938 554336). The seat of the Earl of Powis, this impressive building has been continuously inhabited for over 500 years. It is a restored medieval castle with late 16th-C plasterwork and panelling, and has on display fine paintings, tapestries, early Georgian furniture and relics of Clive of India. The castle is in the centre of

beautiful 18th-C terraced gardens and a park. Programme of events, fine plant shop, excellent tea rooms. *Castle and museum open Easter-Jun, Sep & Oct, Wed-Sun 13.00-17.00; July & Aug, Tue-Sun 13.00-17.00; also B. Hols during season. Garden open same days as museum 11.00-18.00.* Charge.

The Flash Leisure Centre Salop Road, Welshpool (01938 555952). Swimming pool with a flume, bowls hall, fitness suite, sauna and sports hall. Café.

Tourist Information Centre At the Flash Leisure Centre, Welshpool, and reached by following the line of the towpath and crossing over bridge 117, 100yds along the A483 (01938 552043).

● **Welshpool & Llanfair Railway**

The Station, Llanfair Caereinion (01938 810441). This delightful narrow-gauge railway originally opened in 1903, and is now restored and run by enthusiasts. Telephone for train times.

● **Brithdir**

Powys A small main road settlement on the busy A483 with an isolated pub and scattered houses and farms. To the south is the Luggy Aqueduct, a small iron trough carrying the canal over the fast flowing Luggy Brook, built in 1819 by George Buck, who was also responsible for the distinctive paddle gear found at the majority of locks.

BOAT TRIPS & HIRE
Montgomery Canal Cruises Severn Street Wharf, Welshpool (01938 553271). A variety of public cruises are available in the trip boat *Maldwyn*, which can accommodate up to 42 passengers. Also private charter, with food and drink supplied if you wish. For short breaks Anglo-Welsh 4, 6 & 8-berth cruisers are based here, and there is also a 12-seater self-drive narrow boat for day hire.

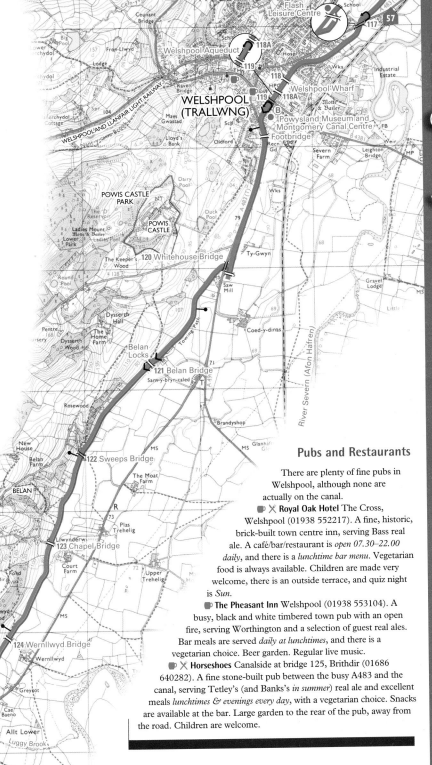

Pubs and Restaurants

There are plenty of fine pubs in
Welshpool, although none are
actually on the canal.

Royal Oak Hotel The Cross,
Welshpool (01938 552217). A fine, historic,
brick-built town centre inn, serving Bass real
ale. A café/bar/restaurant is *open 07.30–22.00
daily*, and there is a *lunchtime bar menu*. Vegetarian
food is always available. Children are made very
welcome, there is an outside terrace, and quiz night
is *Sun*.

The Pheasant Inn Welshpool (01938 553104). A
busy, black and white timbered town pub with an open
fire, serving Worthington and a selection of guest real ales.
Bar meals are served *daily at lunchtimes*, and there is a
vegetarian choice. Beer garden. Regular live music.

Horseshoes Canalside at bridge 125, Brithdir (01686
640282). A fine stone-built pub between the busy A483 and the
canal, serving Tetley's (and Banks's *in summer*) real ale and excellent
meals *lunchtimes & evenings every day*, with a vegetarian choice. Snacks
are available at the bar. Large garden to the rear of the pub, away from
the road. Children are welcome.

Berriew

Continuing south west, the canal runs through woods south of Berriew and then swings back towards the River Severn, as the valley is narrowed by the hills sweeping in from the east. The A483 follows the canal very closely. However, there are some fine glimpses of the River Severn between the tree-lined canal to the east and the rolling hillsides to the west, all covered with broad-leaved woodland. Two locks, at Berriew and Brynderwyn, continue the rise towards Newtown, lifting the canal above the level of the Severn, whose waters flow swiftly alongside from Tan-y-fron to Newtown. The two lock keeper's cottages are fine white-washed houses and at Brynderwyn, a former coal wharf, there is a late 19th-C warehouse still standing. Just past bridge 135 there is a llama paddock, at the base of the wooded hills to the east of the canal, looking decidedly out of place in the more traditional farmscape. It is part of Penllwyn Holiday Lodges, where a lake has been created, adjoining the cut. Several of the bridges beyond Tan-y-fron have their dates of construction cast into them; Glanhafren Bridge (143) was built in 1889 and is comparatively ornate with iron cast balustrades, and bridge 147 has elegant white iron railings displaying the date 1853 and Brymbo. Bridge 142 is one of the few remaining swing bridges on the canal.

● **Berriew**
Powys. PO, tel, stores, garage. The village of Berriew lies to the west, climbing the steep slopes of the fast-flowing river which cascades over rocks beneath the houses. In the centre of the village is a handsome 18th-C single span stone arch across the river; the black and white painted timber-framed and stone houses are ranged on either side. The village is undoubtedly picturesque, with a unity of style, and has been voted the Best Kept Village in Wales numerous times; but this has not spoilt it, for it is still quiet, pretty and self-contained. The church – a Victorian restoration of a medieval building, dedicated to St Bueno (who miraculously brought St Winifred back to life: see St Winifred's Well in the Llanymynech section) – is the centre point of the village, set attractively amongst trees. The vicarage is dated 1616. A two-arched brick aqueduct carries the canal over the beautiful wooded valley of the River Rhiw. Originally built of stone, the aqueduct was reconstructed in 1889 and although it appeared quite sound when the navigation was closed, the canal was piped across it, because of leakage, before the latest renovation work.

Andrew Logan Museum of Sculpture Berriew (01686 640689). Next to the Talbot Hotel by the river Rhiw. Works of popular poetry and metro-politan glamour by the founder, in 1972, of the Alternative Miss World Contest. Nature reserve of flora, fauna, 'planets and gods'. An enlivening and enriching experience. *Open May–Jun, Sep & Oct, Sat, Sun & B. Hols 14.00–18.00; July–Aug, Wed–Sun; Nov & Dec, Sun only; also Easter and B. Hol Mons.* Charge. Café and gift shop.

● **Garthmyl**
Powys. Tel. An old village beside the canal. The original wharf buildings can still be identified, looking rather incongruous as the wharf has long vanished. The concentration of remains, such as kiln banks, warehouses and a maltings, is probably due to the fact that the canal terminated here until the extension of the navigation between 1815 and 1821.

THE QUAY TO THE MARCHES
Prior to the building of the Montgomery Canal, the River Severn was a natural artery for trade, navigated above Shrewsbury as far as Pool Quay. Of course such river transport was unreliable, and low water levels would result in long delays. The beams in the Powis Arms were marked for every day the boatmen were stranded for lack of water.

It was from Swan Wharf, opposite the pub, that Montgomeryshire Oak was shipped downstream to the naval dockyards at Bristol. In 1712 the *Duchess*, owned by George Bradley, was transporting 40 ton loads to Bristol and back. Until the Montgomery & Ellesmere Canal linked with the main inland waterways network in 1833, Pool Quay remained an important transhipment point.

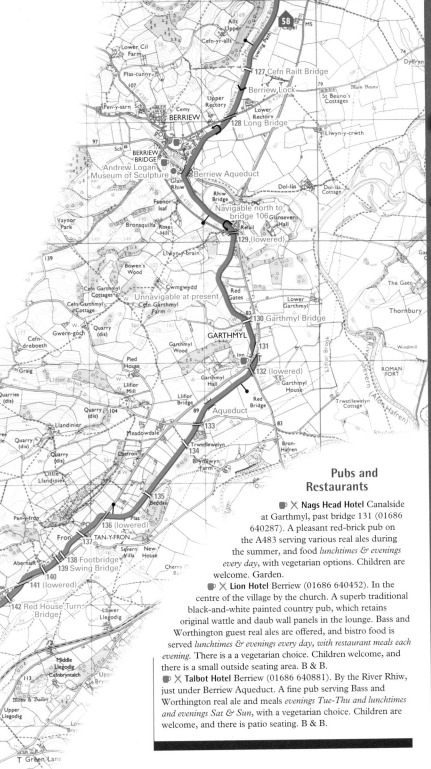

Pubs and Restaurants

🍺 ✕ **Nags Head Hotel** Canalside at Garthmyl, past bridge 131 (01686 640287). A pleasant red-brick pub on the A483 serving various real ales during the summer, and food *lunchtimes & evenings every day*, with vegetarian options. Children are welcome. Garden.

🍺 ✕ **Lion Hotel** Berriew (01686 640452). In the centre of the village by the church. A superb traditional black-and-white painted country pub, which retains original wattle and daub wall panels in the lounge. Bass and Worthington guest real ales are offered, and bistro food is served *lunchtimes & evenings every day, with restaurant meals each evening.* There is a a vegetarian choice. Children welcome, and there is a small outside seating area. B & B.

🍺 ✕ **Talbot Hotel** Berriew (01686 640881). By the River Rhiw, just under Berriew Aqueduct. A fine pub serving Bass and Worthington real ale and meals *evenings Tue-Thu and lunchtimes and evenings Sat & Sun,* with a vegetarian choice. Children are welcome, and there is patio seating. B & B.

Newtown

The canal continues south west towards Newtown along the wooded west side of the Severn valley. Canal and river flow side by side, the river providing the water for the canal via a feeder at Penarth and at one time by a pumping station at Newtown. Five single locks raise the canal to its summit level at Newtown. Aberbechan aqueduct is triple-arched and spans Bechan Brook, where there are the remains of a corn mill and maltings, hidden between the trees. Bridge 153 south of the aqueduct has the place and date of construction – Brymbo 1862 – cast into it. The canal is dry south of Freestone Lock and the course ends short of its original terminus. The once busy basin and the last half mile or so have vanished under a road, so the entry to Newtown must now be made on foot – it is a pleasant walk.

● **Abermule**
Powys. PO, tel, stores, garage. The best feature of the village is the iron bridge carrying the road jointly over the canal and the River Severn. After a plain girder bridge across the canal it develops into a beautiful elegant single-span arch leaping across the river. Into the curve of the arch are cast the words 'This second iron bridge constructed in the county of Montgomeryshire 1852'. By the PO there is a water-pump.

● **Newtown**
Powys. PO, tel, stores, garage, bank, station, cinema, market, leisure centre. Built around the Severn which sweeps through the town in a gentle curve. Prosperous as a woollen manufacturing town from the 18thC; the industry has now ceased. Its growth in the early 19thC

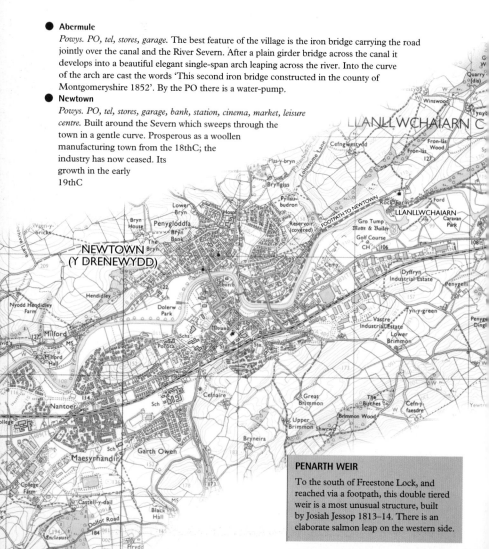

PENARTH WEIR

To the south of Freestone Lock, and reached via a footpath, this double tiered weir is a most unusual structure, built by Josiah Jessop 1813–14. There is an elaborate salmon leap on the western side.

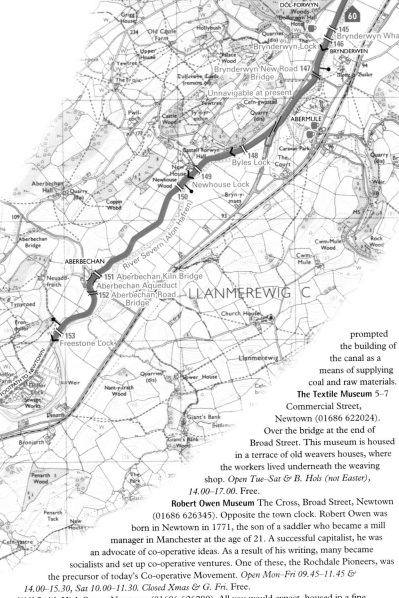

prompted
the building of
the canal as a
means of supplying
coal and raw materials.
The Textile Museum 5–7
Commercial Street,
Newtown (01686 622024).
Over the bridge at the end of
Broad Street. This museum is housed
in a terrace of old weavers houses, where
the workers lived underneath the weaving
shop. *Open Tue–Sat & B. Hols (not Easter),
14.00–17.00.* Free.

Robert Owen Museum The Cross, Broad Street, Newtown
(01686 626345). Opposite the town clock. Robert Owen was
born in Newtown in 1771, the son of a saddler who became a mill
manager in Manchester at the age of 21. A successful capitalist, he was
an advocate of co-operative ideas. As a result of his writing, many became
socialists and set up co-operative ventures. One of these, the Rochdale Pioneers, was
the precursor of today's Co-operative Movement. *Open Mon–Fri 09.45–11.45 &
14.00–15.30, Sat 10.00–11.30. Closed Xmas & G. Fri.* Free.

W H Smith High Street, Newtown (01686 626280). All you would expect, housed in a fine
recreation of the early shop, with a small museum upstairs.

Pubs and Restaurants

Access to Abermule village is via Brynderwyn
Bridge (147) and follow the road, turning
right at the roundabout, for about ¹/₂ mile.
🍺 **Abermule Hotel** Abermule (01686
630676). Friendly and traditional country
pub with an inglenook, serving Brains and

Worthington real ale. Food is served *all day
every day*, children are welcome, and there is
a beer garden.

There are plenty of pubs and hotels to be
found in Newtown.

SHROPSHIRE UNION CANAL

MAXIMUM DIMENSIONS

Autherley to Nantwich, and Middlewich Branch
Length: 72'
Beam: 7'
Headroom: 8'

Nantwich to Ellesmere Port
Length: 72'
Beam: 9'
Headroom: 8'

MANAGER
Autherley Junction to Audlem:
01785 284253
Audlem to Ellesmere Port and
the Middlewich Branch: 01244 390372

MILEAGE

AUTHERLEY JUNCTION (Staffordshire &
Worcestershire
Canal) to Norbury: 15½ miles
Market Drayton: 27 miles

HURLESTON JUNCTION (Llangollen
Canal): 40¾ miles
Barbridge Junction (Middlewich Branch): 42 miles
Chester Junction with Dee Branch: 58 miles

ELLESMERE PORT JUNCTION with
Manchester Ship Canal: 66½ miles
Locks: 47

Middlewich Branch
Middlewich (Trent & Mersey Canal) to
Barbridge Junction: 10 miles
Locks: 4

THE CHESTER CANAL

In 1772 an enabling Act was passed for a canal from the River Dee in Chester to join the Trent & Mersey Canal at Middlewich, with a spur to Nantwich. The building of the Trent & Mersey was the cause of this new venture, for it was seen as a threat to the future of the River Dee Navigation and the port of Chester. The new canal was designed to bolster Chester as an alternative port to Liverpool, and so was planned as a barge canal, with locks 80ft by 14ft 9in. Work started in Chester in the middle of 1772 and progressed slowly. There were engineering and financial problems, and the main line of the new canal was altered to terminate at a basin and warehouses just outside Nantwich: the proposed line to Middlewich was now to be a branch. The Nantwich–Chester link was completed in 1779, but the spur to Middlewich was not built until 54 years later. When the Nantwich–Chester Canal was finished, arguments with the Dee River Company delayed the building of the river lock. By this time competition with the Trent & Mersey was out of the question. Although regular freight and fast passenger services were run, the canal was wholly uneconomic and in 1787 the company collapsed. In 1790 it was revived and the canal repaired, for the directors saw the publication of the plans of the Ellesmere Canal as their last chance to complete the line to Middlewich.

THE BIRMINGHAM & LIVERPOOL JUNCTION CANAL

The future prosperity of the Ellesmere & Chester was limited by the lack of an outlet to the south, without which its trade could never be more than local. So the company was much cheered by the plans for the Birmingham & Liverpool Junction Canal which received its Act in 1825. The line from Nantwich to Autherley, on the Staffordshire & Worcestershire Canal, would give a direct link between Liverpool and the Midlands, and thus with the canal network as a whole. After serious engineering difficulties the canal was opened in 1835, shortly after the opening of the long-planned branch from the Chester Canal to the Trent & Mersey at Middlewich, providing access to Manchester and the Potteries. Railway competition was close at hand by this date, and so the Birmingham & Liverpool Junction and Ellesmere & Chester companies worked closely together to preserve their profits. Ellesmere Port was greatly enlarged, and by 1840 steam haulage was in use on the Wirral line and on the Mersey itself. In 1845 the two companies merged, and then shortly after were reformed as the Shropshire Union Railways & Canal Company.

THE SHROPSHIRE UNION CANAL

The Shropshire Union Railways & Canal Company was formed under the shadow of railway expansion. Its initial plans were to build railways instead of canals, on the principle that it would halve the construction costs to lay a railway along the bed of an existing canal. By 1849 this plan had been abandoned, for the slow development of railways in Wales had shown the company that canals could still be profitable. Throughout the mid 19th-C the Shropshire Union network remained profitable, and did not experience the steady decline of other major canal systems. The London & North Western Railway Company was a major shareholder in the Shropshire Union, and they were happy to let the canals remain as they provided the company with a significant tentacle into Great Western Railway territory. As a result the Shropshire Union was allowed to expand steadily; in 1870 the company owned 213 narrow boats, and in 1889 there were 395. By 1902 this fleet had increased to 450 boats. A few branches were threatened with closure on the grounds of unprofitability, but all remained open. The flourishing trade continued until World War I, which started a pattern of regular heavy losses from which the company was never able to recover. In 1921 the company gave up canal carrying, and sold most of its fleet of boats to private operators. Locks were closed at weekends, and standards of maintenance began to slip. In 1922 the Shropshire Union Company was bought out by the London & North Western Railway, which then was swallowed in turn by the newly-formed London Midland & Scottish Railway. Despite these changes the network remained open, although trade declined rapidly. Many traders were driven away by the lack of maintenance, which meant that most boats could only operate half empty. In 1936 a breach occurred on the Montgomery Canal one mile south of Frankton Junction; the company set out to repair the damage and then changed their minds. (The Weston line had been similarly abandoned after a breach in 1917.) With trade at a standstill there were no complaints, and in 1944 an Act was passed making closure official. This Act also officially abandoned 175 miles of the old Shropshire Union network. Out of this mass closure only the main line and the Middlewich Branch remained, although the Llangollen Branch (see page 17) luckily also escaped closure, being originally retained as a water supply channel. The Montgomery Canal also survives and is now the subject of an exciting restoration project (see page 49).

MEETING ONESELF COMING BACK

When first constructed the Shroppie relied very heavily on Belvide Reservoir – beside the A5 – for its supplies of water. In its original form the reservoir proved woefully inadequate and its capacity was doubled in 1836 to give a total of 70 million cubic metres of water. Thirty-four years later Barnhurst Sewerage Farm opened at Autherley Junction and, when it later became a treatment works, its entire discharge became available to feed both the Shroppie and the Staffs & Worcs Canal. Today there is rarely a problem of water shortage on the Shroppie, which can largely be attributed to the regular habits of the good people of Wolverhampton.

Autherley Junction

The Shropshire Union Canal leaves the Staffordshire & Worcestershire Canal at Autherley Junction, and runs straight along the side of the former Wolverhampton Aerodrome at Pendeford, now covered with houses. Passing the Wolverhampton Boat Club (visiting boaters welcome), the canal soon enters a short cutting, which is through rock and narrow in places. Emerging briefly into the green and quiet countryside that is found along the whole length of this navigation, the canal (having shrugged off the noisy intrusion of the M54 motorway) again plunges into a deep, long cutting that is typical of this particular stretch. The start of this length is beautifully framed by the arch of bridge 8, beguiling the boater into a tree-lined avenue. There are picnic sites by bridges 2 and 3.

NAVIGATIONAL NOTES

The canal is very narrow south of bridges 5 and 6, and between bridges 8 and 9.

● Autherley Junction

An important and busy canal junction, where in 1830 Thomas Telford brought his Birmingham & Liverpool Junction Canal (now part of the Shropshire Union system) to join the much older Staffordshire & Worcestershire Canal (built by James Brindley and opened in 1772). There is a former canal toll office here, also a boatyard and a boatclub. The stop lock has a fall of only about 6in: it was insisted upon by the Staffordshire & Worcestershire Company to prevent the newer canal stealing water from them. Autherley Junction is sometimes confused with Aldersley Junction, 1/2 mile to the south, where the Birmingham Canal Navigations join the Staffordshire & Worcestershire Canal from the east after falling through the Wolverhampton flight of 21 locks.

Boatyards

Ⓑ **Oxley Moor Stop** (Ron Lloyds Boatyard) The Wharf, Oxley Moor Road, Oxley, Wolverhampton (01902 789522). South of Autherley Junction on the Staffordshire & Worcestershire Canal. 🏠 🛈 ⚓ D Pump-out, gas, narrow boat hire, overnight and long-term mooring, winter storage, slipway, crane, boat sales, boat and engine repairs, dry dock, boat building, toilets, telephone, club.

Ⓑ **Water Travel** Autherley Junction, Oxley Moor Road, Wolverhampton (01902 782371). 🏠 🛈 ⚓ D E Pump-out, gas, narrow boat hire, overnight mooring, slipway, chandlery, provisions, books and maps, boat repairs, toilets, solid fuel, gifts. Emergency call-out.

Pubs and Restaurants

🍺 **Pendulum** Autherley (01902 623201). North west of Blaydon Road Bridge. Food *lunchtimes and evenings (not Sun)*. Rotating guest ale. Children and outside seating. Pub games. Safeway supermarket next door.

BOAT TRIPS

Nb. Stafford is a 42-seat boat operating public trips *on 1st Sun of the month* and booked charter trips. Telephone (01902) 789522 for further details.

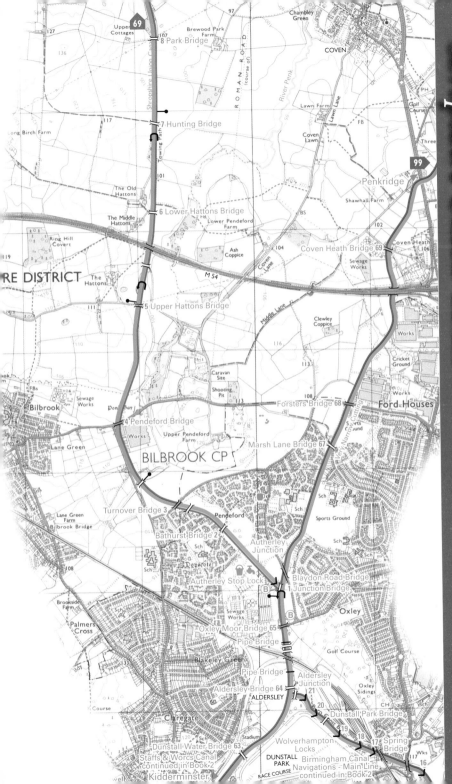

Shropshire Union Canal

Autherley Junction

Brewood

Dirty Lane Bridge 20
Tavern Bridge 19
71
WHEATON ASTON
LAPLEY
Wheaton Aston Lock
7'0"
Wheaton Aston Bridge 18
Sch
Brook House Farm

Leaving the balustraded Avenue Bridge (10), which leads westward to Chillington Hall, the canal curves in a bold cutting past the village of Brewood (moorings by bridge 14) and its attractive wharf – and moves north west along a very straight embankment. The head bank of the big Belvide Reservoir can be seen on the west side; its feeder stream enters the canal just south of Stretton Aqueduct. This solid but elegant cast iron structure carries the canal over the A5. Crossing the aqueduct by boat tends to give the canal traveller an air of great superiority over the teeming motorists below. After another long, wooded cutting the canal reaches Wheaton Aston Lock. This lock marks the end of the long pound from Autherley and the beginning of the 17-mile level that lasts almost to Market Drayton. Reasonably priced diesel can be obtained from Turners Garage by bridge 19, which also holds an amazing stock of boat and bicycle parts.

● **Brewood**
Staffs. PO, tel, stores, bank, takeaway, garage.
The name (pronounced Brood) derives from Celtic Bre, meaning hill, thus giving wood on the hill. It originally consisted of a Roman fort on Beacon Hill to defend Watling Street. Dean Street, below the church, is a gem with a great diversity of façades jostling for attention side by side. Most obvious are the tripartite windows of Dean Street House; although lower down the street are Old Smithy Cottages, built c.1350 and once a hall house open to the roof. The village church is a tall, elegant building which has been greatly restored but still contains a 16th-C font and several 16th-C effigies and 17th-C monuments commemorating the Giffard family of Chillington Hall. Speedwell Castle, on the market square, has a most strikingly ornate façade and is a delightful building (some would say folly) erected by an apothecary around 1740. He is reputed to have won handsomely on a horse named Speedwell and used his winnings to build this dwelling. The chemist shop, nearby, has an 18th-C exterior and in 1828 was the birthplace of Thomas Walker, an eminent Victorian engineer, who built the Severn railway tunnel. The entire market square is allegedly riddled with underground vaults and passages interconnecting Speedwell Castle with the pubs and hotels ringing the square.
Chillington Hall 1 1/2 miles west of the canal, south west of Brewood, this has been the home of the Giffard family since the 12thC. The existing hall was built in the 18thC, and the wooded park in which it stands was designed by

Capability Brown. *Open May–Aug, Thu afternoons.*
Belvide Reservoir A large nature reserve open to naturalists. The Royal Society for the Protection of Birds is developing the reserve to include displays and hides, enabling enthusiasts to have a greater opportunity to observe the many species of birds. There is only private club fishing and no sailing on the reservoir, so as to preserve the bird sanctuary.

● **Stretton**
Staffs. 1 mile north east of Stretton Aqueduct off the A5. The church was rebuilt in the 19thC but retains its original chancel and fragments of medieval glass in the east window.
Stretton Hall Built in 1620 to designs by Inigo Jones. Most interesting features are the vast fireplace with steps up to it for chimney sweep boys, and the remarkable staircase suspended by chains from the roof. The house is private.

● **Lapley**
Staffs. 3/4 mile north east of bridge 17. The central tower of the church dominates the village. It is an interesting building with fine Norman windows, an old Dutch font and traces of medieval paintings on the nave walls. The church as we see it now was completed in the 15thC.

● **Wheaton Aston**
Staffs. PO, tel, stores, butchers, baker, take-away, garage. Overrun by new housing. The village green around the church (rebuilt in 1857) is a memento of a more pleasant past. The garage beside the canal can repair boat engines and also sells chandlery. There is wheelchair access on both sides of the canal at bridge 19.

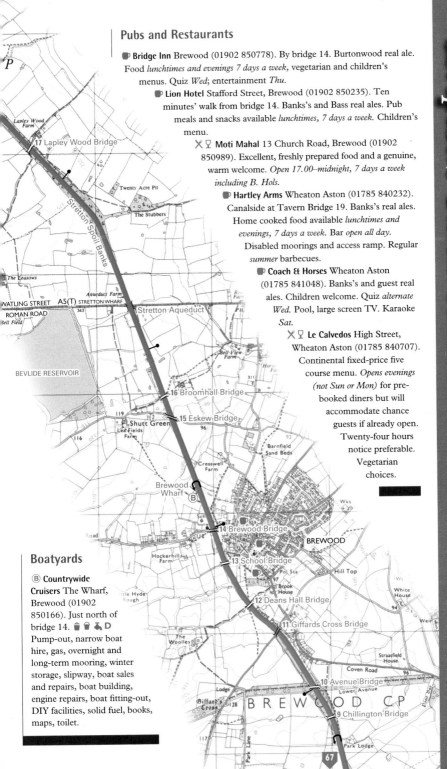

Pubs and Restaurants

⚓ **Bridge Inn** Brewood (01902 850778). By bridge 14. Burtonwood real ale. Food *lunchtimes and evenings 7 days a week*, vegetarian and children's menus. Quiz *Wed*; entertainment *Thu*.

⚓ **Lion Hotel** Stafford Street, Brewood (01902 850235). Ten minutes' walk from bridge 14. Banks's and Bass real ales. Pub meals and snacks available *lunchtimes, 7 days a week*. Children's menu.

✕ ♀ **Moti Mahal** 13 Church Road, Brewood (01902 850989). Excellent, freshly prepared food and a genuine, warm welcome. *Open 17.00–midnight, 7 days a week including B. Hols.*

⚓ **Hartley Arms** Wheaton Aston (01785 840232). Canalside at Tavern Bridge 19. Banks's real ales. Home cooked food available *lunchtimes and evenings, 7 days a week*. Bar *open all day*. Disabled moorings and access ramp. Regular *summer* barbecues.

⚓ **Coach & Horses** Wheaton Aston (01785 841048). Banks's and guest real ales. Children welcome. Quiz *alternate Wed*. Pool, large screen TV. Karaoke *Sat*.

✕ ♀ **Le Calvedos** High Street, Wheaton Aston (01785 840707). Continental fixed-price five course menu. *Opens evenings (not Sun or Mon)* for pre-booked diners but will accommodate chance guests if already open. Twenty-four hours notice preferable. Vegetarian choices.

Boatyards

ⓑ **Countrywide Cruisers** The Wharf, Brewood (01902 850166). Just north of bridge 14. 🚽 🚿 ⚒ D Pump-out, narrow boat hire, gas, overnight and long-term mooring, winter storage, slipway, boat sales and repairs, boat building, engine repairs, boat fitting-out, DIY facilities, solid fuel, books, maps, toilet.

Church Eaton

The canal now proceeds along the very long pound, alternately in cuttings and on embankments. Both offer interest: the cuttings for their rich vegetation, and the embankments for the excellent views over quiet, unspoilt grazing land.

Pubs and Restaurants

 X **Royal Oak** Church Eaton (01785 823078). Banks's, Marston's and Wadworth real ales served together with food *lunchtimes and evenings (not Sun evenings)*. Vegetarians and children catered for. Outside seating.
 Fox Marston (01785 840729). One mile south west of bridge 24. Country pub, indistinguishable from a private cottage with roses clambering up the walls, offering a wide range of real ales – at least six rotating guests. Food *lunchtimes (telephone to check – not Mon) and evenings (not Sun & Mon)*. Vegetarians and children catered for. Garden.

Cruising on the Shropshire Union Canal

● **Church Eaton**

Staffs. Tel. 1 mile north east of bridge 25. Parts of the old village remain, especially at the end of the village street in the vicinity of the fine church: St Editha's, a Norman structure with the spire added to the tower in the 15thC. The east window dates from about 1400 and almost fills the wall.

72

32 Cowley Bridge

31 Cowley Double Road Bridge

30 Castle Cutting Bridge

29 Wood Eaton Bridge

28 Oscote Barn Bridge

27 Park Bridge

26 Turnover Bridge

25 High Onn Bridge

24 Little Onn Bridge

23 Rye Hill Cutting Bridge

22 Rye Hill Bridge

21 Shushions Bridge

20 Dirty Lane Bridge

68

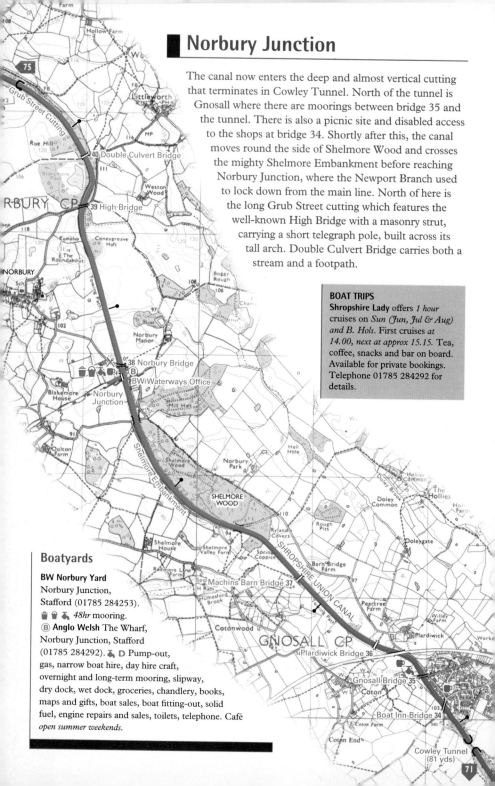

Norbury Junction

The canal now enters the deep and almost vertical cutting that terminates in Cowley Tunnel. North of the tunnel is Gnosall where there are moorings between bridge 35 and the tunnel. There is also a picnic site and disabled access to the shops at bridge 34. Shortly after this, the canal moves round the side of Shelmore Wood and crosses the mighty Shelmore Embankment before reaching Norbury Junction, where the Newport Branch used to lock down from the main line. North of here is the long Grub Street cutting which features the well-known High Bridge with a masonry strut, carrying a short telegraph pole, built across its tall arch. Double Culvert Bridge carries both a stream and a footpath.

BOAT TRIPS
Shropshire Lady offers *1 hour* cruises on *Sun (Jun, Jul & Aug)* and B. Hols. First cruises *at 14.00, next at approx 15.15.* Tea, coffee, snacks and bar on board. Available for private bookings. Telephone 01785 284292 for details.

Boatyards

BW Norbury Yard
Norbury Junction, Stafford (01785 284253). *48hr* mooring.
Ⓑ **Anglo Welsh** The Wharf, Norbury Junction, Stafford (01785 284292). D Pump-out, gas, narrow boat hire, day hire craft, overnight and long-term mooring, slipway, dry dock, wet dock, groceries, chandlery, books, maps and gifts, boat sales, boat fitting-out, solid fuel, engine repairs and sales, toilets, telephone. Café *open summer weekends.*

Cowley Tunnel

This short tunnel was originally intended to be much longer – 690yds – but most of it was opened out at an early stage during construction (in 1831) because of dangerous faults in the rock, and now only 81yds remain. The tunnel is unlined, and to the south of it a steep narrow cutting through solid rock stretches a considerable distance – an awe-inspiring sight.

Gnosall

Staffs. PO, tel, stores, off-licence, takeaways, garage. East of bridge 35. The main feature of interest in the village is the church of St Laurence, a mile east of the canal. It is a 15th-C building with original Norman tower arches. The east window has fine decorated tracery framing modern stained glass.

Shelmore Embankment

The construction of this great embankment, 1 mile long, just south of Norbury Junction, was the source of endless grief and expense to the Birmingham & Liverpool Junction Canal Company in general and to Thomas Telford, the engineer, in particular. It was an enormous task anyway to shift the millions of cubic feet of earth to build the bank; but while the contractors struggled to complete it, the bank slipped and collapsed time and again. By early 1834, Shelmore Embankment was the only unfinished section of the whole canal. It was not until 1835, after 5$1/2$ years' solid work on it and well after Telford's death, that the embankment was completed by William Cubitt and the B&LJ Canal was opened as a through route. There are flood gates at each end, to close off the channel in case of a breach. These were closed each night during World War II as a precaution against bombing.

Norbury Junction

This was once the outlet for the Shrewsbury, Newport and Trench branches on to the rest of the Shropshire Union Canal system. There was a long flight of locks from the junction down to Newport, but these are now closed, except for the top lock which is used as a dock.

Loynton Moss

This is a floating bog with an interesting plant community managed by Staffordshire Wildlife Trust (01889 508534). It can be accessed by a footpath immediately north of bridge 39 which links into a circular walk with interpretation boards. **Keep to the footpath** as the moss is potentially dangerous. There are viewpoints around the site.

Pubs and Restaurants

Boat Inn (01785 822208). Gnosall, by Bridge 34. Recently refurbished canalside pub currently serving Marston's real ale together with rolls and sandwiches. Garden, pub games and bar billiards.

Navigation Gnosall (01785 822327). Canalside, at bridge 35. Rotating guest real ales together with a range of food served in the restaurant and bar *lunchtimes and evenings, 7 days a week during summer.* Vegetarians and children catered for. Garden and play area. Disabled access and facilities.

Royal Oak Gnosall (01785 822362). In the village by the railway bridge. A basic bar, and a comfortable lounge, where you can enjoy Burton, Tetley and guest real ales. Food available *lunchtimes and evenings every day – carvery Sat evenings & Sun lunchtimes.* Children and vegetarians catered for. Garden and play area. Pub games.

Junction Inn Norbury (01785 284288). Canalside, at Norbury Junction. Superbly situated canal pub. Marston's, Banks's and guest real ales, food *lunchtimes and evenings.* Carvery *Sat evenings and Sun lunchtimes.* Good vegetarian selection. Beer garden and children's play area. Pub games. Shop in beer garden selling gifts, clothes and toys.

Measham Teapot Norbury Junction (01785 284292). Serving an inexpensive selection of home-made meals and snacks in an attractive waterside café with an interesting display of Measham teapots. Shropshire cream teas a speciality. *Open Easter–Sep, Sat & Sun.*

High Bridge, High Offley
(see page 72)

Shebdon

The canal moves out of Grub Street cutting, leaving behind the unusual double-arched bridge, containing a small telegraph pole, and, passing the village of High Offley on a hill to the north, continues in a north westerly direction through the quiet open farmland that always accompanies this canal. Along this stretch are two canalside pubs – both amaze the traveller by their very survival, situated as they are on quiet roads and an even quieter canal. The great Shebdon Embankment is heralded by an aqueduct; at the far end is a large ex-chocolate factory (now producing only dried milk), whose goods used to be carried to and from Bournville (on the Worcester & Birmingham Canal) by canal boat.

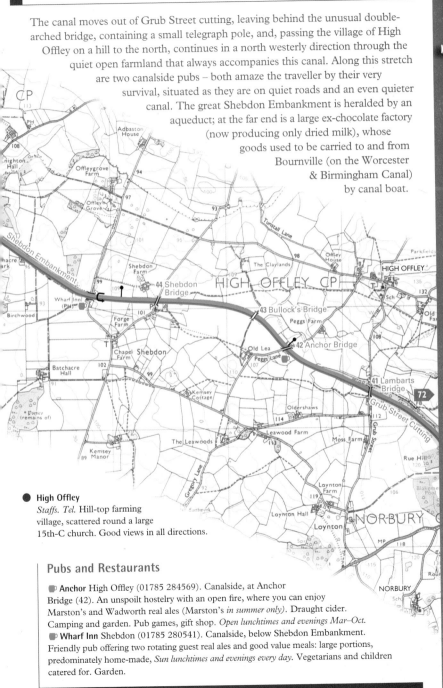

● **High Offley**
Staffs. Tel. Hill-top farming
village, scattered round a large
15th-C church. Good views in all directions.

Pubs and Restaurants

🍺 **Anchor** High Offley (01785 284569). Canalside, at Anchor Bridge (42). An unspoilt hostelry with an open fire, where you can enjoy Marston's and Wadworth real ales (Marston's *in summer only*). Draught cider. Camping and garden. Pub games, gift shop. *Open lunchtimes and evenings Mar–Oct.*
🍺 **Wharf Inn** Shebdon (01785 280541). Canalside, below Shebdon Embankment. Friendly pub offering two rotating guest real ales and good value meals: large portions, predominately home-made, *Sun lunchtimes and evenings every day.* Vegetarians and children catered for. Garden.

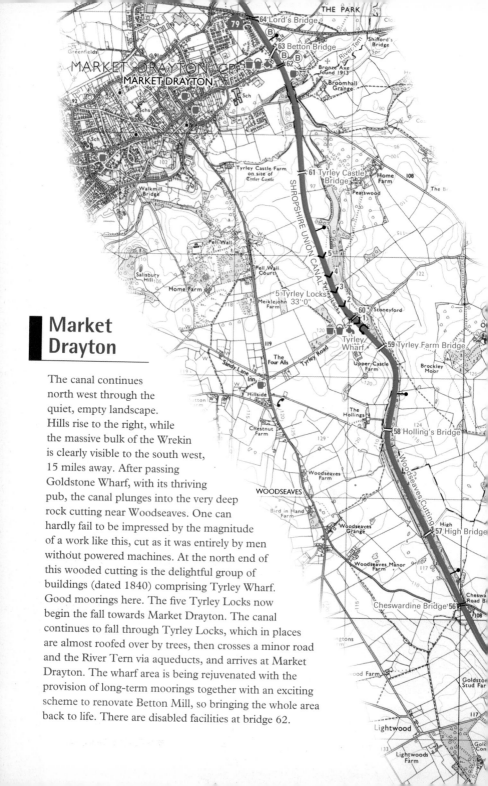

Market Drayton

The canal continues
north west through the
quiet, empty landscape.
Hills rise to the right, while
the massive bulk of the Wrekin
is clearly visible to the south west,
15 miles away. After passing
Goldstone Wharf, with its thriving
pub, the canal plunges into the very deep
rock cutting near Woodseaves. One can
hardly fail to be impressed by the magnitude
of a work like this, cut as it was entirely by men
without powered machines. At the north end of
this wooded cutting is the delightful group of
buildings (dated 1840) comprising Tyrley Wharf.
Good moorings here. The five Tyrley Locks now
begin the fall towards Market Drayton. The canal
continues to fall through Tyrley Locks, which in places
are almost roofed over by trees, then crosses a minor road
and the River Tern via aqueducts, and arrives at Market
Drayton. The wharf area is being rejuvenated with the
provision of long-term moorings together with an exciting
scheme to renovate Betton Mill, so bringing the whole area
back to life. There are disabled facilities at bridge 62.

● **Market Drayton**
Shropshire. MD Wed & Sat. PO, tel, stores, garage, banks, laundrette. On the west bank of the canal, the market centre for the surrounding district, is an attractive town with some splendid old buildings. It received its charter in 13thC but was destroyed by fire in 1651. However, picturesque black-and-white timber framing was again used for the rebuilding, the best of which is the Tudor House Hotel in the market square and the adjacent Sandbrook Vaults (1653) in Shropshire Street. The parish church of St Mary is large and well-sited overlooking the Tern valley and dates from the 12thC. The ivy-clad Corbet Arms Hotel is a fine centre-piece to the main square. The town now claims to be the home of ginger bread – there are two bakeries, one producing the original Billingtons recipe which was sold at a weekly market in the Buttercross. The link may be somewhat tenuous, but is based on the town's connection with Clive of India who was known to have returned from the east with a plentiful selection of spices, one of which could well have been ginger!

Swimming Centre Newtown, Market Drayton (01630 655177). Newly constructed swimming pool offering a variety of activity programmes. Open 7 days a week – times and activities vary from holiday to term-time so telephone for details.

Tourist Information Centre 49 Cheshire Street, Market Drayton (01630 652139). A well stocked centre *open Apr–Oct, 10.00–17.00 (16.00 Sat) & Nov–Mar, 10.00–16.00; closed 13.00–13.30. Also closed Sun & B. Hol Mon & for two weeks over Xmas.* Interesting range of town trails available including a children's version.

Pubs and Restaurants

🍺 ✕ **Wharf Tavern** Goldstone Wharf, Cheswardine (01630 661226). Canalside, at bridge 55. Once a coal wharf and warehouse, now a popular canal venue. Bass real ale, together with meals *lunchtimes and evenings.* (Book for restaurant meals *at weekends.*) Vegetarians catered for. Garden with children's play area.

🍺 **Talbot** Market Drayton (01630 658675). Canalside at bridge 62. Marston's real ale and bar food available *lunchtimes and evenings, 7 days a week.* Vegetarians catered for. Children's room and trampoline. Garden.

🍺 **Stafford Court Hotel** Stafford Street, Market Drayton (01630 652646). West of bridges 62 & 63. Serving Banks's and Marston's real ales, bar meals and *Sunday lunches.* Children welcome. Outside seating.

🍺 ✕ **Corbet Arms Hotel** High Street, Market Drayton (01630 652037). A Georgian coaching inn with a very forward lady ghost in room 7. Tetley's real ale, bar and restaurant meals *L & D, 7 days a week (not Sun evenings).* Quiz *Wed & Fri.* Also Henry's Night Club – *Thu, Fri & Sat evenings.*

🍺 **Crown** Queen Street, Market Drayton (01630 655675). This single room pub serves Marston's real ale and food *lunchtimes and evenings (not Sun evenings).*

🍺 **Jack Hanby's** Stafford Street, Market Drayton (01630 652530). Real ales from the not too distant Hanby Brewery dispensed in an open-plan bar. Beer garden and pub games. *Open all day.*

There are many other good pubs in Market Drayton.

NAVIGATIONAL NOTES

Woodseaves cutting is very narrow; there is not always room to pass another craft.

Boatyards

See page 78 for details.

Adderley

Immediately north of Market Drayton coal is available from H. Orwell and Son, established at Victoria Wharf since 1888 (01630 652472). Soon the canal regains its peaceful isolation, passing through a pleasant wooded cutting (which is alleged by the superstitious to shelter a vociferous ghost) before arriving at the five Adderley Locks: the middle of the three main groups of locks between Autherley and Nantwich.

● **Adderley**
Shropshire. PO, tel, stores. A rather under-populated village, bisected by the now closed railway and flanked by the large Shavington and Adderley Parks. The unusual church, set by itself, was rebuilt of red sandstone in 1801 in neo-classical

style. In 1958 a large portion of the church was closed to reduce maintenance costs, including the tower dated 1712, the transepts and the chancel. As a result the much smaller interior is better suited to contemporary needs and feels more like a large formal drawing room than a church.

Boatyards

Ⓑ **Holidays Afloat** Newcastle Road, Market Drayton (01630 652641). Gas, overnight mooring, long-term mooring, winter storage, slipway, crane, boat & engine sales, boat & engine repairs (including outboards), chandlery, maps, gifts, solid fuel.

Ⓑ **Betton Mill** Betton Road, Market Drayton (01630 655929). D Boat sales, engine sales and

repairs, boat repairs, boat building and fitting-out, solid fuel. *24 hour* emergency call out (07973 708906). Note: the site also accommodates craft units in the converted mill and Peter Roden Marine Engineer (01270 524383).

Ⓑ **Tom's Moorings** Lord's Bridge, Market Drayton (01543 414808). 🚿 🚽 🔥 Pump-out, overnight mooring, long-term mooring.

Adderley Locks

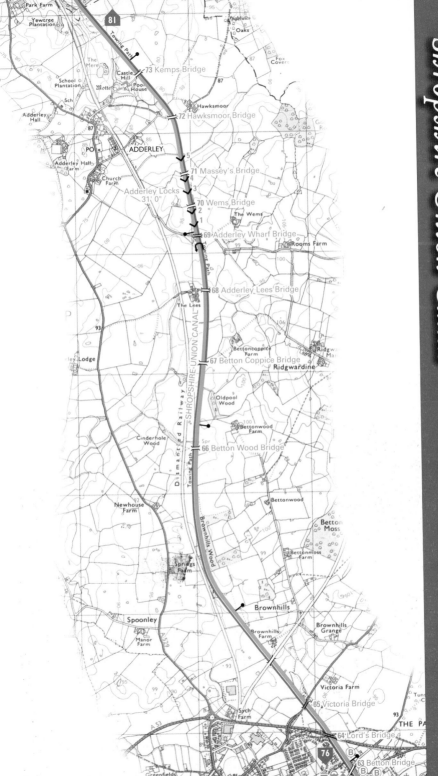

81

73 Kemps Bridge

72 Hawksmoor Bridge

5

71 Massey's Bridge

4

3

Adderley Locks 31' 0"

2

1

70 Wems Bridge

69 Adderley Wharf Bridge

68 Adderley Lees Bridge

67 Betton Coppice Bridge

Ridgwardine

66 Betton Wood Bridge

SHROPSHIRE UNION CANAL

Dismantled Railway

Towing Path

Brownhills Wood

Brownhills

65 Victoria Bridge

64 Lord's Bridge

76

63 Betton Bridge

62

Audlem

Adderley Locks are shortly followed by the 15 locks in the Audlem flight, lowering the canal by over 90ft to the dairylands of southern Cheshire. The locks are close together, well maintained, and provide over two hours' energetic navigating. There is an attractive cottage at the top lock, the wharf has a craft shop, and there are two pubs near bridge 78, along with a general store. The bottom of the locks is marked by a restored canal stable (base of the Day-Star Theatre Company) and just to the north a minor aqueduct over the infant River Weaver. The canal flows northwards through an undisturbed stretch of pastoral land. Cows graze either side, clearly intent on maintaining Cheshire's reputation as a prime dairy county. It is chilling to reflect that in 1968 hardly a single beast was left alive for miles around here after the ravages of foot and mouth disease.

Pubs and Restaurants

Bridge 12 Shropshire Street, Audlem (01270 811267). Canalside at bridge 78. A friendly traditional pub with a children's room. Enjoy a pint of Marston's or Bateman real ale here, and food *lunchtimes and evenings*. Garden. Disabled access.

Shroppie Fly The Wharf, Audlem (01270 811772). This converted warehouse serves Flowers, Castle Eden and Boddingtons real ales from a bar built like a narrow boat, complete with cratch. Extensive range of interesting food *lunchtimes and evenings, 7 days a week*. Vegetarian and children's menus. Canalside seating. Pool, darts, dominoes, table football. Useful book exchange for boaters. *Open all day in summer*.

Lord Combermere The Square, Audlem (01270 811316). Handy for those who fancy choosing between a pint of Courage, Marston's, Ruddles or John Smith's real ale. An assortment of rooms lead off the bar area, through an assortment of doors. Food *lunchtimes and evenings*. Garden, pub games and winter fires.

Old Priest House Coffee Shop (Beaman's Shop) The Square, Audlem (01270 812263). A traditional old sweet shop, walls lined with wooden shelves and a myriad selection of sweetie jars together with home-made preserves and ice-cream. The coffee shop sells tea, coffee, snacks and toasties. *Open 09.00–18.00, 7 days a week (10.00 on Sun)*.

The Shroppie Fly at Audlem

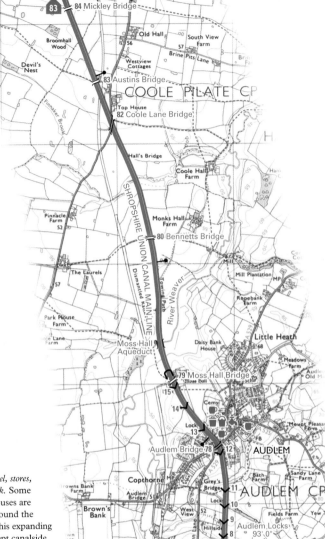

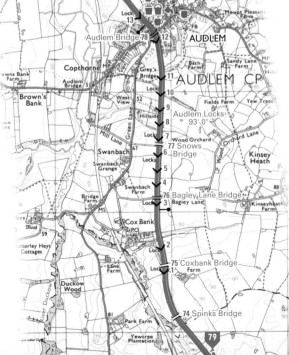

Shropshire Union Canal *Audlem*

● **Audlem**

Ches. PO, tel, stores, garage, bank. Some pleasant houses are grouped around the church in this expanding and well-kept canalside village. The massive shape of the 15th-C church seems to spill down from its hillock in battlemented layers. The colonnaded structure at its foot was once a butter market. The mellow old buildings on the canal wharf have been well renovated and there are good moorings by the old wharf crane, rescued from the nearby railway goods yard.

Nantwich

Hack Green Locks briefly interrupt the navigation. The railway which once accompanied the canal has long since closed, although the line crossing from Shrewsbury to Nantwich and Crewe is still open. At the end of this section, the tower of Nantwich church is clearly visible to the east, while Dorfold Park appears on the left. There are good moorings between Hack Green top lock and Burrows Bridge (85). Swinging round Dorfold Park on a long embankment, the canal crosses the Nantwich–Chester road on a fine cast iron aqueduct and soon reaches an oblique canal junction at Nantwich Basin: this is where Telford's narrow Birmingham & Liverpool Junction Canal joins the older Chester Canal. The stop-gates to be seen at each end of the embankment are a precaution against flooding in the event of a breach or damage to the aqueduct. The wide bridgehole at the next and all subsequent bridges reveals the difference in gauge of the two canals. The Chester Canal's width is complemented by its sweeping course, as it curves gracefully round the hillside towards Hurleston Junction.

NAVIGATIONAL NOTES

If you are heading southwards and wish to take on water at bridge 92, slow down well in advance. The water point is immediately south of the bridge.

Dorfold Hall ¼ mile south west of Nantwich Basin. Built by Ralph Wilbraham in 1616, this beautiful Jacobean house is approached along an avenue of trees. The panelled rooms contain fine furnishings and family portraits. *Open Apr–Oct, Tue & B. Hol Mon 14.00–17.00.* Charge.

● **Nantwich**
Ches. MD Thu, Sat. All services. A very fine old town, prosperous since Roman times because of its salt springs, which made it the country's main salt-mining centre until the 19thC. The town was devastated by fire in 1583 but rebuilt in fine Tudor style. Many of the half-timbered houses still remain: two especially interesting buildings on the road into town from the basin are the Cheshire Cat Inn and a tiny cottage built in 1502 and restored in 1971. On Beam Street are the Tollemache Almshouses, built in 1638 by Sir Edmund Wright who became Lord Mayor of London in 1641.
Church of St Mary Church Lane, Nantwich (01270 625268). Focal point of the town centre, it is a large and magnificent red sandstone church which stands behind its former grave-yard, now an open green. It dates from the 14thC, though it was greatly restored in 1885. It has an unusual octagonal tower and the vaulted chancel contains 20 ornate 14th-C choir stalls with canopies. Fine collection of kneelers. *Open all year.* Donation. **Visitor Centre** *open Mar–Dec, weekdays 10.00–16.30.* Refreshments. For guided party tours telephone (01270) 820534.
Hack Green Secret Nuclear Bunker Hack Green, Nantwich (01270 623353). Described as: 'A unique and exciting day out . . . discovering the secret world of Nuclear Government', this highly unusual attraction, beside bridge 85 would have become home to the select few in the event of a nuclear strike. Experience a four minute

warning, dispatch your children on the Soviet Spy Mouse Trail or drop into the NAAFI style canteen for your survival rations. Too sinister for some; for others the chance to see the under-ground paraphernalia required to support existence in the face of nuclear holocaust. *Open Apr–Sep & most weekends throughout the winter, 10.00–17.00.* Regular booked *evening* tours – telephone for details. Charge.
Nantwich Museum Pillory Street (01270 627104). An insight into the life and times of an historic market town. Roman and medieval treasures and a cheese-making display. Details on the Civil War Battle of Nantwich. *Open daily (except Wed & Sun), 10.30–16.30.* Free.
Players Theatre Love Lane, Nantwich (01270 624556). Regular productions *throughout the year.*
Tourist Information Centre Church House, Church Walk, Nantwich (01270 610983). *Open Mon–Sat & B. Hols.*

● **Acton**
Ches. Tel. A small village with a large church of red stone and an old pub with a mounting block outside.

● **Nantwich Basin**
A busy canal basin, once the terminus of the isolated Chester Canal from Nantwich to Ellesmere Port. When the B & LJ Canal was first authorised in 1826, Telford intended to bring it from Hack Green across Dorfold Park and straight into Nantwich Basin; but the owner of the park refused to allow it and forced the company to build the long embankment right round the park and the iron aqueduct over the main road. This proved a difficult and costly diversion since, as at Shelmore, the embankment repeatedly collapsed. Today the old canalside cheese warehouses are still in existence and there is a boatyard and a hire base here.

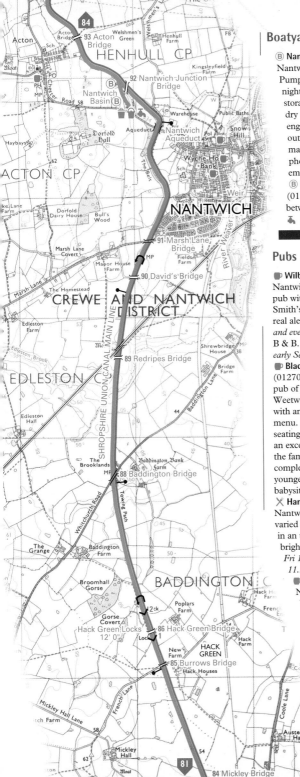

Boatyards

Ⓑ **Nantwich Canal Centre** Basin End, Nantwich (01270 625122). 🛢️🚿⚓ **D** Pump-out, gas, day craft hire, overnight and long-term mooring, winter storage, crane, boat sales and repairs, dry dock, wet dock, boat fitting-out, engine sales and repairs (including outboards), chandlery, books, maps and gifts, groceries, café, telephone, solid fuel, laundrette, toilet, emergency call out. *Open 7 days.*

Ⓑ **Simolda** Basin End, Nantwich (01270 624075). On the canal, between bridge 92 and the aqueduct. ⚓ (close by) Narrow boat hire.

Pubs and Restaurants

🍺 **Wilbraham Arms** 58 Welsh Row, Nantwich (01270 626419). Comfortable pub with an elegant frontage. John Smith's, Weetwood and Coach House real ales; draught cider. Food *lunchtimes and evenings,* pub games and open fires. B & B. Host to a real cider festival *in early Sep.*

🍺 **Black Lion** 39 Welsh Row, Nantwich (01270 628711). Cosy, timber-framed pub of great character dispensing Weetwood and Titanic real ales together with an appetising, though limited, bar menu. Pub games, open fires, outside seating and a children's room make this an excellent (though busy) venue for all the family. Live music *at weekends* completes the atmosphere (but leave younger children behind in the care of a babysitter). *Open all day.*

✕ **Hannah Restaurant** 4 Oatmarket, Nantwich (01270 610199). A tasty and varied selection of Indian cuisine served in an unusual setting amidst cheerful, brightly-painted furniture. *Open Sun-Fri 11.30-14.00 & 18.00-midnight; Sat 11.30-23.45.*

🍺 **Vine Inn** 42 Hospital Street, Nantwich (01270 624172). Bass, Worthington and guest real ales served in an old pub that seems to dive below street level. Food available *lunchtimes (daily) and evenings (Wed-Sat).* Pub games.

🍺 **Star** Acton (01270 627296). Bass real ale and bar food *lunchtimes Mon–Sat.* Vegetarian snacks. Children welcome. Outside seating. Venue for local football, darts and dominoes teams.

Barbridge Junction

At Hurleston Junction the Llangollen Canal branches off up four narrow locks on its way to North Wales (see page 18). Meanwhile the main line of the Shropshire Union soon reaches Barbridge (PO, tel, stores, off-licence) where there is a junction with the Middlewich Branch. This branch connects the Shropshire Union system to the Trent & Mersey Canal. The canal moves almost westwards now alongside a busy main road, passing an enormous

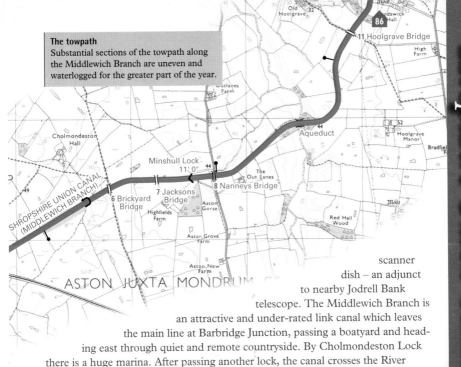

The towpath
Substantial sections of the towpath along
the Middlewich Branch are uneven and
waterlogged for the greater part of the year.

Shropshire Union Canal

Barbridge Junction

scanner
dish – an adjunct
to nearby Jodrell Bank
telescope. The Middlewich Branch is
an attractive and under-rated link canal which leaves
the main line at Barbridge Junction, passing a boatyard and heading east through quiet and remote countryside. By Cholmondeston Lock
there is a huge marina. After passing another lock, the canal crosses the River
Weaver on an aqueduct as it approaches the village of Church Minshull, where
L.T.C Rolt and *Cressy* spent an enjoyable sojourn, commending the local pub.

Boatyards

Ⓑ **Barbridge Marine** Wardle, Nantwich
(01270 528682). 🚽 🚿 ⛽ Gas, overnight
mooring, long-term mooring, winter storage,
slipway, cradle, boat sales and repairs, engine
sales and repairs, outboard specialist,
chandlery, books and maps, boat building,
upholstery, refits, toilet.

Ⓥ **Venetian Marine** Cholmondeston Lock,
Nantwich (01270 528251/528318). 🚽 🚿 ⛽
D Gas, pump-out, long-term mooring, slipway, winter storage, dry dock, wet dock, boat
building, boat sales and repairs, engine sales
and repairs, groceries, large chandlery, books
and maps, gifts, café, telephone, toilets.

Pubs and Restaurants

🍺 **Barbridge Inn** Chester Road, Barbridge
(01270 528443). A busy, brewery chain pub,
offering Boddingtons, Cains and guest real ales.
Food available *all day, every day*. Children and
vegetarians catered for. Canalside garden.
🍺 **Jolly Tar** Barbridge Junction (01270 528283).
Greenalls and Bass real ales together with grills
and a range of home-made pub food served
*lunchtimes and evenings (7 days a week) and all
day Sat & Sun in summer.* Children's menu and
outside play area including bouncy castle. Live
music *Wed.* Pool, darts and dominoes.

Middlewich

This is a quiet stretch of canal passing through rich farmland interspersed with woods. There are superb views to the west over the River Weaver and Winsford Top Flash. At bridge 22A the main London-Glasgow electric railway line makes a noisy crossing. The canal then descends through two locks to Middlewich, where it joins the Trent & Mersey. This last few yards of the Middlewich Branch used to belong to the Trent & Mersey, and the bridge over the entrance to the branch is grandiosely inscribed Wardle Canal 1829. There are good moorings at the boatyard to the left of the junction.

Boatyards

ⓑ **Kings Lock Boatyard** Booth Lane, Middlewich (01606 737564). 🛁 D Gas, overnight mooring, long-term mooring, winter storage, slipway, crane, engine sales and repairs (including outboards), boat repairs, chandlery (including mail order), books, maps, gifts, solid fuel. *Emergency call-out.*

ⓑ **Andersen Boats** Wych House, St Anne's Road, Middlewich (01606 833668). Pump-out, gas, narrow boat hire, boat building, boat fitting-out, DIY, books and maps. Useful DIY shop nearby.

ⓑ **Middlewich Narrowboats** Canal Terrace, Middlewich (01606 832460). 🛁 🚻 ⚓ D Pump-out, gas, narrow boat hire, overnight mooring (*not Fri*), long-term mooring, dry dock, groceries, chandlery, books and maps, engine repairs, toilets, laundry service, breakdown service, grit blasting, hull & cabinside painting. *Closed Sun.* Useful tool hire shop next door.

Pubs and Restaurants

🍺 ✕ **Big Lock** Middlewich (01606 833489). Canalside. Variously a bottle-making factory and canal-horse stables, this pub now serves Ruddles, Courage and Webster's real ales (and guests) together with bar snacks and an à la carte menu. Food available *L & D, 7 days a week*. Children and vegetarians catered for. Garden area and *weekend music in winter*

🍺 ✕ **Boars Head** Kinderton Street, Middlewich (01606 833191). Large rambling pub offering Robinson's real ale and bar snacks *from 12.00–21.00*. Children's room in hotel next door together with restaurant serving meals *lunchtimes and evenings*. Patio. B & B.

🍺 **Newton Brewery Inn** Middlewich (01606 833502). ¼ mile south of Big Lock. Marston's real ale served in a small friendly pub with an attractive garden running down to the towpath. Selection of meals and snacks *lunchtimes and evenings (not Sun evenings)*. Children welcome.

🍺 **Cheshire Cheese** Lewin Street, Middlewich (01606 832097). Basic but welcoming traditional pub offering Cains, John Smith's and Burtonwood real ales (plus two guests weekly) together with inexpensive bar snacks *lunchtimes and evenings*. Beer garden. Children welcome.

🍺 **Kings Lock** Middlewich (01606 833537). Overlooking the lock. Bar food *lunchtimes and evenings*. Canalside seating. B & B.

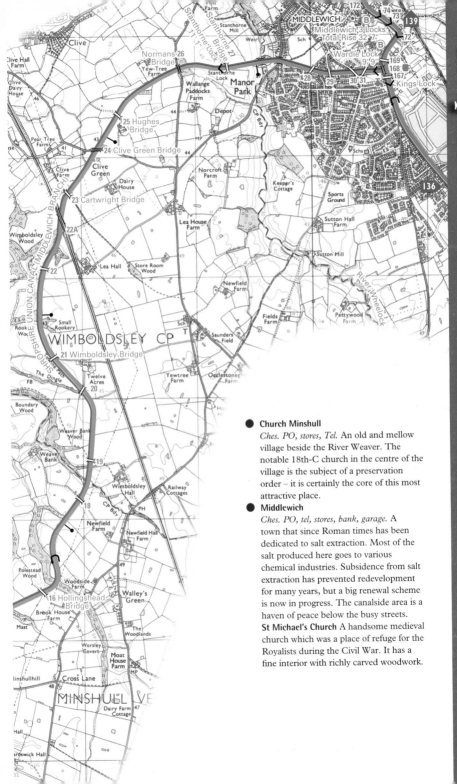

Shropshire Union Canal

Middlewich

● **Church Minshull**
Ches. PO, stores, Tel. An old and mellow
village beside the River Weaver. The
notable 18th-C church in the centre of the
village is the subject of a preservation
order – it is certainly the core of this most
attractive place.

● **Middlewich**
Ches. PO, tel, stores, bank, garage. A
town that since Roman times has been
dedicated to salt extraction. Most of the
salt produced here goes to various
chemical industries. Subsidence from salt
extraction has prevented redevelopment
for many years, but a big renewal scheme
is now in progress. The canalside area is a
haven of peace below the busy streets.
St Michael's Church A handsome medieval
church which was a place of refuge for the
Royalists during the Civil War. It has a
fine interior with richly carved woodwork.

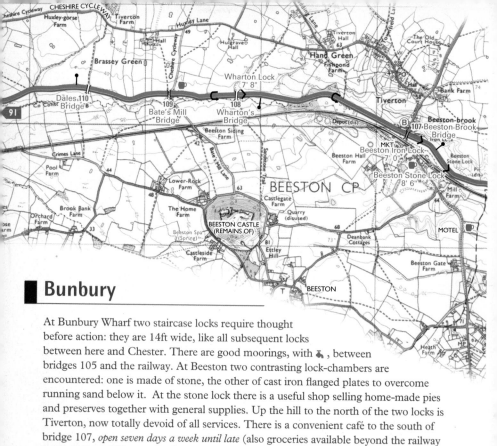

Bunbury

At Bunbury Wharf two staircase locks require thought before action: they are 14ft wide, like all subsequent locks between here and Chester. There are good moorings, with ♨, between bridges 105 and the railway. At Beeston two contrasting lock-chambers are encountered: one is made of stone, the other of cast iron flanged plates to overcome running sand below it. At the stone lock there is a useful shop selling home-made pies and preserves together with general supplies. Up the hill to the north of the two locks is Tiverton, now totally devoid of all services. There is a convenient café to the south of bridge 107, *open seven days a week until late* (also groceries available beyond the railway bridge). From Wharton Lock an excellent view is obtained of the massive bulk of Beeston Castle, a landmark which can be seen from places up to 30 miles away. As one moves westward, the romantic-looking turrets of neighbouring Peckforton Castle (of somewhat younger origins) come into view.

Boatyards

Ⓑ**Chas Hardern Beeston** Castle Wharf, Nr Tarporley (01829 732595). 🛉 🛉 ♨ D Pump-out, gas, coal, narrow boat hire, chandlery, books and maps, gifts, boat fitting-out, boat and engine repairs.
Ⓑ**Anglo Welsh** The Canal Wharf, Bunbury (01829 260638). 🛉 🛉 ♨ D E Pump-out, gas, narrow boat hire, day hire craft, overnight mooring, long-term mooring, winter storage, slipway, crane, provisions, books and maps, boat and engine sales and repairs, wet dock, DIY facilities, groceries, café, gifts, solid fuel, telephone, toilet. *24hr emergency call-out.*

● **Calveley**
Ches. Tel, stores, garage.
● **Bunbury**
Ches. PO, tel, stores, garage, butcher. A mile south west of Bunbury Locks. The church is an outstanding building: supremely light, airy and spacious, it stands as a fine monument to workmanship of the 14th and 15thC.

Bunbury Mill Bunbury (01829 261422). Up the hill from Bunbury Wharf, towards the village. Guided tours around a fully restored watermill, working until 1960 when it was destroyed by a massive flood. *Open Easter–Sep, Sun & Wed (also Mon & Fri B. Hols) 14.00-17.00. Last admission 16.30.* Nominal charge. Informal groups and parties catered for. Details may change, so telephone if possible.

Beeston Castle Beeston, Tarporley (01829 260464). The impressive ruins of a 13th-C castle built by the Earl of Chester in 1337. Situated on top of a steep hill dominating the surrounding countryside, it was in an ideal, almost unassailable position. *Open daily.* Charge.

Peckforton Castle Stone House Lane, Peckforton (01829 260930). Built in the 1840s with fine views out over the Cheshire plain.

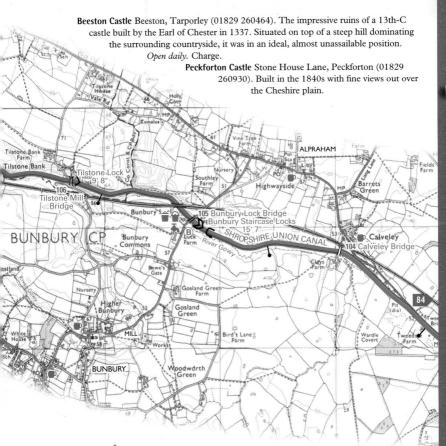

Pubs and Restaurants

Davenport Arms Calveley (01829 260430). Near the wharf. Rotating guest real ales in a friendly pub five minutes from the canal. Home-made bar food *lunchtimes and evenings.* Children and vegetarians catered for. Beer garden. *Regular* live music nights from the guitar-playing landlord, and others.

Dysart Arms Bunbury (01829 260183). By the church. Once a farmhouse with stone flagged floors it now serves Bass, Worthington and two guest real ales. Large range of food available *lunchtimes and evenings, 7 days a week in summer; lunches at weekends and evening meals daily in winter.* Children welcome when eating or in the attractive gardens. Pub games.

Nags Head Bunbury (01829 260027). In centre of the village. An attractively decorated façade with a horse's head picked out in a central plaster frieze. Greenalls real ales, food, beer garden.

Wild Boar Hotel Beeston (01829 260309). ¹/₂ mile past Beeston Castle Hotel, on A49. Restaurant in a large Tudor building serving food *L & D, 7 days a week.* Vegetarians and children catered for. Garden. B & B.

Beeston Castle Hotel Beeston (01829 260234). Below bridge 107. Worthington and Bass real ales and an attractive restaurant serving meals (*L & D*) in this market-side hotel. A la carte menu (booking *at weekends*) and snacks in the bar. Vegetarians and children catered for. Garden. B & B.

Shady Oak Nr Beeston (01829 733159). Canalside, at Bate's Mill Bridge. Friendly, canalside pub (beside Bate's Mill Bridge) serving Courage and Theakston real ales and home-cooked food *all day, every day.* Groups and parties catered for.

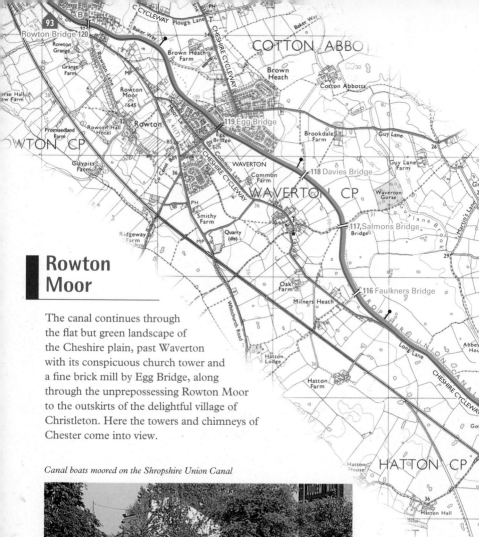

Rowton Moor

The canal continues through the flat but green landscape of the Cheshire plain, past Waverton with its conspicuous church tower and a fine brick mill by Egg Bridge, along through the unprepossessing Rowton Moor to the outskirts of the delightful village of Christleton. Here the towers and chimneys of Chester come into view.

Canal boats moored on the Shropshire Union Canal

Pubs and Restaurants

STOP

🍺 **Poacher's Pocket** Tattenhall Road, Tattenhall (01829 771010). South of Crow's Nest Bridge 113. Value for money concept pub where portions can easily outstrip the capacity of an ordinary digestive system. Inexpensive home-cooked food available *all day, every day*, including a range of vegetarian options. Children's indoor activity centre and outdoor play area. Banks's and Camerons real ales. Garden.

Battle of Rowton Moor It was here, 3 miles from Chester, that one of the last major battles of the Civil War took place in 1645. The Parliamentarians completely routed the Royalists who, still under fierce attack, retreated to Chester. It is said that King Charles I watched the defeat from the walls of Chester, but it is more probable that he saw only the final stages under the walls of the city. Charles fled, leaving 800 prisoners and 600 dead and wounded.

● **Waverton**
Ches. PO, tel, stores. The sturdy church tower carries a pleasing, modest spire. Inside the church, which was greatly restored by the Victorians, the low aisle arches lend a certain cosiness to the building.

Boatyards

Ⓑ **The Workshop** The Moorings, Rowton Bridge, Christleton, Chester (01244 332633). Overnight mooring, long-term mooring, winter storage, slipway, engine sales and repairs (including outboards). *Emergency call out.*

Chester

Leaving Christleton the canal passes a useful
stores beside bridge 121, and a garage selling
gas and *red* diesel west of bridge 123, before
dropping into the ancient city of Chester
through five locks; none of these have top
gate paddles, and they all take rather long to
fill. The canal goes straight through the
middle of the town. Passing the site of an
old lead works, and a great variety of bridges,
the navigation approaches the old city and
suddenly curves round into a very steep
rock cutting. Soon the Northgate Locks
(a staircase) are reached: at the bottom is a
sharp right turn to Tower Wharf, a good
place to tie up for the night. Here the line
of the original Chester Canal once led
straight down, via a further two locks (long
since abandoned), into the River Dee. There
is a boatyard at the head of the arm leading
down into the Dee and a handy store on the
off-side next to bridge 128.

Boatyards

ⓑ **David Jones Boatbuilders** Upper Cambrian
View, Chester (01244 376363). At junction with
Dee Branch. ⚒ Winter storage, slipway.
Shipwrights, wood and steel boats built, all repairs
and specialise in classic craft. *Emergency call out.
Open Mon–Fri, weekends by appointment.*
ⓑ **BW Chester Yard** Tower Wharf, Chester
(01244 390372). 🚽 ⚒ Slipway. Dry dock (book-
ings & charge) and pump-out (charge).

● **Cristleton**
Ches. PO, tel, stores. A very pleasant village near the
canal, well worth visiting.
● **Chester**
Ches. MD Tue, Thu. All services. There is a wealth
of things to see in this Roman city. It is in fact an
excellent town to see on foot, because of the amazing
survival of almost all the old city wall. This provides
Chester with its best and rarest feature – one can walk
right round the city on this superb footpath, over the
old city gates and past the defensive turrets, including
King Charles' Tower above the canal. Other splendid
features are the race course – the Roodee – (just outside the city wall and therefore well inside the modern
town) where Chester Races are held each year in *May,
Jul, Aug and Sep* – it can easily be overlooked for free
from the road that runs above and beside it – the superb
old cathedral, the bold new theatre, the Rows (unique
double-tier medieval shopping streets), and the immense
number of old and fascinating buildings throughout the town.

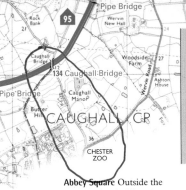

Abbey Square Outside the
cathedral, opposite the Victorian town
hall, the square is entered through a
massive gateway built in 1377.
Chester Cathedral Northgate Street,
Chester (01244 324756). A magnificent
building of dark red stone on the site of a
10th-C minster. In 1092 the Earl of Chester
and St Anselm founded a Benedictine
abbey which was dissolved in 1540, but in
the following year it was made a cathedral
and the seat of a bishop. In 1742 Handel
gave his first public performance of the
Messiah in the cathedral and a copy of his
marked score is on display. *Open daily.*
Church of St John the Baptist St John's
Street. Impressive 12th-C church that was
built on the site of an earlier Saxon church.
Chester Castle Grosvenor Road, Chester
(01244 327617). The original timber
structure, c.1069, was replaced by stone
walls and towers by Henry III.
Unfortunately, in 1789 the defensive
walls were removed to make way for the
incongruous Thomas Harrison group of
buildings, which include the Grand
Entrance and Assize Courts.

The main part of the castle is occupied by
troops of the Cheshire Regiment, but the
13th-C Agricola Tower is open to the public.
Chester Toy Museum 13A Lower Bridge Street,
Chester (01244 346297). Pure childhood
nostalgia. *Open daily 10.00–17.00.* Charge.
Chester Visitor & Craft Centre Vicars Lane,
Chester (01244 351609). Working craft shops
and café. Brass rubbing, video theatre and Hall
of Names. *Open Mon–Sat 09.00–17.30 & Sun
10.00–17.00 (10.00–16.00 winter).* Free.
Dewa Roman Experience Pierpoint Lane,
Bridge Street, Chester (01244 343407).
Reconstruction of Roman Chester. Shop and
tearoom. *Open daily 09.00–17.00.* Charge.
Heritage Centre Bridge Street Row, Chester
(01244 321616). Story of Chester, its
buildings and its inhabitants. *Open Sat & Sun.*
Charge.
Museum of the Cheshire Regiment Situated
inside the tower of the castle. *Open daily
09.00–17.00. Closed Xmas – New Year.*
Grosvenor Museum Grosvenor Street, Chester
(01244 321616). Award-winning museum that
introduces Chester's past, in particular the
Roman fortress of Deva and its inhabitants.

● **Northgate Locks**
Hewn out of solid rock, these three staircase locks lower the canal by 33ft,
an impressive feat of engineering and a suitable com-
plement to the deep
rock cutting
nearby.

The Dee Branch

This branch into the tidal River Dee runs through three wide locks from the boatyard near Tower Wharf. There used to be a large basin below the second lock, but this has now been filled in. The bottom lock and bridge are new, having been built to replace an old single-tracked swing bridge on a main road. There is a very sharp bend into the branch from Tower Wharf.

Anyone wishing to take a boat into the River Dee *must* give *7 days* notice to BW on (01244) 390372 during office hours. Charge. (The bottom lock has to be kept padlocked to prevent silting up at high water.) It is practicable to enter or leave the River Dee at this point for *only four hours either side of high water*, since there is insufficient water at the entrance for the rest of the time.

Pubs and Restaurants

● ✕ **Old Trooper** Christleton Bridge, nr Chester (01244 335784). A Beefeater pub/restaurant (*L & D*) serving Boddingtons, Wadworth and Flowers real ales. Vegetarians and children catered for.

There are many pubs in Chester including:

● **Fortress & Firkin** Cow Lane, Chester. Canalside next to bridge 123E. The usual selection of real ales from the Firkin Brewery range, together with inexpensive bar meals and snacks available *throughout the day*. Outside seating.

● **Albion** Albion Street, Chester (01244 340345). City centre pub of great character, serving *lunchtime and evening* food *(not Mon evenings)* and Greenalls, Cains and guest real ales. Open fire. *Open all day Fri.*

● **Olde Custom House** Watergate Street, Chester (01244 324435). Comfortable city pub, not far from the racecourse, serving Banks's and Marston's real ales together with food *lunchtimes and evenings*. Outside seating. *Open all day.*

● **Union Vaults** Egerton Street, Chester (01244

322170). Plassey and Greenalls real ales dispensed in this friendly local, together with a regular *Sun evening* folk club. Children's room, outside seating and pub games. *Open all day.*

● ✕ **Mill Hotel** Milton Street, Chester (01244 350035). Boddingtons, Cains, Weetwood and an interesting and ever-changing range of guest real ales. Bar and restaurant food *L & D until 22.30*. Children and vegetarians catered for. No smoking area and small canalside patio. Disabled access. B & B. *L & D* canal cruises.

● **Telford's Warehouse** Tower Wharf, Chester (01244 390090). Canalside on the wharf beside the BW office. A regular music venue, host to a varied range of bands, catering for most tastes. An altogether most interesting setting for both the entertainment and for the consumption of an inexpensive selection of homemade bar meals and snacks, together with Courage, Theakston and guest real ales. Also the Gallery Restaurant – home to regular art exhibitions – offers a similar well-priced and interesting menu as the pub.

The Wirral

Sweeping northwards along the lock-free pound from Chester to the Mersey, the canal enters open country for the last time as it crosses the Wirral. The handsome stone railway viaduct over the navigation carries the Chester–Birkenhead line, while beyond long term moorings are very much in evidence at Top Farm, stretching almost to bridge 135. Stoak (or Stoke – alternative spelling) is now surrounded by canal and motorway. The church is conspicuous from the navigation; north of the village, the distant oil refineries and chimneys herald the industrial activity along Merseyside. The docks and basins of the port itself, where the Shropshire Union Canal meets the Manchester Ship Canal, are – or were – very extensive. Telford's famous warehouses in which the narrow boats and barges were loaded and discharged under cover were regrettably set alight by local hooligans and had to be demolished in the interests of safety. But now part of the old dock complex is the home of the Boat Museum, a large sub-aqua centre and the headquarters of the British Sub-Aqua Club. The sprawling museum site, making excellent use of the multitude of different buildings once part of the docks complex, plays host to a wide range of festive activity from boating jamborees to a variety of musical events. It has more than once been the venue for an excellent weekend of Cajun music and dance; the boats forming a strikingly colourful backdrop to non-stop revelling. Whatever one's interests, making the journey beyond Chester is always well worthwhile. There is still access for boats from the Shropshire Union through several wide locks down into the

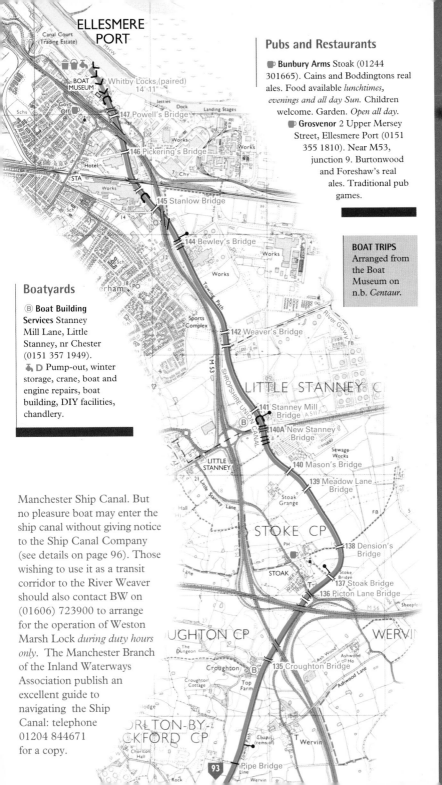

Pubs and Restaurants

Bunbury Arms Stoak (01244 301665). Cains and Boddingtons real ales. Food available *lunchtimes, evenings and all day Sun.* Children welcome. Garden. *Open all day.*

Grosvenor 2 Upper Mersey Street, Ellesmere Port (0151 355 1810). Near M53, junction 9. Burtonwood and Foreshaw's real ales. Traditional pub games.

BOAT TRIPS
Arranged from the Boat Museum on n.b. *Centaur.*

Boatyards

Ⓑ **Boat Building Services** Stanney Mill Lane, Little Stanney, nr Chester (0151 357 1949). ♿ **D** Pump-out, winter storage, crane, boat and engine repairs, boat building, DIY facilities, chandlery.

Manchester Ship Canal. But no pleasure boat may enter the ship canal without giving notice to the Ship Canal Company (see details on page 96). Those wishing to use it as a transit corridor to the River Weaver should also contact BW on (01606) 723900 to arrange for the operation of Weston Marsh Lock *during duty hours only.* The Manchester Branch of the Inland Waterways Association publish an excellent guide to navigating the Ship Canal: telephone 01204 844671 for a copy.

Ellesmere Port Bottom Lock Entry into the Manchester Ship Canal from the Shropshire Union is restricted by a swing bridge over the first lock (adjacent to the Holiday Inn) which is not under the control of BW. Boaters wishing to enter the canal must first contact Ellesmere Port & Neston Borough Council (0151 356 6433) to make arrangements for the bridge to be swung. Any difficulties in obtaining assistance should be referred to the BW Chester office on 01244 390372.

Manchester Ship Canal Harbour Master, Queen Elizabeth II Dock, Eastham, Wirral (0151 327 1461). The ship canal currently carries an increasing annual tonnage of approximately 2,500 vessel movements per year. A great deal of it is hazardous, petrochemical traffic and therefore a no smoking regime is enforced. The canal company is happy to allow pleasure boat use on the understanding that certain conditions are adhered to. It is not a navigation for the novice boater and should be viewed as a transit corridor for the experienced boat owner (not hire boater) to access the River Weaver, the River Mersey, the Shropshire Union Canal or the cruising waterways above Pomona Lock.

1 The boat must carry £1 million third party insurance cover.
2 The boat is subject to an annual Certificate of Seaworthiness.
3 The appropriate fee is paid, currently set at £15.10 plus £15.10 for each lock used.
4 The boater must contact the harbourmaster in advance of passage to obtain copies of:
   a) Pleasure Craft Transit Notes
   b) Port of Manchester Navigation Bylaws.
   At this juncture one can discuss appropriate times of arrival and departure to coincide with scheduled shipping movements.
5 At all times the boater is required to act in a responsible manner and be aware that this is a daytime transit route only, with no lay-by facilities. One should familiarise oneself with the geography of the canal before setting out.
6 VHF radio equipment is desirable (the Manchester Ship Canal Company call and operate on channel 14) and if not available a mobile phone should be considered essential.

Weston Marsh Lock Access to the River Weaver via Weston Marsh Lock is during the following duty hours and only after prior notice to BW at Northwich (01606 723900): *Mon–Thu 08.00–16.00, Fri 08.00–15.00.* The lock may be available on some summer weekends *(end of May B. Hol–Sep)*. Contact BW for further details.

● **Stoak**
Ches. Tel. There is little of interest in this scattered village, except a pleasant country pub and a small, pretty church.
Chester Zoo Chester (01244 380280). ½ mile south of Caughall Bridge (134). Wide variety of animals, shown as much as possible without bars and fences, enhanced by attractive flower gardens and its own miniature canal. Largest elephant house in the world. *Open daily 10.00–dusk. Closed Xmas.* Charge.

● **Ellesmere Port**
Ches. MD Fri. All services. An industrial town of little interest apart from the fine Victorian railway station.
Blue Planet Aquarium Longlooms Road, Little Stanney, Ellesmere Port (0151 357 8800). West of bridge 140A and M53 junction 10. New aquarium with two floors of interactive exhibits, themed restaurant, Caribbean reef, Amazon Jungle and Oil-Rig shop. An excellent all-weather attraction, but entry will cost a family of four more than £20.
The Boat Museum Ellesmere Port (0151 355 5017). Established in the old Ellesmere Port basins. Exhibits, models and photos trace the development of the canal system from early times to its heyday in the 19thC. Vessels on display in the basin include a diverse and widely representative array of narrow boats, a tunnel tug, a weedcutter plus some larger vessels. Restored period cottages. An exciting and expanding venture in a splendid setting beside the ship canal, and not to be missed. Our canal heritage is still alive. *Open Apr–Oct, daily10.00–17.00; Nov–Mar, Sat–Wed & Sun 10.00–16.00. Closed Xmas Day and Boxing Day.* Charge. Pump-out available.
Stanlow Abbey Beside the Mersey, 1½ miles east of the canal on Stanlow Point. Remains of the Cistercian abbey founded in 1178 by John, Baron of Halton. Now isolated by the ship canal.
Port Sunlight Village, the Heritage Centre and the Lady Lever Art Gallery Port Sunlight, the Wirral (0151 644 6466 & 0151 478 4136). Picturesque style 19th-C model village built by the soap baron William Hesketh Lever for his workers, together with a collection of art treasures in a sumptuous gallery, dedicated to his wife. Village *always open*; Heritage centre *open daily 10.00-16.00 in summer; Mon-Fri in winter.* Gallery *open Mon-Sat 10.00-17.00 & Sun 12.00-17.00.* Charge for Gallery. Train from Ellesmere Port to Port Sunlight for village and to Bebington for gallery.

STAFFORDSHIRE & WORCESTERSHIRE CANAL: NORTH

MAXIMUM DIMENSIONS
Length: 70'
Beam: 7'
Headroom: 6' 6"

MANAGER
01785 284253

MILEAGE
AUTHERLEY JUNCTION to
GREAT HAYWOOD JUNCTION: 20½ miles

Locks: 12

Construction of this navigation was begun immediately after that of the Trent & Mersey, to effect the joining of the rivers Trent, Mersey and Severn. Engineered by James Brindley, the Staffordshire & Worcestershire was opened throughout in 1772, at a cost of rather over £100,000. It stretched 46 miles from Great Haywood on the Trent & Mersey to the River Severn, which it joined at Stourport. The canal was an immediate success. It was well placed to bring goods from the Potteries down to Gloucester, Bristol and the West Country; while the Birmingham Canal, which joined it halfway along at Aldersley Junction, fed manufactured goods northwards from the Black Country to the Potteries via Great Haywood. In 1815 the Worcester & Birmingham Canal opened, offering a more direct but heavily locked canal link between Birmingham and the Severn. The Staffordshire & Worcestershire answered this threat by gradually extending the opening times of the locks until, by 1830, they were open 24 hours a day. When the Birmingham & Liverpool Junction Canal was opened from Autherley to Nantwich in 1835, traffic bound for Merseyside from Birmingham naturally began to use this more direct, modern canal. The Staffordshire & Worcestershire lost a great deal of traffic over its length as most of the boats now passed along only the ½-mile stretch of the Staffordshire & Worcestershire Canal between Autherley and Aldersley Junctions. The company levied absurdly high tolls for this tiny length. The B & LJ Company therefore co-operated with the Birmingham Canal Company in 1836 to promote in Parliament a Bill for the Tettenhall & Autherley Canal and Aqueduct. This project was to be a canal flyover, going from the Birmingham Canal right over the profiteering Staffordshire & Worcestershire and locking down into the Birmingham & Liverpool Junction Canal. The Staffordshire & Worcestershire company had to give way, and reduced its tolls to an acceptable level.

In spite of this set back, the Staffordshire & Worcestershire maintained a good profit, and high dividends were paid throughout the rest of the 19thC. From the 1860s onwards, railway competition began to bite, and the company's profits began to slip. Several modernisation schemes came to nothing, and the canal's trade declined. Now the canal is used almost exclusively by pleasure craft. It is covered in full in guide 2 of this series.

Autherley Junction

Autherley Junction is marked by a big white bridge on the towpath side. The stop lock just beyond marks the entrance to the Shropshire Union: there is a useful boatyard just to the north of it. Leaving Autherley, the Staffordshire & Worcestershire runs through a very narrow cutting in rock: there is only room for boats to pass in the designated places, so a good look out should be kept for oncoming craft. After passing the motorway and a rather conspicuous sewage works at Coven Heath, the navigation leaves behind the suburbs of Wolverhampton and enters pleasant farmland. The bridges need care: although the bridgeholes are reasonably wide, the actual arches are rather low.

● **Autherley Junction**
A busy canal junction with a full range of boating facilities close by.

● **Coven**
Staffs. PO, tel, stores, garage, fish & chips. The only true village on this section, Coven lies beyond a dual carriageway north west of Cross Green Bridge. There are a large number of shops, including a laundrette.

Gailey Lock (see page 100)

Boatyards

Ⓑ **Water Travel** Autherley Junction, Oxley Moor Road, Wolverhampton (01902 782371). 🛉 ⚓ D Pump-out, gas, narrow boat hire, slipway, boat and engine repairs, chandlery, toilets.

The towpath
This is generally in good condition.

BOAT TRIPS
n.b. Stafford Public trips on the *first Sun each month*, plus private charter. For details telephone (01902) 789522.

Pubs and Restaurants

🍺 ✕ **Anchor Inn** (01902 790466). Canalside by Cross Green Bridge. A large family-friendly pub with a roof-top terrace, tastefully decorated with wood and stained glass. Morland's and Tetleys real ale, and meals are *available all day*, with vegetarian options. The food is good, and includes a balti choice. Children's menu, garden and good moorings.

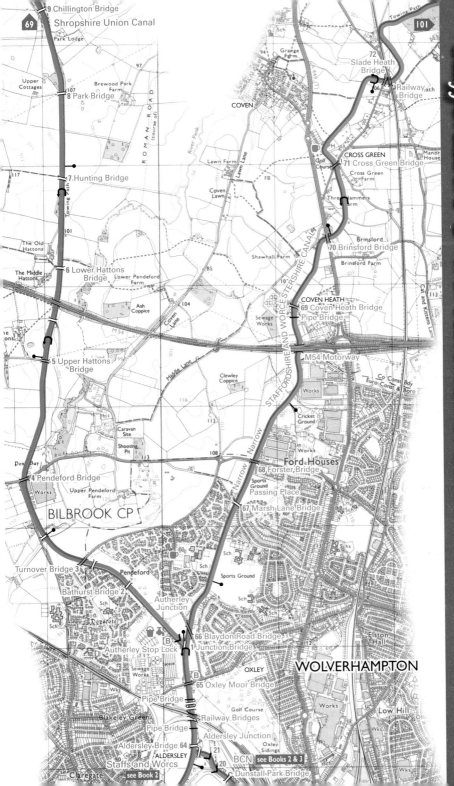

69

101

9 Chillington Bridge
Shropshire Union Canal

Park Lodge

Upper Cottages

107
8 Park Bridge
Brewood Park Farm

97

94

Grange Farm

72 Slade Heath Bridge

Railway Bridge

Towing Path

COVEN

PO

117

7 Hunting Bridge

Towing Path

River Penk

Lawn Farm

Lawn Lane

101

CROSS GREEN
71 Cross Green Bridge

Golf Course

Cross Green Farm

Three Hammers Farm

The Old Hattons

FB

Coven Lawn

The Middle Hattons

6 Lower Hattons Bridge

Lower Pendeford Farm

BS

Shawhall Farm

STAFFORDSHIRE AND WORCESTERSHIRE CANAL

Brinsford

70 Brinsford Bridge

Brinsford Farm

Ash Coppice

104

Coven Lane

10

COVEN HEATH
69 Coven Heath Bridge
Pipe Bridge

Manor House

Cat and Kittens Lane

113

5 Upper Hattons Bridge

M54

Sewage Works

M54 Motorway

Co Const Bdy
Euro Const & Boro

116

Middle Lane

Clewley Coppice

113

Works

Cricket Ground

Works

Caravan Site

Shooting Pit

113

108

Narrow

Narrow

Ford Houses

Pon Bar

4 Pendeford Bridge

Works

Upper Pendeford Farm

68 Forster Bridge

Sports Ground
Passing Place

67 Marsh Lane Bridge

BILBROOK CP

Sports Ground

Elston Hall

Turnover Bridge 3

Pendeford

Bathurst Bridge 2

Autherley Junction

66 Blaydon Road Bridge

WOLVERHAMPTON

Autherley Stop Lock

1 Junction Bridge

B

OXLEY

65 Oxley Moor Bridge

Sewage Works

Pipe Bridge

Works

Low Hill

Blakeley Green

Pipe Bridge

Railway Bridges

Golf Course

Oxley Sidings

Aldersley Bridge 64

Aldersley Junction

21

BCN
see Books 2 & 3

Staffs and Worcs
see Book 2

ALDERSLEY

20

Clareene

Dunstall Park Bridge

Gailey Wharf

The considerable age of this canal is shown by its extremely twisting course, revealed after passing the railway bridge. There are few real centres of population along this stretch, which comprises largely former heathland. Hatherton Junction marks the entrance of the former Hatherton Branch of the Staffordshire & Worcestershire Canal into the main line. This branch used to connect with the Birmingham Canal Navigations. It is closed above the derelict second lock, although the channel remains as a feeder for the Staffordshire & Worcestershire Canal. There is a marina at the junction. A little further along, a chemical works is encountered, astride the canal in what used to be woodlands. Gailey Wharf is about a mile further north: it is a small canal settlement that includes a boatyard and a large, round, toll keeper's watch-tower, containing a useful canal shop. The picturesque Wharf Cottage opposite has been restored as a bijou residence. The canal itself disappears under Watling Street and then falls rapidly through five locks towards Penkridge. These locks are very attractive, and some are accompanied by little brick bridges. The M6 motorway comes alongside for 1/2 mile, screening the reservoirs which feed the canal.

Pillaton Old Hall South east of bridge 85. Only the gate house and stone built chapel remain of this late 15th-C brick mansion built by the Littleton family, although there are still traces of the hall and courtyard. The chapel contains a 13th-C wooden carving of a saint. Visiting is by appointment only: telephone (01785) 712200. The modest charge is donated to charity.

Gailey and Calf Heath reservoirs 1/2 mile east of Gailey Wharf, either side of the M6. These are feeder reservoirs for the canal, though rarely drawn on. The public has access to them as nature reserves to study the wide variety of natural life, especially the long-established heronry which is thriving on an island in Gailey Lower reservoir. In Gailey Upper, fishing is available to the public from the riparian owner. In Gailey Lower a limited number of angling tickets are available on a season ticket basis each year from BW. There is club sailing on two of the reservoirs.

Boatyards

ⓑ **Otherton Boat Haven** Otherton Hall Farm, Offerton (01785 712515). 🛁 🚽 🔧 D Pump-out, gas, overnight and long-term mooring, crane, boat and engine sales and repairs, toilets.

ⓑ **Gailey Marine** The Wharf, Watling Street, Standeford (01902 790612). 🛁 🚽 🔧 Pump-out, gas, narrow boat hire, long-term mooring, boat & engine repairs, boatbuilding, public telephone. Boat building on site at J.D. Boat Services, contact as above. Gifts and provisions opposite in the Roundhouse.

ⓑ **Calf Heath Marina** (01902 790570). 🔧 D Pump-out, gas, overnight and long-term moorings, telephone, toilet.

Pubs and Restaurants

✕ ♀ **Misty's Bar & Restaurant** Calf Heath Marina (01902 790570). Licensed restaurant, serving excellent and reasonably priced food *L & D*. Children welcome, garden.

🍺 **Spread Eagle** Watling Street, Gailey (01902 790212). About 1/2 mile west of Gailey Wharf. A large road house serving Banks's real ale and food *lunchtimes and evenings*. Enormous garden.

🍺 **Cross Keys** Filance Lane (01785 712826). Canalside, at Filance Bridge (84). Once a lonely canal pub, now it is modernised and surrounded by housing estates. Family orientated, it serves Banks's, Bass, M & B and Worthington real ale and food *lunchtimes and evenings*. Garden, with *summer* barbeques. 🔧 There is a useful Spar shop 100yds north, on the estate.

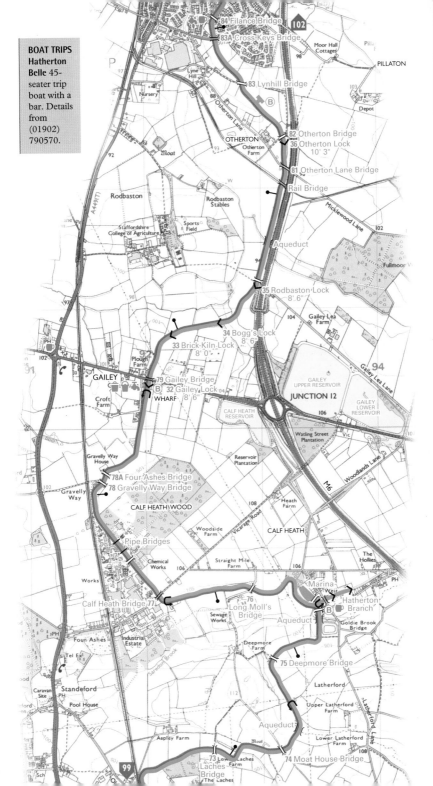

BOAT TRIPS
Hatherton Belle 45-seater trip boat with a bar. Details from (01902) 790570.

84 Filance Bridge
102
83A Cross Keys Bridge
Moor Hall Cottages
98
PILLATON

83 Lynhill Bridge

82 Otherton Bridge
36 Otherton Lock 10' 3"

OTHERTON
Otherton Farm
81 Otherton Lane Bridge

Rail Bridge

Micklewood Lane
102

Rodbaston
Rodbaston Stables

Aqueduct

Staffordshire College of Agriculture
Sports Field

Fullmoor

35 Rodbaston Lock 8' 6"

Gailey Lea Farm
104

34 Bogg's Lock 8' 6"
33 Brick Kiln Lock 8' 0"
Plough Farm

94
Gailey Lea Lane

GAILEY UPPER RESERVOIR

JUNCTION 12

GAILEY
79 Gailey Bridge
32 Gailey Lock 8' 6"
WHARF
Croft Farm

CALF HEATH RESERVOIR

GAILEY LOWER RESERVOIR
106

Watling Street Plantation

Gravelly Way House

Reservoir Plantation

78A Four Ashes Bridge
78 Gravelly Way Bridge
Gravelly Way
102

CALF HEATH WOOD

Woodside Farm

Heath Farm

108

CALF HEATH

M6

Woodlands Lane

Pipe Bridges

Chemical Works
106

Straight Mile Farm
106

The Hollies
PH

Works
105

Calf Heath Bridge 77
76 Long Moll's Bridge
Sewage Works
Aqueduct

Marina
Weir
Hatherton Branch
Goldie Brook Bridge

Four Ashes
Industrial Estate

Deepmore Farm

75 Deepmore Bridge

Latherford
Upper Latherford Farm

Standeford
Pool House

Aqueduct
Moat

Lower Latherford Farm
108

99
73 Low Laches Bridge
The Laches
74 Moat House Bridge

Penkridge

The navigation now passes through Penkridge and is soon approached by the little River Penk: the two water courses share the valley for the next few miles. Apart from the noise of the motorway this is a pleasant valley: there are plenty of trees, a handful of locks and the large Teddesley Park alongside the canal. At Acton Trussell the M6 roars off to the north west and once again peace returns to the waterway.

Grange Farm
Wesleigh Farm
Brookflat
Barnhurst Farm
Barnhurst Farm
104
Roseford 94 Bridge
Roseford Farm
Acton Gate
Ivy House Farm
Actonmill Farm
Hill Lane
78
Wattle Lane
ACTON AND BED
JUNCTION 13
A449(T)
STAFFORDSHIRE AND WORCESTERSHIRE CANAL
93 Acton Bridge
Acton Trussell Farm
ACTON TRUSSELL
Rowley Moor
Dunston Farm
School
99
Meadow
92 Acton Moat Bridge
82
Plushes Farm
91
Cockpit Plantation
Home Farm
Shutt Hill Lock 41
6' 0"
River Penk
91 Shutt Hill Bridge
Moat House Farm
Wellington Belt
Adams Barn
Acton Pasture Barn
Staffordshire Way
Drayton Manor
M6
Sewage Works
103
Honey Pots
Park Gate Lock 40
7' 6"
Lower Drayton
90 Park Gate Bridge
B
TEDDESLEY PARK
The Beeches
102
Parkgate Farm
94
Lower Drayton Farm
95
Lodgerail Pool
89 Teddesley Park Bridge
WOOD BANK
M6 Motorway Bridge
Longford Bridge 88
Wood Bank Farm
Hayes Wood
87 Broom Bridge
39 Longford Lock
10' 0"
97
Bangley Park
Hazel
Dumb Shay
The Roller Mill
Sch
Viaduct
Market
Sch
The Marsh
Little Marshe
Wolgarston
86 Penkridge Bridge
38 Penkridge Lock 9' 3"
103
Quarry Heath
B5012
Sch
85 Princefield Bridge
Leisure Centre
Quarry Heath Farm
Station
Pinfold Lane
B
Filance Lock 37
10' 3"
PENKRIDGE
Littlestones Bridge
Nursery
The Deanery
101
84 Filance Bridge
83A Cross Keys Bridge

Penkridge

Staffs. MD Mon. PO, tel, stores, garage, bank, station. Above Penkridge Lock is a good place to tie up in this relatively old village. It is bisected by a trunk road, but luckily most of the village lies to the east of it. The church of St Michael is tall and sombre, and is well kept. A harmonious mixture of styles, the earliest dates from the 11thC, but the whole was restored in 1881. There is a fine Dutch 18th-C wrought iron screen brought from Cape Town, and the tower is believed to date from about 1500. There are fine monuments of the Littletons of Pillaton Hall

(see the previous section), dating from 1558 and later.

Teddesley Park On the east bank of the canal. The Hall, once the family seat of the Littletons, was used during the last war as a prisoner-of-war camp, but has since been demolished. Its extensive wooded estate still remains.

Acton Trussell

Staffs. PO, tel, stores. A village overwhelmed by modern housing: much the best way to see it is from the canal. The church stands to the south, overlooking the navigation. The west tower dates from the 13thC, topped by a spire built in 1562.

Boatyards

Ⓑ **Teddesley Boat Company** Park Gate Lock, Teddesley Road, Penkridge (01785 714692). D Pump-out, gas, narrow boat hire, day boat hire, overnight & long-term mooring, winter storage, crane, boat & engine sales & repairs, boat building.

Closed Sun. For chandlery telephone (01785) 712437.

Ⓑ **Tom's Moorings** Cannock Road, Penkridge (01543 414808). Above Penkridge Lock. ♿ Pump-out, gas, overnight and long-term mooring.

The Moat House, Acton Trussell

Pubs and Restaurants

🍺 **The Boat** Cannock Road (01785 714178). Canalside, by Penkridge Lock. A mellow and friendly red-brick pub dating from 1779, with plenty of brass and other bits and pieces in the homely bars. Ansells, Marston's and Morland's and food *lunchtimes and evenings (not Sunday evenings).* Children welcome.

🍺 **Star** Market Place, Penkridge (01785 712513). A fine old pub, tastefully renovated and serving Banks's real ale and bar meals *lunchtimes and evenings,* with a vegetarian menu. Outside seating. Children welcome.

🍺 **White Hart** Stone Cross, Penkridge (01785 712242). This historic former coaching inn, visited by Mary, Queen of Scots, and Elizabeth I, has an impressive frontage, timber framed with three gables. It serves Banks's

and Bass real ale and meals *lunchtimes and evenings, along with traditional Siunday lunch.* Garden.

🍺 **Railway** Wolverhampton Road, Penkridge (01785 712685). Tetley's, Banks's, Porter and guest real ales are available in this listed and historic main road pub, along with meals *lunchtimes and evenings, including special Sunday lunches,* with a vegetarian choice. Children welcome. Garden. Karaoke nights.

🍺 ✕ **The Moat House** Bridge 92, Acton Trussell (01785 712217). Attractive 14th-C pub with a conservatory and 6 acres of land-scaped garden. Banks's and Marston's real ale. Restaurant meals *L & D* and bar meals *lunchtimes Mon–Sat and evenings Sun–Fri,* including a vegetarian menu. Children welcome. Pleasant moorings. B & B.

Tixall

Continuing north along the shallow Penk valley, the canal soon reaches Radford Bridge, the nearest point to Stafford. It is about 1 1/2 miles to the centre of town: there is a frequent bus service. A mile further north the canal bends around to the south east and follows the pretty valley of the River Sow. At Milford the navigation crosses the Sow via an aqueduct – an early structure by James Brindley, carried heavily on low brick arches. Dredging around here revealed the presence of great numbers of fresh water mussels. Tixall Lock offers some interesting views in all directions: the castellated entrance to Shugborough Railway Tunnel at the foot of the thick woods of Cannock Chase and the distant outline of Tixall Gatehouse. The canal now completes its journey to the Trent & Mersey Canal at Great Haywood. It is a length of waterway quite unlike any other. Proceeding along this very charming valley, the navigation enters Tixall Wide – an amazing and delightful stretch of water more resembling a lake than a canal, and navigable to the edges. The Wide is noted for its kingfisher population. On the low hill to the north is the equally remarkable Tixall Gatehouse, while woods across the valley conceal Shugborough Hall. The River Trent is met, on its way south from Stoke-on-Trent, and crossed on an aqueduct.

There is a wharf, and fresh produce can be purchased at the farm near here: gifts are sold in the old canal toll booth. The Trent & Mersey Canal is entered through an elegantly arched bridge, the subject of a very famous photograph taken by the canal historian Eric de Maré.

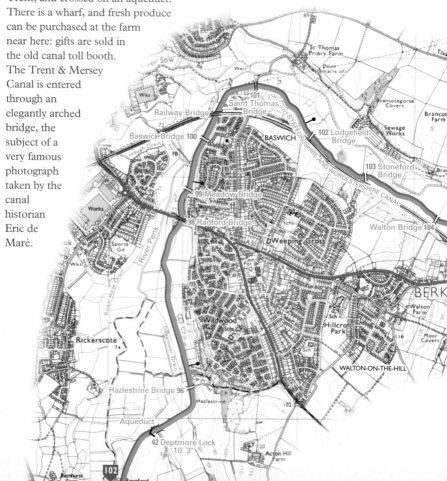

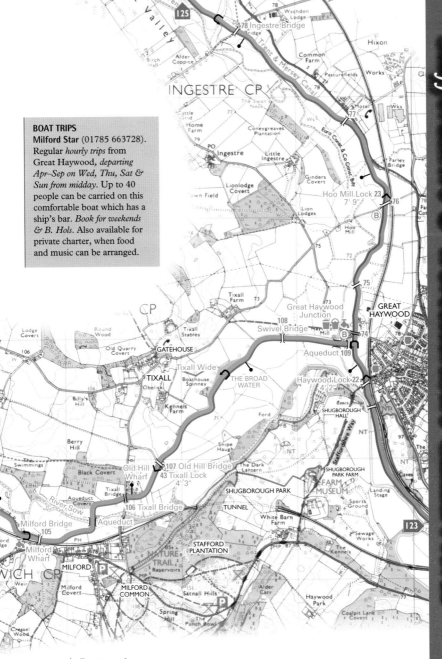

BOAT TRIPS
Milford Star (01785 663728).
Regular *hourly trips* from
Great Haywood, *departing
Apr–Sep on Wed, Thu, Sat &
Sun from midday*. Up to 40
people can be carried on this
comfortable boat which has a
ship's bar. *Book for weekends
& B. Hols*. Also available for
private charter, when food
and music can be arranged.

Boatyards

Ⓑ **Anglo Welsh** The Canal Wharf, Mill Lane, Great Haywood (01889
881711). Pump-out, gas, narrow boat hire, day hire craft, overnight
mooring, long term mooring, boat and engine repairs, toilets, gifts.

● Stafford

Staffs. MD Tue, Fri, Sat. All services. This town is well worth visiting, since there is a remarkable wealth of fine old buildings. These include a handsome City Hall complex of ornamental Italianate buildings, c.1880. The robust-looking gaol is nearby; and the church of St Mary stands in very pleasing and spacious grounds. There are some pretty back alleys: Church Lane contains a splendid-looking eating house, and at the bottom of the lane a fruiterer's shop is in a thatched cottage built in 1610.

The Shire Hall Gallery Market Square, Stafford (01785 278345). A stimulating variety of work by local artists, craftsmen, printmakers, jewellers, photographers and others. *Open Mon–Sat 10.00–17.00.*

Tourist Information Centre The Ancient High House, Greengate Street, Stafford (01785 240204).

● The Stafford Branch

Just west of bridge 101 there was once a lock taking a branch off the Staffordshire & Worcestershire to Stafford. One mile long, it was unusual in that it was not a canal but the canalised course of the River Sow.

● Milford

Staffs. PO, tel, stores, garage. Best reached from Tixall Bridge (106). Milford Hall is hidden by trees.

● Tixall

Staffs. Tel, stores. Just to the east are the stables and the gatehouse of the long-vanished Tixall Hall. This massive square Elizabethan building dates from 1598 and is fully four storeys high. It stands alone in a field and is considered to be one of the most ambitious gatehouses in the country. The gatehouse is now available for holiday lets: telephone the Landmark Trust (01628 825925) for details.

● Great Haywood

Staffs. PO, tel, stores. Centre of the Great Haywood and Shugborough Conservation Area, the village is not particularly beautiful, but it is closely connected in many ways to Shugborough Park, to which it is physically linked by the very old Essex Bridge, where the crystal clear waters of the River Sow join the Trent on its way down from Stoke.

Shugborough Hall *National Trust property.* Walk south along the road from bridge 106 to the A513 at Milford Common. The main entrance is on your left. The present house dates from 1693, but was substantially altered by James Stuart around 1760 and by Samuel Wyatt around the turn of the 18thC. The Trust has leased the whole to Staffordshire County Council who now manage it. The house has been restored at great expense. There are some magnificent rooms and treasures inside.

Museum of Staffordshire Life This excellent establishment, Staffordshire's County Museum, is housed in the old stables adjacent to Shugborough Hall. Open since 1966, it is superbly laid out and contains all sorts of exhibits concerned with old country life in Staffordshire.

Shugborough Park There are some remarkable sights in the large park that encircles the hall. Thomas Anson, who inherited the estate in 1720, enlisted in 1744 the help of his famous brother, Admiral George Anson, to beautify and improve the house and the park. In 1762 he commissioned James Stuart, a neo-Grecian architect, to embellish the grounds. 'Athenian' Stuart set to with a will, and the spectacular results of his work can be seen scattered round the park.

The Park Farm Designed by Samuel Wyatt, it contains an agricultural museum, a working mill and a rare breeds centre. Traditional country skills such as bread-making, butter-churning and cheese-making are demonstrated.

Shugborough Hall, Grounds, Museum and Farm (01889 881388). *Open late Mar–late Sep, daily 11.00–17.00.* Charge. Parties must book.

Pubs and Restaurants

🍺 **Clifford Arms** Main Road, Great Haywood (01889 881321). Friendly village local with a real fire, once a coaching house, now serving Bass real ale and bar and restaurant meals *lunchtimes and evenings every day.* Garden.

🍺 **Fox & Hounds** Main Road, Great Haywood (01889 881252). Plush village pub serving Ansells, Marston's, Tetley's and guest real ales. Food *lunchtimes and evenings.* Vegetarians are catered for. Garden. Children welcome.

✕ ♀ **Lockhouse Restaurant** Trent Lane, Great Haywood (01889 881294). Home-cooked L *every day* and D *Wed–Sat only* (booking advisable). Vegetarians catered for. Marston's real ale. Just a couple of minutes walk from the centre of the village.

▌TRENT & MERSEY CANAL

MAXIMUM DIMENSIONS

Derwent Mouth to Burton upon Trent
Length: 72'
Beam: 10'
Headroom: 7'

Burton upon Trent to south end of Harecastle Tunnel
Length: 72'
Beam: 7'
Headroom: 6' 3"

Harecastle Tunnel
Length: 72'
Beam: 7'
Headroom: 5' 9"

North end of Harecastle Tunnel to Croxton Aqueduct
Length: 72'
Beam: 7'
Headroom: 7'

Croxton Aqueduct to Preston Brook Tunnel
Length: 72'
Beam: 8' 2"
Headroom: 6' 3"

MANAGER:

Derwent Mouth to Colwich: (01283) 790236
Colwich to Trentham: (01785) 284253
Trentham to Preston Brook: (01782) 785703

MILEAGE

DERWENT MOUTH to
Swarkestone Lock: 7 miles
Willington: $12^1/_4$ miles
Horninglow Wharf: $16^1/_2$ miles
Barton Turn: $21^1/_4$ miles
Fradley, junction with Coventry Canal: $26^1/_4$ miles
Great Haywood, junction with Staffordshire & Worcestershire Canal: 39 miles
Stone: $48^1/_2$ miles
Stoke Top Lock, junction with Caldon Canal: 58 miles
Harding's Wood, junction with Macclesfield Canal: $63^3/_4$ miles
King's Lock, Middlewich, junction with Middlewich Branch: $76^1/_4$ miles
Anderton Lift, for River Weaver: $86^1/_2$ miles

PRESTON BROOK north end of tunnel and Bridgewater Canal: $93^1/_2$ miles

Locks: 76

This early canal was originally conceived partly as a roundabout link between the ports of Liverpool and Hull, while passing through the busy area of the Potteries and mid-Cheshire, and terminating either in the River Weaver or in the Mersey. Its construction was promoted by Josiah Wedgwood (1730–95), the famous potter, aided by his friends Thomas Bentley and Erasmus Darwin. In 1766 the Trent & Mersey Canal Act was passed by Parliament, authorising the building of a navigation from the River Trent at Shardlow to Runcorn Gap, where it would join the proposed extension of the Bridgewater Canal from Manchester.

The ageing James Brindley was appointed engineer for the canal. Construction began at once and in 1777 the Trent & Mersey Canal was opened. In the total 93 miles between Derwent Mouth and Preston Brook, the Trent & Mersey gained connection with no fewer than nine other canals or significant branches.

By the 1820s the slowly-sinking tunnel at Harecastle had become a serious bottleneck. Thomas Telford recommended building a second tunnel beside the old one. His recommendation was eventually accepted by the company and the whole tunnel was completed in under three years, in 1827.

Although the Trent & Mersey was taken over in 1845 by the new North Staffordshire Railway Company, the canal flourished until World War I. Today it is assured (by statute) of its future as a pleasure cruising waterway. Look out for the handsome cast iron mileposts, which actually measure the mileage from Shardlow, not Derwent Mouth. There are 59 originals, from the Rougeley and Dixon foundry in Stone, and 34 replacements, bearing the mark T & MCS 1977 of the Trent & Mersey Canal Society.

Shardlow

The Trent & Mersey Canal begins at Derwent Mouth, some 2½ miles upstream of the point where

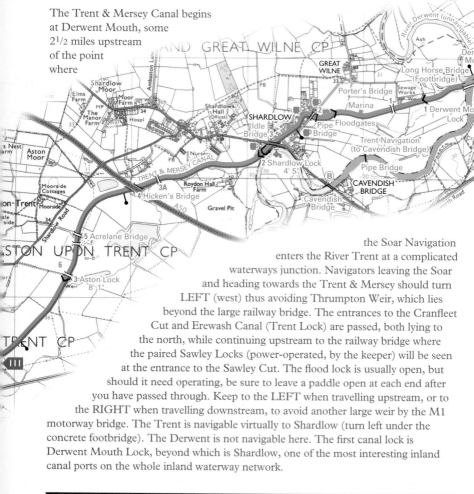

the Soar Navigation enters the River Trent at a complicated waterways junction. Navigators leaving the Soar and heading towards the Trent & Mersey should turn LEFT (west) thus avoiding Thrumpton Weir, which lies beyond the large railway bridge. The entrances to the Cranfleet Cut and Erewash Canal (Trent Lock) are passed, both lying to the north, while continuing upstream to the railway bridge where the paired Sawley Locks (power-operated, by the keeper) will be seen at the entrance to the Sawley Cut. The flood lock is usually open, but should it need operating, be sure to leave a paddle open at each end after you have passed through. Keep to the LEFT when travelling upstream, or to the RIGHT when travelling downstream, to avoid another large weir by the M1 motorway bridge. The Trent is navigable virtually to Shardlow (turn left under the concrete footbridge). The Derwent is not navigable here. The first canal lock is Derwent Mouth Lock, beyond which is Shardlow, one of the most interesting inland canal ports on the whole inland waterway network.

NAVIGATIONAL NOTES

Those heading towards the River Trent should not pass Shardlow floodgates if the warning light shows red.

● **Sawley Cut**
In addition to a large marina and a well-patronised BW mooring site, the Derby Motor Boat Club has a base on the Sawley Cut where well over 100 boats are kept. There are windlasses for sale at Sawley Lock, as well as the more conventional facilities.

● **Shardlow**
Derbs. PO, tel, stores, garage. Few canal travellers will want to pass through Shardlow without stopping. Everywhere there are living examples of large-scale canal architecture, as well as old-established necessities such as canal pubs. By the lock is the biggest and best of these buildings – the 18th-C Trent Mill, now the Clock Warehouse, which has a large central arch where boats once entered to unload. Restored in 1979, it still retains all its original proud elegance.

Shardlow Heritage Centre Adjacent to the Clock Warehouse (01332 792935). *Open Apr-Oct, Fri-Sun 12.00-17.00.* Modest entry charge.

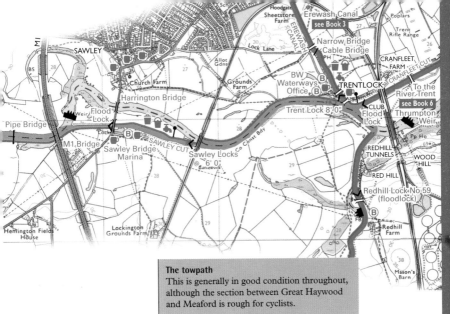

The towpath
This is generally in good condition throughout, although the section between Great Haywood and Meaford is rough for cyclists.

Boatyards

Ⓑ ✕ **Sawley Bridge Marina** Long Eaton, Nottingham (01159 734278). 🚽 🚿 ♨ P D Pump-out, gas, extensive moorings both overnight and long-term, slipway, crane, boat and engine sales and repairs, telephone, toilets, showers, chandlery, coffee shop, solid fuel, laundrette.

Ⓑ ✕ ♀ **Shardlow Marina** London Road, Shardlow (01332 792832). On the River Trent. 🚽 🚿 ♨ D Pump-out, gas, overnight and long-term mooring, winter storage, slipway, boat sales, toilets & showers, chandlery, licensed bar and restaurant.

Pubs and Restaurants

🍺 **Clock Warehouse** London Road, Shardlow (01332 792844). Mansfield real ale, and food *lunchtimes and evenings every day*, with a vegetarian menu. Children welcome, garden and adventure playground.

🍺 **Navigation** By bridge 3, London Road, Shardlow (01332 792918). Six guest real ales, and bar meals *lunchtimes and evenings*, with a vegetarian menu. Garden with play area and aviary. Regular quiz nights.

🍺 **Malt Shovel** By Bridge 2, The Wharf, Shardlow (01332 799763). Friendly canalside pub, built in 1779. Marston's real ale. Excellent and inventive food *lunchtimes only (not Sun)*, with a vegetarian menu. Children welcome. Outside seating by the canal.

🍺 **New Inn** The Wharf, Shardlow, next to

the Malt Shovel (01332 793331). Bass and guest real ales and bar meals *lunchtimes every day, and evenings Tue-Sat*, with a vegetarian options available. Garden and outside seating. Children welcome.

✕ ♀ **The Thai Kitchen** Shardlow (01332 792331). Authentic Thai food in a restaurant haunted by the 'lady in grey'. Children welcome *lunchtimes and early evening*. Outside seating. *L & D (no L Mon)*. B & B.

🍺 **Old Crown** Cavendish Bridge, Shardlow (01332 792392). Bass, Marston's and four guest real ales in a friendly old riverside pub, decorated with old advertsing ephemera. Bar meals *lunchtimes only* and snacks with vegetarian options. Children welcome *at lunchtime only*. Garden with play area. B & B.

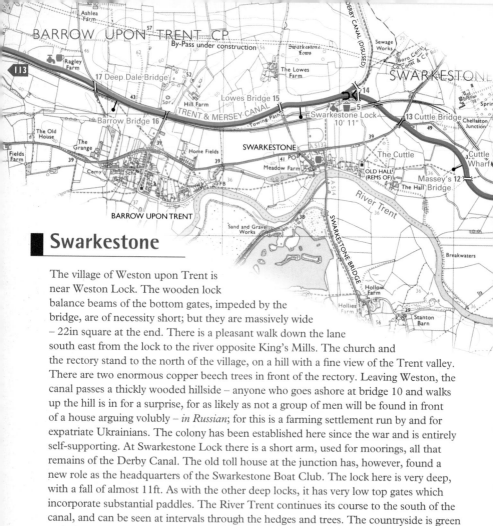

Swarkestone

The village of Weston upon Trent is
near Weston Lock. The wooden lock
balance beams of the bottom gates, impeded by the
bridge, are of necessity short; but they are massively wide
– 22in square at the end. There is a pleasant walk down the lane
south east from the lock to the river opposite King's Mills. The church and
the rectory stand to the north of the village, on a hill with a fine view of the Trent valley.
There are two enormous copper beech trees in front of the rectory. Leaving Weston, the
canal passes a thickly wooded hillside – anyone who goes ashore at bridge 10 and walks
up the hill is in for a surprise, for as likely as not a group of men will be found in front
of a house arguing volubly – *in Russian*; for this is a farming settlement run by and for
expatriate Ukrainians. The colony has been established here since the war and is entirely
self-supporting. At Swarkestone Lock there is a short arm, used for moorings, all that
remains of the Derby Canal. The old toll house at the junction has, however, found a
new role as the headquarters of the Swarkestone Boat Club. The lock here is very deep,
with a fall of almost 11ft. As with the other deep locks, it has very low top gates which
incorporate substantial paddles. The River Trent continues its course to the south of the
canal, and can be seen at intervals through the hedges and trees. The countryside is green
and pleasant, with only the occasional freight train rumbling by to disturb the peace.

● **Weston upon Trent**
Derbs. PO, tel, stores. A scattered village that is in
fact not very close to the Trent. The isolated
church is splendidly situated beside woods on
top of a hill, its sturdy tower crowned by a short
14th-C spire. Inside are fine aisle windows of the
same period. The lock gardens make the
approach from the canal particularly attractive.

● **Swarkestone**
Derbs. PO, tel, stores. The main feature of
Swarkestone is the 18th-C five-arched stone
bridge over the main channel of the River Trent.
An elevated causeway then carries the road on
stone arches all the way across the Trent's flood
plain to the village of Stanton by Bridge. It was
at Swarkestone that Bonnie Prince Charlie, in
the rising of 1745, gave up his attempt for the

throne of England and returned to his defeat at
Culloden. In a field nearby are the few remains
of Sir Richard Harpur's Tudor mansion, which
was demolished before 1750. The Summer
House, a handsome, lonely building, overlooks a
square enclosure called the Cuttle Jacobean in
origin, it is thought that it may have been the
scene of bull-baiting, although it seems more
likely it was just a 'bowle alley'. Restored by
the Landmark Trust, two people may now
have holidays here – telephone (01628) 825925
for details. The Harpurs moved to Calke
following the demolition of their mansion
after the Civil War. The pub in the village, and
monuments in the church, which is tucked
away in the back lanes, are a reminder of the
family.

● **Barrow upon Trent**
Derbs. Tel, stores. A small, quiet village severed from the canal by the busy
A514. A lane from the church leads down to the river. Until recently the
old hall stood next to the church, very much the focus of the village. But
now bright modern houses stand in its place and the surviving lodge
house looks uncomfortably irrelevant. Opposite is a mellow
terrace of old workmen's cottages.

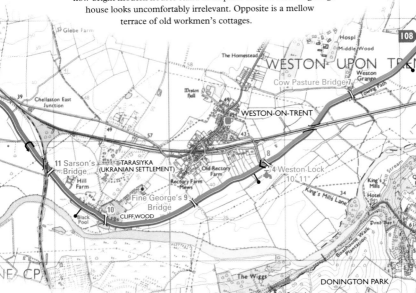

Pubs and Restaurants

◖ **Old Plough** Main Street, Weston upon
Trent (01332 700331). An attractive pub
serving Marston's and a guest real ale. There
is an exciting range of food, with a good
choice for vegetarians and children, available
lunchtimes and evenings every day. Outside
seating. Children welcome.

◖ **Crew & Harpur Arms** Swarkestone, by the
river bridge (01332 700641). Marston's and
guest real ales and bar meals served *all day
12.00–22.00 (21.00 Sun)*, with vegetarian
menu in this handsome pub. Riverside seating

and garden, and Billy Bear's children's play
area.

✕ **Swarkestone Tea Rooms** The Lock Cottage
(01283 790236).

◖ **Ragley Boat Stop** Deepdale Lane, off Sinfin
Lane, Barrow-on-Trent (01332 703919). A
large pub 300 yards west of bridge 17, serving
Courage and Marston's real ale. Food is
available *lunchtimes and evenings and all day
Sun.* Extensive vegetarian and children's
menu. Outside seating in a 3-acre garden.
Children welcome. Good moorings with ♨.

A HOP, A SKIP, AND A JUMP TO DERBY

The Derby Canal, which left the Trent & Mersey at Swarkestone and joined the
Erewash at Sandiacre, has long been disused. One condition of its building, and a
constant drain on its profits, was the free carriage of 5000 tons of coal to Derby each
year, for the use of the poor.
But one of the most unusual loads was transported on 19 April 1826, when 'a fine
lama, a kangaroo, a ram with four horns, and a female goat with two young kids,
remarkably handsome animals' arrived in Derby by canal 'as a present from Lord
Byron to a Gentleman whose residence in the neighbourhood, all of which had been
picked up in the course of the voyage of the *Blonde* to the Sandwich Islands in the
autumn of 1824'.

Willington

Just by bridge 18 is Arleston House, an attractive old building with ground floor walls of stone and the upper tiers of brick. This is followed by Stenson Lock, the last of the wide locks until Middlewich – it has a massive fall of 12ft 4in. Stenson is a small farming centre, always a popular mooring spot and now benefiting from the large marina. After passing through a railway bridge, the canal changes course and heads off

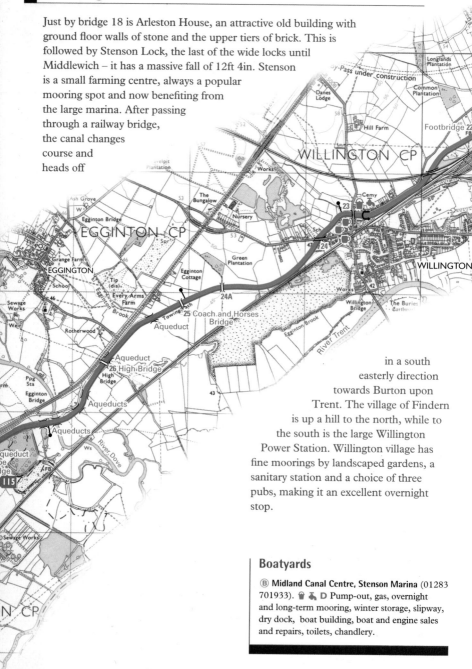

in a south easterly direction towards Burton upon Trent. The village of Findern is up a hill to the north, while to the south is the large Willington Power Station. Willington village has fine moorings by landscaped gardens, a sanitary station and a choice of three pubs, making it an excellent overnight stop.

Boatyards

ⓑ **Midland Canal Centre, Stenson Marina** (01283 701933). 🛢 🔧 D Pump-out, gas, overnight and long-term mooring, winter storage, slipway, dry dock, boat building, boat and engine sales and repairs, toilets, chandlery.

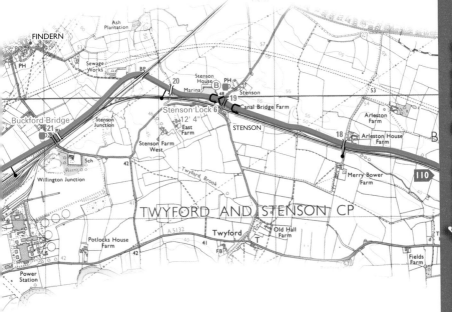

Repton

Derbs. PO. 1½ miles south east of Willington (over the River Trent) is Repton, one of the oldest towns in England. It was once the capital of Mercia and the crypt below St Wystan's Church was built in the 10thC. One of the finest examples of Saxon architecture in the country, this crypt was completely forgotten until the end of the 18thC when a man fell into it while digging a grave. Repton public school dates from 1551 and there is much of historical interest in the school and the town.

Willington

Derbs. PO, tel, stores, fish & chips. The railway bisects this busy little village by an embankment, which has three pubs, all huddled together.

Findern

Derbs. PO, tel, stores. A small, quiet village where Jedekiah Strutt, the inventor of the ribbed stocking frame, served a seven-year apprenticeship with the local wheelwright. At one time the village green was no more than a waste patch used by cars as a short cut, and a parking place. When suggestions were made to turn it into a formal cross roads, the indignant Women's Institute galvanised the villagers into actually uprooting all traces of tarmac from the green and turfing the whole area properly.

Egginton

Derbs. PO, tel, stores. A quiet village lying off the A38. The church, set apart from the village, is pleasingly irregular from the outside, with a large chancel and squat tower.

Pubs and Restaurants

Bubble Inn (01283 703113) Alongside Stenson Lock and Marina, this modern pub in a converted barn serves Marston's and other Courage real ales and bar meals *all day.* Children welcome. Garden.

Canal Turn Heath Lane, Findern (01283 701714). Canalside, at bridge 21. A basic but friendly family pub. Garden.

Rising Sun The Green, Willington (01283 702116). Marston's real ale. Reasonably priced bar food available at *lunchtimes (not Sun).* Bar games, and seats outside.

Green Dragon The Green, Willington (01283 702327). A popular and welcoming pub, with plenty of low beams, serving Marston's, Ind Coope (Burton), Tetley's and guest real ales. Food available *lunchtimes and evenings every day,* including vegetarian menu. Garden. Children welcome.

Burton upon Trent

A twelve-arched stone aqueduct carries the canal over the River Dove, beside a handsome four-arched bridge, no longer in use. The canal passes along one side of Burton, without entering the town. Many of the old canalside buildings have been demolished, but the waterside has been nicely tidied up, making the passage very pleasant. The lovely aroma of malt and hops is strongest to the west of the town, where the canal passes between the Marston and Bass breweries. Dallow Lock is the first of the narrow locks, an altogether easier job of work than the wider ones to the east. Shobnall Basin is now used by a boatyard, and visitor moorings nearby are available from which to explore the town. The A38 then joins the canal, depriving the navigator of any peace. Up on the hills to the north west is the well-wooded Sinai Park – the moated 15th-C house here, now a farm, used to be the summer home of the monks from Burton Abbey. There is a fine canalside pub at bridge 34, and a shop selling provisions, home-made cakes and crafts. It is *open Easter-Oct, every day 09.00–18.00*. The canal enters the new National Forest at bridge 30, and will leave it just beyond Alrewas. The Bass Millenium Woodland, to the west of Branston Lock, is part of this major project.

● **Burton upon Trent**
Staffs. MD Thu, Fri, Sat. All services. Known widely for its brewing industry, which originated here in the 13thC, when the monks at Burton Abbey discovered that an excellent beer could be brewed from the town's waters, because of their high gypsum content. At one time there were 31 breweries producing three million barrels of ale annually: alas, now only a few remain. The advent of the railways had an enormous effect on the street geography of Burton, for gradually a great network of railways took shape, connecting with each other and with the main line. These branches were mostly constructed at street level, and until recent years it was common for road traffic to be held up by endless goods trains chugging all over the town. Little of this system remains. The east side of the town is bounded by the River Trent, on the other side of which are pleasant hills. The main shopping centre lies to the east of the railway station.
The Bass Museum Horninglow Street, ¾ mile from Horninglow Basin. All aspects of brewing during the late 19thC. Also a preserved steam engine, café and shop. Conducted tours around the brewery. *Open every day 10.00–17.00 (last admission 16.00). Closed Xmas.* Admission charge.

Marston's Brewery Visitor Centre Shobnall Road, Burton upon Trent (01283 507391). *You must telephone and book in advance* to tour the brewery, see the Burton Union system, visit the cooperage, enjoy some food and sample the beers, which include Marston's Pedigree, Oyster Stout, Banks's Bitter, plus specials such as India Pale Ale and Owd Roger. *Tours Mon-Fri 11.00, 12.30, 14.30 (also Mon-Thu 18.30).* Charge.
Brewhouse Arts Centre Union Street car park (01283 516030). Live entertainment in a 230-seat theatre, plus a gallery and bistro bar.
Tourist Information Centre 183 High Street, Burton upon Trent (01283 516609/ 508589).
● **Shobnall Basin**
This is all that remains of the Bond End Canal, which gave the breweries the benefit of what was modern transport, before the coming of the railways.
● **Branston**
Staffs. PO, tel, stores, garage, butcher, Chinese take-away, fish & chips. This is apparently the place where the famous pickle originated.

Boatyards

ⓑ **Jannel Cruisers** Shobnall Marina, Shobnall Road, Burton upon Trent (01283 542718). In Shobnall Basin. 🚿 🚽 ♨ D Pump-out, gas, narrow boat hire, overnight mooring, long-term mooring, winter storage, slipway, dry dock, chandlery, books and maps, boat building, boat sales, engine sales and repairs, toilets.

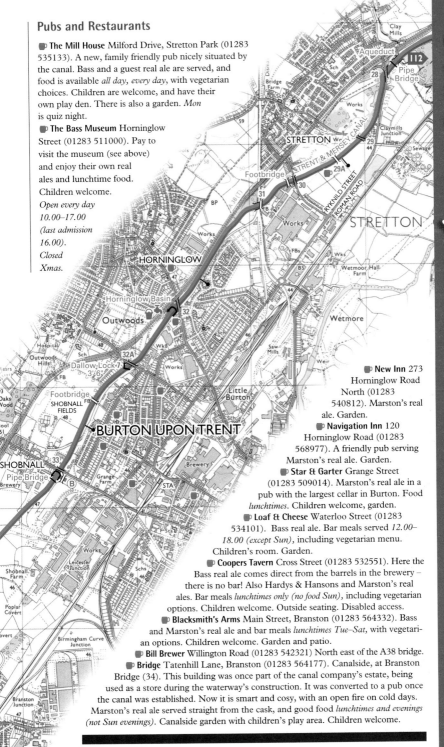

Pubs and Restaurants

The Mill House Milford Drive, Stretton Park (01283 535133). A new, family friendly pub nicely situated by the canal. Bass and a guest real ale are served, and food is available *all day, every day*, with vegetarian choices. Children are welcome, and have their own play den. There is also a garden. *Mon* is quiz night.

The Bass Museum Horninglow Street (01283 511000). Pay to visit the museum (see above) and enjoy their own real ales and lunchtime food. Children welcome. *Open every day 10.00–17.00 (last admission 16.00). Closed Xmas.*

New Inn 273 Horninglow Road North (01283 540812). Marston's real ale. Garden.

Navigation Inn 120 Horninglow Road (01283 568977). A friendly pub serving Marston's real ale. Garden.

Star & Garter Grange Street (01283 509014). Marston's real ale in a pub with the largest cellar in Burton. Food *lunchtimes*. Children welcome, garden.

Loaf & Cheese Waterloo Street (01283 534101). Bass real ale. Bar meals served *12.00–18.00 (except Sun)*, including vegetarian menu. Children's room. Garden.

Coopers Tavern Cross Street (01283 532551). Here the Bass real ale comes direct from the barrels in the brewery – there is no bar! Also Hardys & Hansons and Marston's real ales. Bar meals *lunchtimes only (no food Sun)*, including vegetarian options. Children welcome. Outside seating. Disabled access.

Blacksmith's Arms Main Street, Branston (01283 564332). Bass and Marston's real ale and bar meals *lunchtimes Tue–Sat*, with vegetarian options. Children welcome. Garden and patio.

Bill Brewer Willington Road (01283 542321) North east of the A38 bridge.

Bridge Tatenhill Lane, Branston (01283 564177). Canalside, at Branston Bridge (34). This building was once part of the canal company's estate, being used as a store during the waterway's construction. It was converted to a pub once the canal was established. Now it is smart and cosy, with an open fire on cold days. Marston's real ale served straight from the cask, and good food *lunchtimes and evenings (not Sun evenings)*. Canalside garden with children's play area. Children welcome.

Barton Turn

Beside Tatenhill Lock there is an attractive cottage: at the tail of the lock is yet another of the tiny narrow brick bridges that are such an engaging feature of this navigation. Note the very fine National Forest seat just north of the lock – there is another at Bagnall Lock, along with a 'living willow' sculpture. After passing flooded gravel pits and negotiating another tiny brick arch at bridge 36, the canal and the A38, the old Roman road, come very close together – thankfully the settlement of Barton Turn has been passed, leaving the main street (the old Roman road of Ryknild Street) wide and empty. It is with great relief that Wychnor Lock, with its diminutive crane and ware-house, is reached – here the A38 finally parts company with the canal, and some peace returns. To the west is the little 14th-C Wychnor church. Before Alrewas Lock the canal actually joins the River Trent – there is a large weir which should be given a wide berth. The canal then winds through the pretty village of Alrewas, passing the old church, several thatched cottages and a brick bridge.

● **Barton-under-Needwood**
Staffs. PO, tel, stores, bank, garage. Many years ago, when there were few roads and no canals in the Midlands, the only reasonable access to this village was by turning off the old Roman road, Ryknild Street: hence, probably, the name Barton Turn. The village is indeed worth turning off for, although unfortunately it is nearly a mile from the canal. A pleasant footpath from Barton Turns Lock leads quietly to the village, which is set on a slight hill. Its long main street has many attractive pubs. The church is battlemented and surround-ed by a very tidy churchyard. Pleasantly uniform in style, it was built in the 16thC by John Taylor, Henry VIII's private secretary, on the site of his cottage birthplace. The former Royal Forest of Needwood is to the north of the village.
● **Wychnor**
Staffs. A tiny farming settlement around the church of St Leonards, which was built in Early English Decorated style. Parts date from around 1200: the tower is probably 17th-C.
● **Alrewas**
Staffs. PO, tel, stores, garage, butcher, chemist, tea room, fish & chips. Away from the A513, this is an attractive village whose rambling back lanes harbour some excellent timbered cottages. The canal's unruffled passage through the village gives the place a restful air, and the presence of the church and its pleasant churchyard adds to this impression. The River Trent touches the village, feeding the old Cotton Mill, and provides it

with a fine background which is much appreciated by fishermen. The somewhat unusual name Alrewas, pronounced olrewus, is a corruption of the words Alder Wash – a reference to the many alder trees which once grew in the often-flooded Trent valley and gave rise to the basket weaving for which the village was once famous.
Alrewas Church A spacious building of mainly 13th-C and 14th-C construction, notable for the unmatching nave arches (octagonal and quatre-foil) and the old leper window, which is now filled by modern stained glass.

Boatyards

Boat Doctor (01332 771622). Emergency marine engineer with *24 hour* emergency breakdown call out.
Ⓑ **Wychnor Moorings** Wychnor, Burton upon Trent (07778 668388).
🛢 💧 ⚓ Pump-out, gas, long-term mooring, coal.

NAVIGATIONAL NOTES

In times of flood great caution should be exercised along the stretch immediately north of Alrewas lock – keep well over to the towpath side at all times.

Pubs and Restaurants

🍺 **Three Horseshoes** Station Road, Barton-under-Needwood (01283 716268). A quiet pub, with no juke box or pool table, but with extremely friendly staff serving a changing range of real ales and excellent bar meals *lunchtimes and evenings*, with vegetarian options.

Good selection of single malt whiskys. Children are welcome. Garden, and regular entertainment.

✕ **Little Chef** Canalside at Barton, and very handy (01283 716135). *Open 07.00– 22.00 daily*. Vegetarian options.

🍺 **Shoulder of Mutton** Main Street, Barton-under-Needwood (01283 712568). A 17th-C pub serving Bass, Worthington and a guest real ale and bar meals *lunchtimes and evenings (not Sun evenings)*, with a vegetarian menu. Function room. Children welcome, and a garden with a play area.

🍺 **Barton Turns** Barton Turn, just opposite Barton Lock (01283 712142). A basic but friendly pub serving Marston's real ale and bar meals *lunchtimes and evenings*, with vegetarian menu. Breakfast is also available. Small garden, and occasional live music.

🍺 **Crown** Post Office Road, Alrewas, near bridge 46 (01283 790328). Marston's, Bass and guest real ales and food *lunchtimes and evenings every day*, with a vegetarian menu. Children welcome. Garden.

🍺 **The Old Boat** Canalside at Alrewas, Kings Bromley Road (01283 791468). With a boat-themed and quirky interior, this relaxed and popular pub offers excellent meals *lunchtimes and evenings every day*, with vegetarian options, along with Ushers real ale. Children (and also dogs) welcome. Pleasant garden with play area. Regular entertainment. Moorings. Fishing facilities.

🍺 **George & Dragon** Main Street, Alrewas (01283 791476). Marston's real ale and bar meals *lunchtimes and evenings (not Sun)* with vegetarian menu, in an old village local. Garden. Children welcome.

🍺 **William IV** William IV Road, Alrewas (01283 790206). Marston's real ale, with bar meals *lunchtimes and evenings every day*, with a vegetarian menu. Children welcome. Patio. Regular *Sunday* quiz nights.

✕ 🍷 **Rafters Restaurant** Claymar Hotel, Alrewas (01283 790202). A welcoming and informal restaurant with a fine collection of Royal commorative mugs. Marston's real ale, bar meals and an à la carte menu served *evenings and Sun lunchtimes*. Children welcome, and a garden.

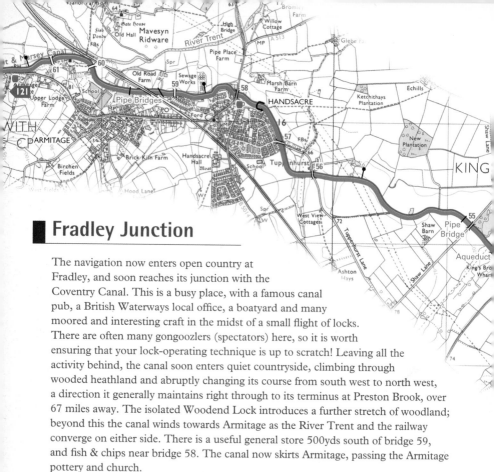

Fradley Junction

The navigation now enters open country at
Fradley, and soon reaches its junction with the
Coventry Canal. This is a busy place, with a famous canal
pub, a British Waterways local office, a boatyard and many
moored and interesting craft in the midst of a small flight of locks.
There are often many gongoozlers (spectators) here, so it is worth
ensuring that your lock-operating technique is up to scratch! Leaving all the
activity behind, the canal soon enters quiet countryside, climbing through
wooded heathland and abruptly changing its course from south west to north west,
a direction it generally maintains right through to its terminus at Preston Brook, over
67 miles away. The isolated Woodend Lock introduces a further stretch of woodland;
beyond this the canal winds towards Armitage as the River Trent and the railway
converge on either side. There is a useful general store 500yds south of bridge 59,
and fish & chips near bridge 58. The canal now skirts Armitage, passing the Armitage
pottery and church.

NAVIGATIONAL NOTES

West of bridge 61 the canal is very narrow, due to the removal of Armitage Tunnel, and
wide enough for one boat only. Check that the canal is clear before proceeding.

Boatyards

ⓑ **BW Waterways Office** Fradley Junction
(01283 790236). 🛉 🚿 ⚓ Overnight mooring,
long-term mooring, toilets.
ⓑ **Swan Line Cruisers** Fradley Junction (01283

790332). ⚓ D Pump-out (*not weekends*), gas,
narrow boat hire, overnight mooring, dry dock,
groceries, chandlery, books and maps, boat
building, boat sales, engine sales and repairs.

● **Fradley Junction**
A long-established canal centre where the
Coventry Canal joins the Trent & Mersey. Like
all the best focal points on the waterways, it is
concerned solely with the life of the canals, and
has no relationship with local roads or even with

the village of Fradley. The junction bristles with
boats for, apart from it being an inevitable
meeting place for canal craft, there is a boatyard,
a British Waterways maintenance yard, BW
moorings, a boat club and a popular pub – all in
the middle of a five-lock flight.

● **Kings Bromley**

Staffs. PO, tel, stores. A village 1½ miles north of bridge 54, along the A515. There are some pleasant houses and an old mill to be seen here, as well as what is reputed to have been Lady Godiva's early home. The Trent flows just beyond the church, which contains some old glass and a 17th-C pulpit and font. A large cross in the southern part of the churchyard is known locally as Godiva's cross.

● **Armitage**

Staffs. PO, tel, stores, garage. A main road village, whose church is interesting: it was rebuilt in the 19thC in a Saxon/Norman style, which makes it rather dark. The font is genuine Saxon, however, and the tower was built in 1690. The organ is 200 years old, and enormous: it came from Lichfield Cathedral and practically deafens the organist at Armitage. The town is widely known for its Armitage Shanks water closets.

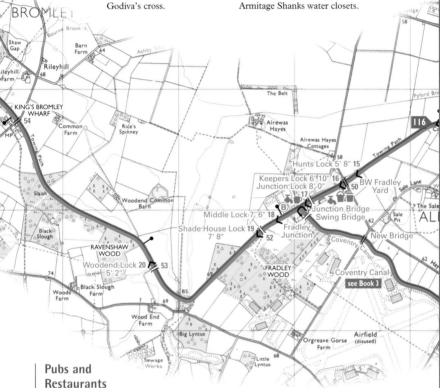

Pubs and Restaurants

● **Swan** Fradley Junction (01283 790330). Canalside, the focus of the junction and justly famous. There is a fine public bar with a coal fire and pub games, a comfortable lounge, and a cellar bar. Ansells, Ind Coope (Burton) and Marston's real ales are offered, and bar meals are served *lunchtimes and evenings every day.*

● **Crown** The Green, Handsacre (01543 490239). At bridge 58. A welcoming 300-year-old pub serving Bass, Marston's and Worthington real ale. Reasonably priced but good bar food *lunchtimes only Tue-Sat,* with a vegetarian menu. Grocer and fish & chips nearby. Family and games room, and a garden. Regular quiz nights. Good moorings.

✗ ☐ **Tom Cobleigh's Spode Cottage** Armitage (01543 490353). A very popular restaurant in a timbered 17th-C farmhouse, sensitively converted. Imaginative menu, vegetarians catered for, and Bass, Marston's, Worthington and a guest real ale to enjoy. *Open every day Mon–Sat 11.00–23.00 and Sun 12.00–22.30.* Booking advisable at weekends. Children welcome *until 21.30.* Large garden.

● **Plum Pudding** Canalside, west of Armitage, Rugeley Road, Armitage (01543 490330). A well kept pub serving Marston's, Tetley's and guest real ales, with bar meals *lunchtimes and evenings, restaurant meals evenings,* and including a vegetarian menu. Outside seating and garden. Children welcome *for meals only.*

Rugeley

The A513 crosses the canal on
a new bridge where the short, 130yds
long, Armitage Tunnel used to run before its
roof was removed in 1971 to combat the subsidence
effects of coal being mined nearby. There is a distinguished
restaurant just across the road here, very much a rarity on canals
in general and this area in particular. To the west stands Spode House,
a former home of the pottery family. The huge power station at Rugeley,
tidied up now, comes into view – and takes a long time to recede. There are
pleasant moorings at Rugeley, by bridge 66, with the town centre and shops
only a short walk away. North of the town, the canal crosses the River Trent via a
substantial aqueduct. The canal now enters an immensely attractive area full of
interest. Accompanied by the River Trent, the canal moves up a narrowing valley
bordered by green slopes on either side, Cannock Chase being clearly visible to the
south. Wolseley Hall has gone, but Bishton Hall (now a school) still stands: its very
elegant front faces the canal near Wolseley Bridge.

● **Spode House** Spode House and Hawkesyard
Priory stand side by side. The priory was founded
in 1897 by Josiah Spode's grandson and his niece
Helen Gulson when they lived at Spode House.
● **Rugeley**
Staffs. PO, tel, stores, garage, banks, station, cinema.
An unexciting place with a modern town centre
and a dominating power station. There are two
churches by bridge 67; one is a 14th-C ruin, the
other is the parish church built in 1822 as a
replacement.

● **Cannock Chase**
An area of outstanding natural beauty and
officially designated as such in 1949. The Chase
is all that remains of what was once a Norman
hunting ground known as the King's Forest of
Cannock. Flora and fauna are abundant and
include a herd of fallow deer whose ancestors have
grazed in this area for centuries. Shugborough
Park is at the north end of the Chase.

Cannock Chase

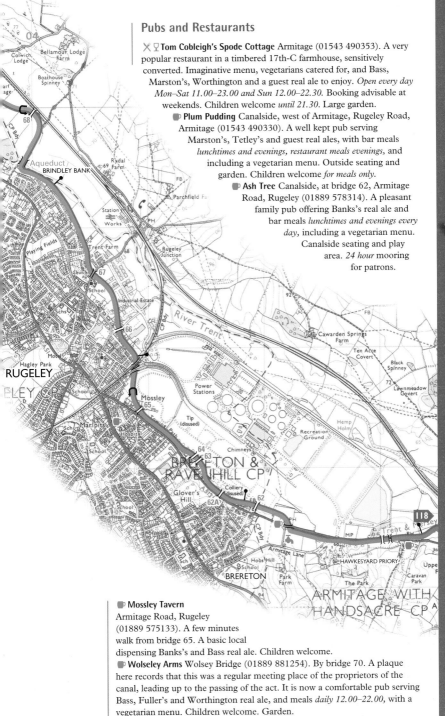

Pubs and Restaurants

✗ ♀ **Tom Cobleigh's Spode Cottage** Armitage (01543 490353). A very popular restaurant in a timbered 17th-C farmhouse, sensitively converted. Imaginative menu, vegetarians catered for, and Bass, Marston's, Worthington and a guest real ale to enjoy. *Open every day Mon–Sat 11.00–23.00 and Sun 12.00–22.30*. Booking advisable at weekends. Children welcome *until 21.30*. Large garden.

Plum Pudding Canalside, west of Armitage, Rugeley Road, Armitage (01543 490330). A well kept pub serving Marston's, Tetley's and guest real ales, with bar meals *lunchtimes and evenings, restaurant meals evenings*, and including a vegetarian menu. Outside seating and garden. Children welcome *for meals only*.

Ash Tree Canalside, at bridge 62, Armitage Road, Rugeley (01889 578314). A pleasant family pub offering Banks's real ale and bar meals *lunchtimes and evenings every day*, including a vegetarian menu. Canalside seating and play area. *24 hour* mooring for patrons.

Mossley Tavern Armitage Road, Rugeley (01889 575133). A few minutes walk from bridge 65. A basic local dispensing Banks's and Bass real ale. Children welcome.

Wolseley Arms Wolsey Bridge (01889 881254). By bridge 70. A plaque here records that this was a regular meeting place of the proprietors of the canal, leading up to the passing of the act. It is now a comfortable pub serving Bass, Fuller's and Worthington real ale, and meals *daily 12.00–22.00*, with a vegetarian menu. Children welcome. Garden.

Great Haywood

The pleasant surroundings continue as the canal passes Colwich. As the perimeter of Shugborough Park is reached the impressive façade of the Hall can be seen across the parkland. Haywood Lock and a line of moored craft announce the presence of Great Haywood and the junction with the Staffordshire & Worcestershire Canal (see page 105), which joins the Trent & Mersey under a graceful and much photographed towpath bridge: just the other side there is a useful boatyard. Beyond the junction the Trent valley becomes much broader and more open. There is another boatyard by Hoo Mill Lock.

● **Great Haywood**
Staffs. PO, tel, stores. Centre of the Great Haywood and Shugborough Conservation Area, the village is not particularly beautiful, but it is closely connected in many ways to Shugborough Park, to which it is physically linked by the very old Essex Bridge, where the crystal clear waters of the River Sow join the Trent on its way down from Stoke. Haywood Lock is beautifully situated between this packhorse bridge (which is an Ancient Monument) and the unusually decorative railway bridge that leads into Trent Lane. The lane consists of completely symmetrical and very handsome terraced cottages: they were built by the Ansons to house the people evicted from the former Shugborough village, the site of which is now occupied by the Arch of Hadrian within the park, built to celebrate Anson's circumnavigation of the globe in 1740–4. There is an interesting-looking Roman Catholic church in Great Haywood: the other curious feature concerns the Anglican church. About 100yds south of Haywood Lock is an iron bridge over the canal. This bridge, which now leads nowhere, used to carry a private road from Shugborough Hall which crossed both the river and the canal on its way to the church just east of the railway. This was important to the Ansons, since the packhorse bridge just upstream is not wide enough for a horse and carriage, and so until the iron bridge was built the family had to *walk* the 300yds to church on Sunday mornings!
Shugborough Hall *National Trust property.* Walk west from Haywood Lock and through the park. The present house dates from 1693, but was substantially altered by James Stuart around 1760 and by Samuel Wyatt around the turn of the 18thC. It was at this time that the old village of Shugborough was bought up and demolished by the Anson family so that they should enjoy more privacy and space in their park. Family fortunes fluctuated greatly for the Ansons, the Earl of Lichfield's family; eventually crippling death duties in the 1960s brought about the transfer of the estate to the National Trust. The Trust has leased the property to Staffordshire County Council who now manage the whole estate. The house has been restored at great expense. There are some magnificent rooms and many treasures inside.
Museum of Staffordshire Life This excellent establishment, Staffordshire's County Museum, is housed in the old stables adjacent to Shugborough Hall. Open since 1966, it is superbly laid out and contains all sorts of exhibits concerned with old country life in Staffordshire. Amongst other things it contains an old fashioned laundry, the old gun-room and the old estate brew-house, all completely equipped. Part of the stables contains harness, carts, coaches and motor cars. There is an industrial annexe up the road, containing a collection of preserved steam locomotives and some industrial machinery.
Shugborough Park There are some remarkable sights in the large park that encircles the hall. Thomas Anson, who inherited the estate in 1720, enlisted in 1744 the help of his famous brother, Admiral George Anson, to beautify and improve the house and the park. And in 1762 he commissioned James Stuart, a neo-Grecian architect, to embellish the park. 'Athenian' Stuart set to with a will, and the spectacular results of his work can be seen scattered round the park. The stone monuments that he built have deservedly extravagant names like the Tower of the Winds, the Lanthorn of Demosthenes and so on.
The Park Farm Designed by Samuel Wyatt, it contains an agricultural museum, a working mill and a rare breeds centre. Traditional country skills such as bread-making, butter-churning and cheese-making are demonstrated.
Shugborough Hall, Grounds, Museum and Farm (01889 881388). *Open late Mar–late Sep, daily 11.00–17.00.* Parties must book.

Boatyards

Ⓑ **Anglo Welsh** The Canal Wharf, Mill Lane, Great Haywood (01889 881711).
🚽 🚿 ⛽ D Pump-out, gas, narrow boat hire, day hire craft, overnight mooring, long term mooring, boat and engine repairs, toilets, gifts.
Ⓑ **Hoo Mill Boatyard** Hoo Mill Lane, Great Haywood (01889 882611) ⛽ D Pump-out, gas, narrow boat hire, long-term mooring, winter storage, dry dock, boatbuilding, boat and engine sales and repairs, toilets, showers, laundrette, chandlery.

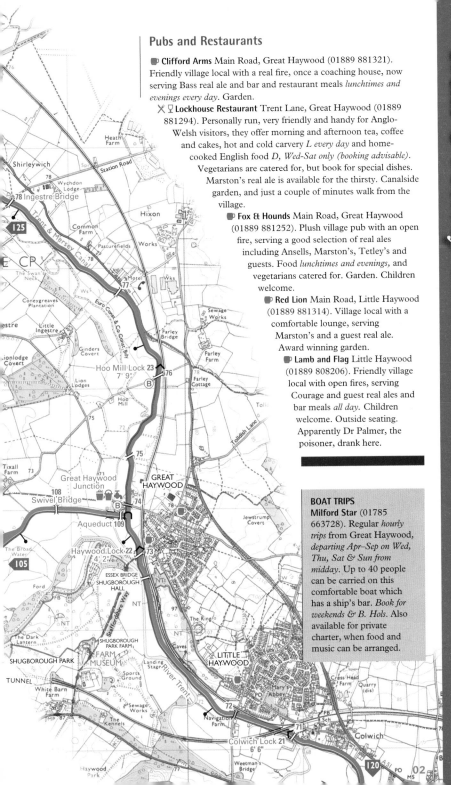

Pubs and Restaurants

Clifford Arms Main Road, Great Haywood (01889 881321). Friendly village local with a real fire, once a coaching house, now serving Bass real ale and bar and restaurant meals *lunchtimes and evenings every day.* Garden.

Lockhouse Restaurant Trent Lane, Great Haywood (01889 881294). Personally run, very friendly and handy for Anglo-Welsh visitors, they offer morning and afternoon tea, coffee and cakes, hot and cold carvery *L every day* and home-cooked English food *D, Wed-Sat only (booking advisable).* Vegetarians are catered for, but book for special dishes. Marston's real ale is available for the thirsty. Canalside garden, and just a couple of minutes walk from the village.

Fox & Hounds Main Road, Great Haywood (01889 881252). Plush village pub with an open fire, serving a good selection of real ales including Ansells, Marston's, Tetley's and guests. Food *lunchtimes and evenings,* and vegetarians catered for. Garden. Children welcome.

Red Lion Main Road, Little Haywood (01889 881314). Village local with a comfortable lounge, serving Marston's and a guest real ale. Award winning garden.

Lamb and Flag Little Haywood (01889 808206). Friendly village local with open fires, serving Courage and guest real ales and bar meals *all day.* Children welcome. Outside seating. Apparently Dr Palmer, the poisoner, drank here.

BOAT TRIPS
Milford Star (01785 663728). Regular *hourly trips* from Great Haywood, *departing Apr–Sep on Wed, Thu, Sat & Sun from midday.* Up to 40 people can be carried on this comfortable boat which has a ship's bar. *Book for weekends & B. Hols.* Also available for private charter, when food and music can be arranged.

Weston upon Trent

The canal now leaves behind the excitement of Great Haywood to continue its quiet north westerly passage through a broad valley towards Stone and Stoke-on-Trent. Hoo Mill Lock is a busy spot with many moored boats, and a useful boatyard. North of the lock a busy road joins the hitherto quiet canal for a while. To the west is Ingestre Hall: beyond here the locks are broadly spaced and, although roads are never far away, the atmosphere is one of remoteness and peace. The village of Weston upon Trent is pretty, and there are pleasant pubs to visit.

● **Great Haywood**
See previous section.
Ingestre Hall (01889 270225). ½ mile south west of bridge 78. Originally a Tudor building, the Hall was rebuilt in neo-Gothic style following a disastrous fire in 1820. The house is surrounded by large attractive gardens. It is now a residential arts centre *not open to the public.*
Battle of Hopton Heath This was fought 1½ miles west of Weston. An inconclusive Civil War battle on 19 March 1643, it reflected the strategic importance to both sides of Stafford, only 4 miles south west of the battlefield. In the engagement, 1800 Parliamentarians met 1200 Royalists (mostly cavalry). Supported by Roaring Meg – a 29-pound cannon – the Royalists took the initiative, making several bold and effective cavalry charges against the enemy. However, the Roundheads' musketry fought back strongly, and after the Royalist leader (the Earl of Northampton) was killed, the Cavaliers weakened and fell back. Eventually both sides were exhausted and nightfall brought an end to the battle. Casualties – at under 200 – were surprisingly light, and neither side could claim victory. The Cavaliers returned to Stafford, but two months later they lost the town for good to the Roundheads.

● **Weston upon Trent**
Staffs. PO, tel, stores. A pretty village of cottages and new houses, stretching away from St Andrew's church.

Great Haywood Junction Bridge (see page 123)

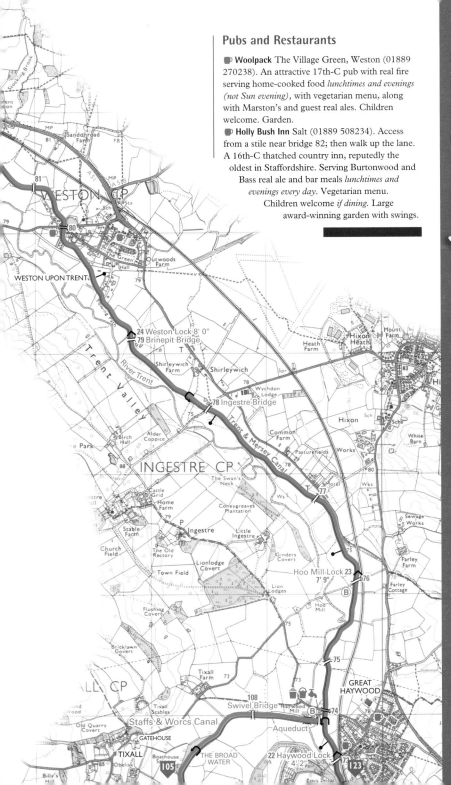

Pubs and Restaurants

🍺 **Woolpack** The Village Green, Weston (01889 270238). An attractive 17th-C pub with real fire serving home-cooked food *lunchtimes and evenings (not Sun evening),* with vegetarian menu, along with Marston's and guest real ales. Children welcome. Garden.

🍺 **Holly Bush Inn** Salt (01889 508234). Access from a stile near bridge 82; then walk up the lane. A 16th-C thatched country inn, reputedly the oldest in Staffordshire. Serving Burtonwood and Bass real ale and bar meals *lunchtimes and evenings every day.* Vegetarian menu. Children welcome *if dining.* Large award-winning garden with swings.

Stone

The wooded Sandon Park rises steeply on the north bank as the canal continues in a north westerly direction, passing through quiet meadows to the little village of Burston. The 100-year-old tower of Aston Church is prominent as the canal continues up through the quiet water meadows of the Trent valley. Soon Stone is entered; below the bottom lock is a good place to moor – a fine old canal pub by the lockside, children's playground and shops are close by. These locks are deeper than most on the narrow canals – their average rise is about 10ft. Just above the second lock there is a boatyard and three dry docks: there is another boatyard a few yards further on. Lock 29 is accompanied by a little tunnel under the road for boat horses.

Pubs and Restaurants

Dog & Doublet Inn Sandon (01889 508331). Marston's real ale and bar food *lunchtimes and evenings,* with a vegetarian menu. Children welcome. Garden with children's playthings. B & B.

✕ Greyhound Burston (01889 508263). A 10-minute walk up the lane east of bridge 86. Burtonwood and local guest real ales. Good bar and restaurant food, *lunchtimes and evenings and all day Sun,* with a vegetarian menu. Garden with play area, and a games room. Children welcome.

Three Crowns Little Stoke, Stone (01785 812977). A welcoming stone and thatch pub with open fires, dating from the 1700s, where the food is highly recommended. You can enjoy a meal from *12.00-21.30 every day,* and there are vegetarian choices. Real ales are Bass, Fuller's and Worthington. Children are welcome, and there is a garden.

Star Inn Stone bottom lock, Stafford Street (01785 813096). Well kept Banks's, Camerons, Marston's and guest real ales are served in this superb traditional lock-side pub, which apparently dates from the 14th-C and claims to be the oldest on the waterways, and where none of the rooms are on the same level. Good food is served *all day every day.* Children welcome. An excellent canal pub, with outside seating.

Crown & Anchor Station Road, Stone (01785 285401). Thatched pub serving Bass and Worthington real ale and meals *lunchtimes Sun-Wed, and lunchtimes and evenings Thu-Sat,* with a vegetarian menu. Outside seating. Children welcome.

Royal Exchange Radford Street, Stone (01785 615415). Basic pub serving inexpensive *lunchtime* bar meals and snacks with a vegetarian choice. Children welcome. Outside seating.

Rising Sun Newcastle Road, Stone 901785 813494). Bass, Marston's and Morrells real ale. Food available *lunchtimes Tue-Sun, and evenings Tue-Sat.* Children welcome. Picnic area.

Sandon

Staffs. PO, tel, stores. A small estate village clustered near the main gates to Sandon Park. The main road bisecting the place is enough to send any canal boatman scurrying back to the safety of the pretty Sandon Lock. There is a pub, however, opposite the park gates. All Saints Church, up the hill, is 13th-C to 15th-C with a Norman font and a 17th-C wall painting.

Burston

Staffs. Tel. A hamlet apparently untouched by modern times, in spite of the proximity of three transport routes. Most of the village is set around the village pond. A surprisingly quiet place.

Stone

Staffs. MD Tue, Thu. PO, tel, stores, garage, bank, station, laundrette. A very busy and pleasant town with excellent boating and shopping facilities. The old priory church began to fall down in 1749, so in 1753 an Act of Parliament was obtained to enable the parishioners to rebuild it. The new church, St Michael's in Lichfield Road, was consecrated in 1758, having cost £5000: it is a handsome building in open ground, on a slope at the east end of the town.

Boatyards

Ⓑ **Canal Cruising Co** Crown Street, Stone (01785 813982). 🚽 🛠 **D** Pump-out, gas, narrow boat hire, dry dock, boat repairs, boat building and painting. Supermarket adjacent, telephone nearby. 🚽 100yds along from boatyard.

Ⓑ **Stone Boatbuilding** Newcastle Road, Stone (01785 812688). 🚽 🚽 🛠 **D** Gas, winter storage, slipway, crane, boat building, boat and engine sales, boat repairs, outboard engine repairs, telephone, toilets, chandlery.

Ⓑ **Staffordshire Narrowboats** The Wharf, Newcastle Road, Stone (01785 816871). 🚽 🛠 Pump-out, narrow boat hire, overnight and long-term mooring, small selection of books and maps. 🚽 nearby.

The Star Inn at Star Lock, Stone

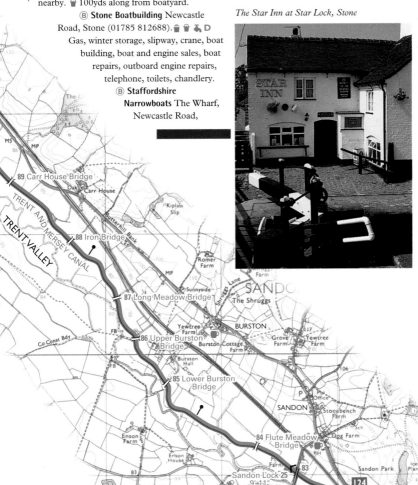

Barlaston

The Stone Locks are soon followed by another flight of four, climbing up the valley to Meaford. The present Meaford Locks replaced an earlier staircase of three, the remains of which can be seen by lock 33. Here the railway line draws alongside. The valley widens out now and becomes flatter and less rural. The railway flanks the canal as it approaches straggling Barlaston (PO). Just before Trentham Lock, where there are good moorings, is the Wedgwood Pottery, set back from the canal. The factory is conveniently served by Wedgwood Halt. North of Hem Heath Bridge, where there is also a PO, delicatessen and useful shop in the petrol station, looms Stoke-on-Trent.

Wedgwood Factory The Wedgwood Group is the largest china and earthenware manufacturer in the world. It was started in 1759 in Burslem by the famous Josiah Wedgwood, the Father of English Potters, who came from a small pottery family. By 1766 he was sufficiently prosperous to build a large new house and factory which he called Etruria – a name suggested by his close friend Dr Erasmus Darwin – and to use the canal, of which he was a promoter, for transport. It was here that he produced his famous Jasper unglazed stoneware with white classical portraits on the surface. He revolutionised pottery making with his many innovations and after his death in 1795 the company continued to expand. In the 1930s the Wedgwoods decided to build a new factory because mining subsidence had made Etruria unsuitable. The Etruria factory has unfortunately since been demolished but the large new factory began production in 1940 in Barlaston and is still the centre of the industry, with six electric tunnel ovens which produce none of the industrial smoke that is commonly associated with the Potteries. The Wedgwood Museum at Barlaston has a vast range of exhibits of Wedgwood pottery. The works is only a few yards from the canal, accessible from bridge 104. The Visitor Centre is *open daily, Mon–Fri 09.00–17.00, Sat 10.00–17.00, Sun 10.00–16.00* and a small charge is made. There are demonstrations, a shop, a museum and refreshments. Parties of 12 people and over must book (01782 204218). A stop here should be on every canal traveller's itinerary.

Traditional canal boat decoration

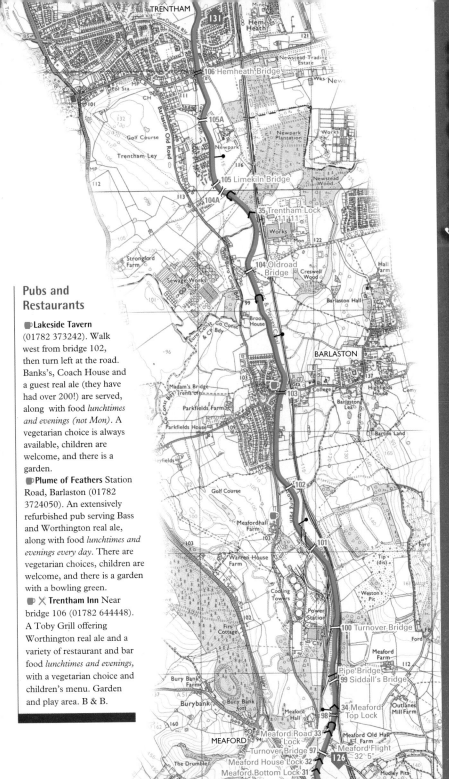

Pubs and Restaurants

🍺**Lakeside Tavern**
(01782 373242). Walk
west from bridge 102,
then turn left at the road.
Banks's, Coach House and
a guest real ale (they have
had over 200!) are served,
along with food *lunchtimes
and evenings (not Mon)*. A
vegetarian choice is always
available, children are
welcome, and there is a
garden.

🍺**Plume of Feathers** Station
Road, Barlaston (01782
3724050). An extensively
refurbished pub serving Bass
and Worthington real ale,
along with food *lunchtimes and
evenings every day*. There are
vegetarian choices, children are
welcome, and there is a garden
with a bowling green.

🍺✕**Trentham Inn** Near
bridge 106 (01782 644448).
A Toby Grill offering
Worthington real ale and a
variety of restaurant and bar
food *lunchtimes and evenings*,
with a vegetarian choice and
children's menu. Garden
and play area. B & B.

Stoke-on-Trent

This is a built-up length of canal, passing right through Stoke-on-Trent with all its factories and warehouses. Signs of the pottery industry still remain amidst much rebuilding. Its most remarkable manifestation are the bottle kilns – the brick furnaces shaped like gigantic bottles about 30ft high that still stand, cold and disused (but, happily, to be preserved), at the side of the canal. The Caldon Canal (see page 9) leaves the main line just above Stoke Top Lock. A statue of James Brindley, who built the Trent & Mersey Canal, was erected near the junction, on the Caldon Canal, in 1989. The Trent & Mersey then passes a marina and a pleasant pub, built for the National Garden Festival, before heading towards the south portal of the great Harecastle Tunnel.

● **Stoke-on-Trent**
Staffs. MD Wed, Fri, Sat. All services. The city was formed in 1910 from a federation of six towns (Burslem, Fenton, Hanley, Longton, Stoke and Tunstall) but became known as the Five Towns in the novels of Arnold Bennett. The thriving pottery industries are the source of the city's great prosperity – one to visit is the famous Spode China works which is right in the centre of the town in Church Street. The Town Hall, in Glebe Street, is an imposing and formal 19th-C building. Opposite the Town Hall is the parish church of St Peter, which contains a commemorative plaque to Josiah Wedgwood. Festival Park has been built on the site of the old Shelton Steelworks, with a dry ski slope, Waterworld and a multi-screen cinema amongst other attractions. You can catch the Wedgwood Express bus to visit many of the attractions from The Moat House Hotel, north of bridge 117.
City Museum and Art Gallery Bethesda Street, Hanley (01782 202173). As one might expect, it contains one of the world's most outstanding collections of ceramics, including work from Egypt, Persia, China, Greece and Rome. The historical development of pottery manufacture in Stoke-on-Trent is also traced from Roman times to the present day. *Open Mon–Sat 10.00–17.00 and Sun 14.00–17.00.* Free. Café on site.
Churchill China (Queens) Whieldon Road, Stoke (01782 745899). Close to bridge 112, this factory shop sells fine bone china and giftware. *Open Mon–Sat 09.00–17.00.*
Jesse Shirley's Etruscan Bone & Flint Mill Lower Bedford Street, Etruria (01782 287557). At the junction with the Trent & Mersey. This is a Victorian steam-powered potter's miller's works built in 1857 and which ground bone, flint and stone for the pottery industry, until closure in 1972. It has now been restored as part of an industrial complex incorporating a blacksmith's shop with working steam-powered machinery. Originally the raw materials and ground products were transported by canal, and present-day canal travellers will find plenty of moorings available. *Open for guided tours Wed–Sun 10.00–16.00(closed Mon & Tue).* Also operate special steam days *Apr–Dec, first weekend each month.* Charge. Tea room and shop.
Tourist Information Centre Quadrant Road, Hanley, Stoke on Trent (01782 236000).

Pubs and Restaurants

● ✕ **China Gardens** Canalside at Stoke Marina, Etruria (01782 260199). Large lounge, a carvery restaurant and a special family room. Local celebrities are featured in their Etruria Hall of Fame. Bass and Worthington real ale and meals *lunchtimes and evenings,* with a vegetarian menu. Garden with playground, and moorings.
● **Shelton Bar** 67 Etruria Old Road (01782 279330). West of bridge 117A. A warm and friendly pub in a listed building, serving Bass real ale and a wide range of food *lunchtimes and evenings.* Children welcome, garden and moorings.
● **Bird in Hand** Etruria Vale Road, Etruria (01782 205048). Close to the junction, this is a popular canal enthusiasts' pub serving Banks's real ale and bar snacks. Children welcome. Garden.

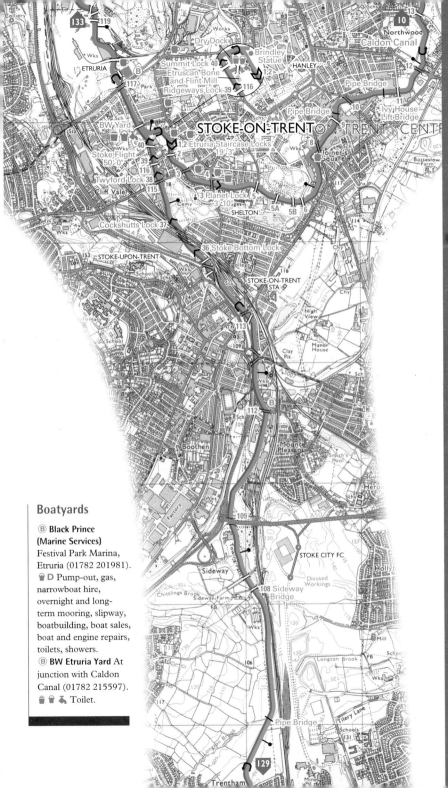

Boatyards

Ⓑ **Black Prince
(Marine Services)**
Festival Park Marina,
Etruria (01782 201981).
🚽 D Pump-out, gas,
narrowboat hire,
overnight and long-
term mooring, slipway,
boatbuilding, boat sales,
boat and engine repairs,
toilets, showers.
Ⓑ **BW Etruria Yard** At
junction with Caldon
Canal (01782 215597).
🚽 🚽 ♨ Toilet.

Harecastle Tunnel

The canal continues for a while through an industrial area, mostly connected with the pottery business and its needs, passing a large boatyard and a couple of pubs. Before long the navigation passes the expansive Westport Park Lake before abandoning its very twisting course and making a beeline for Harecastle Hill and the 2926yd tunnel through it. Only one of the tunnels is navigable now. The odd colour of the water here is caused by local ironstone strata.

NAVIGATIONAL NOTES

HARECASTLE TUNNEL Do not enter in an unpowered craft. Passage is prohibited unless the tunnel is manned. The maximum convoy length is eight boats. Follow tunnel-keepers instructions at all times. *Updated tunnel opening times can be obtained on (01782) 785703.*

● The Three Harecastle Tunnels

There are altogether three parallel tunnels through Harecastle Hill. The first, built by James Brindley, was completed in 1777, after 11 years' work. To build a 9ft wide tunnel 1³/₄ miles long represented engineering on a scale quite unknown to the world at that time, and the world was duly impressed. Since there was no towpath in the tunnel the boats – which were of course all towed from the bank by horses at that time – had to be legged through by men lying on the boat's cabin roof and propelling the boat by walking along the tunnel roof. The towing horse would, in the meantime, have to be walked over the top of the hill. This very slow means of propulsion, combined with the great length of the narrow tunnel and the large amount of traffic on the navigation, made Harecastle a major bottle-neck for canal boats. So in 1822 the Trent & Mersey

Canal Company called in Thomas Telford, who recommended that a second tunnel be constructed alongside the first one. This was done: the new tunnel was completed in 1827, with a towpath (now removed), after only three years' work. Each tunnel then became one-way until in the 20thC Brindley's bore had sunk so much from mining subsidence that it had to be abandoned. Its entrance can still be seen to the west of the newer tunnel mouth. An electric tug was introduced in 1914 to speed up traffic through Telford's tunnel; this service was continued until 1954. The third tunnel through Harecastle Hill was built years after the other two, and carried the Stoke-Kidsgrove railway line. It runs 40ft above the canal tunnels and is slightly shorter. This tunnel was closed in the 1960s: the railway line now goes round the hill and through a much shorter tunnel. Thus two out of the three Harecastle tunnels are disused.

Harecastle Tunnel – the northern portal

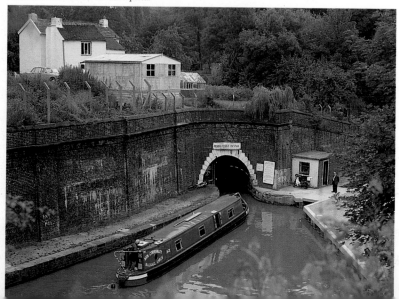

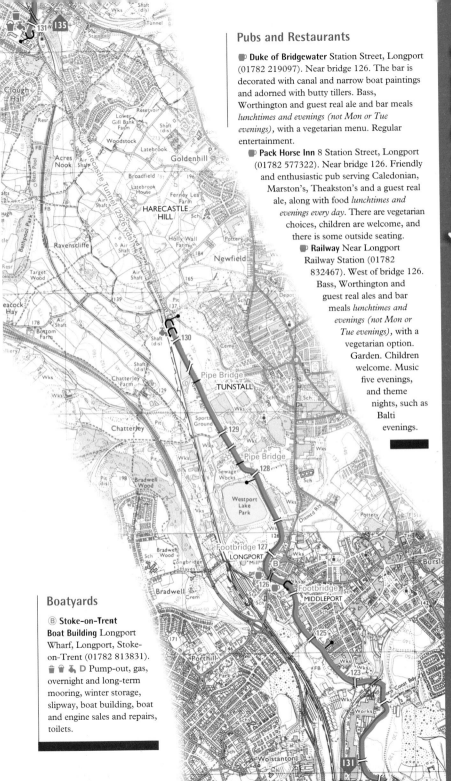

Pubs and Restaurants

🍺 **Duke of Bridgewater** Station Street, Longport (01782 219097). Near bridge 126. The bar is decorated with canal and narrow boat paintings and adorned with butty tillers. Bass, Worthington and guest real ale and bar meals *lunchtimes and evenings (not Mon or Tue evenings)*, with a vegetarian menu. Regular entertainment.

🍺 **Pack Horse Inn** 8 Station Street, Longport (01782 577322). Near bridge 126. Friendly and enthusiastic pub serving Caledonian, Marston's, Theakston's and a guest real ale, along with food *lunchtimes and evenings every day*. There are vegetarian choices, children are welcome, and there is some outside seating.

🍺 **Railway** Near Longport Railway Station (01782 832467). West of bridge 126. Bass, Worthington and guest real ales and bar meals *lunchtimes and evenings (not Mon or Tue evenings)*, with a vegetarian option. Garden. Children welcome. Music five evenings, and theme nights, such as Balti evenings.

Boatyards

ⓑ **Stoke-on-Trent Boat Building** Longport Wharf, Longport, Stoke-on-Trent (01782 813831). 🚿 🚽 🔧 **D** Pump-out, gas, overnight and long-term mooring, winter storage, slipway, boat building, boat and engine sales and repairs, toilets.

Harding's Wood Junction

At the north end of Harecastle Tunnel (2926yds long) the navigation passes Kidsgrove station and a coal yard: beyond is Harding's Wood Junction with the Macclesfield Canal, which crosses the T & M on Poole Aqueduct. The canal continues to fall through a heavily locked stretch sometimes called 'heartbreak hill' but known to the old boatmen as the 'Cheshire Locks'. Two minor aqueducts are encountered, but the locks are all pairs of narrow locks, side by side. At Hassall Green are a *PO, tel, and stores* incorporating a canal shop, restaurant and boatyard services.

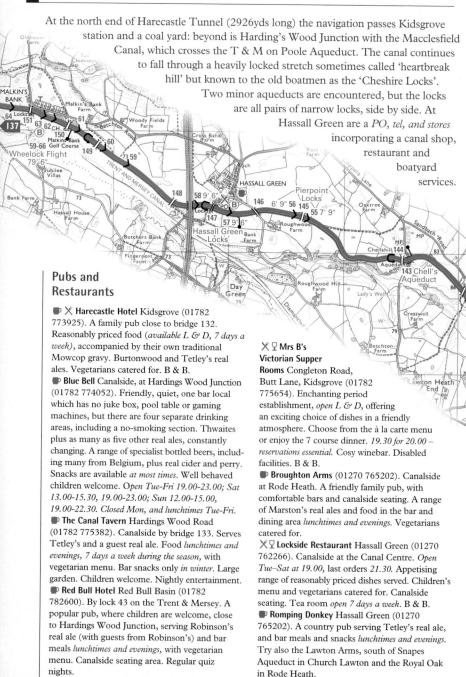

Pubs and Restaurants

🚢 ✕ **Harecastle Hotel** Kidsgrove (01782 773925). A family pub close to bridge 132. Reasonably priced food (*available L & D, 7 days a week*), accompanied by their own traditional Mowcop gravy. Burtonwood and Tetley's real ales. Vegetarians catered for. B & B.

🚢 **Blue Bell** Canalside, at Hardings Wood Junction (01782 774052). Friendly, quiet, one bar local which has no juke box, pool table or gaming machines, but there are four separate drinking areas, including a no-smoking section. Thwaites plus as many as five other real ales, constantly changing. A range of specialist bottled beers, including many from Belgium, plus real cider and perry. Snacks are available *at most times*. Well behaved children welcome. O*pen Tue-Fri 19.00-23.00; Sat 13.00-15.30, 19.00-23.00; Sun 12.00-15.00, 19.00-22.30. Closed Mon, and lunchtimes Tue-Fri.*

🚢 **The Canal Tavern** Hardings Wood Road (01782 775382). Canalside by bridge 133. Serves Tetley's and a guest real ale. Food *lunchtimes and evenings, 7 days a week during the season*, with vegetarian menu. Bar snacks only *in winter*. Large garden. Children welcome. Nightly entertainment.

🚢 **Red Bull Hotel** Red Bull Basin (01782 782600). By lock 43 on the Trent & Mersey. A popular pub, where children are welcome, close to Hardings Wood Junction, serving Robinson's real ale (with guests from Robinson's) and bar meals *lunchtimes and evenings*, with vegetarian menu. Canalside seating area. Regular quiz nights.

✕ 🍷 **Mrs B's Victorian Supper Rooms** Congleton Road, Butt Lane, Kidsgrove (01782 775654). Enchanting period establishment, *open L & D*, offering an exciting choice of dishes in a friendly atmosphere. Choose from the à la carte menu or enjoy the 7 course dinner. *19.30 for 20.00 – reservations essential.* Cosy winebar. Disabled facilities. B & B.

🚢 **Broughton Arms** (01270 765202). Canalside at Rode Heath. A friendly family pub, with comfortable bars and canalside seating. A range of Marston's real ales and food in the bar and dining area *lunchtimes and evenings*. Vegetarians catered for.

✕ 🍷 **Lockside Restaurant** Hassall Green (01270 762266). Canalside at the Canal Centre. *Open Tue–Sat at 19.00*, last orders *21.30.* Appetising range of reasonably priced dishes served. Children's menu and vegetarians catered for. Canalside seating. Tea room *open 7 days a week.* B & B.

🚢 **Romping Donkey** Hassall Green (01270 765202). A country pub serving Tetley's real ale, and bar meals and snacks *lunchtimes and evenings.* Try also the Lawton Arms, south of Snapes Aqueduct in Church Lawton and the Royal Oak in Rode Heath.

● **Kidsgrove**
Staffs. MD Tue. All services. Originally an iron and coal producing town, Kidsgrove was much helped by the completion of the Trent & Mersey Canal. James Brindley is buried here.

● **Rode Heath**
PO, tel, stores. A useful shopping area right by bridge 140. There is a butcher's shop at bridge 139.

Rode Heath Rise Once the site of a salt works, it has now been landscaped and restored as a wildflower meadow. Ring 01477 534115 for further information

NAVIGATIONAL NOTES

HARECASTLE TUNNEL Do not enter in an unpowered craft. With the complete removal of the towpath, headroom is no longer the problem it it once was. A one-way system operates, so follow the instructions of the tunnel keepers. *Updated tunnel opening times can be obtained by phoning 01782 785703.*

Boatyards

Ⓑ **David Piper** Red Bull Basin, Church Lawton, Kidsgrove (01782 784754). By Red Bull Aqueduct. **D** Pump-out, gas, overnight and long-term storage, winter storage, slipway, boat & engine sales & repairs, boat building, chandlery.

Ⓑ **Smithsons Solid Fuel and Caravan Centre** Kidsgrove (01782 787887). Near bridge 132. **D** Calor gas, solid fuel, lubricants and caravan fittings which can be used as chandlery.

Ⓑ **Canal Centre** Hassall Green, Sandbach (01270 762266). **D** Pump-out, gas, overnight and long-term mooring, winter storage, groceries, books and maps. Also post office, general store, off-licence, gifts, licensed restaurant and tea room, B & B, paraffin, coal. *Closed Sun.*

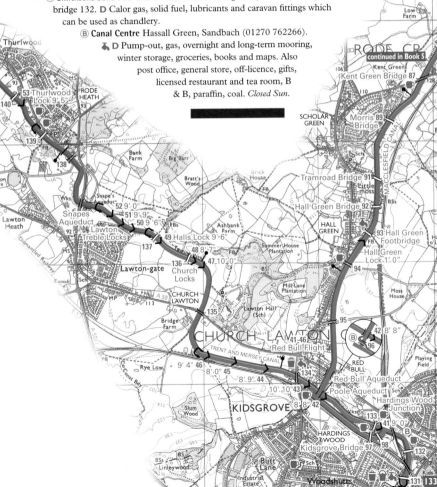

Wheelock

The canal now descends the Wheelock flight of eight locks, which are the last paired locks one sees when travelling north- wards. The countryside continues to be quiet and unspoilt but unspectacular. The pair of locks halfway down the flight is situated in the little settlement of Malkin's Bank, over-looked by terraced houses. The boatman's co-op used to be here, in the small terrace of cottages. The adjoining boatyard now specialises in the restoration of traditional working boats. At the bottom of the flight is the village of Wheelock; west of here the navigation curls round the side of a hill before entering the very long-established salt-producing area that is based on Middlewich. The 'wild' brine pumping and rock-salt mining that has gone on hereabouts has resulted in severe local subsidence; the effect on the canal has been to necessitate the constant raising of the banks as lengths of the canal bed sink. This of course means that the affected lengths tend to be much deeper than ordinary canals. Non-swimmers beware of falling overboard. The navigation now begins to lose the rural character it has enjoyed since Kidsgrove. Falling through yet more locks, the canal is joined by a busy main road (useful for fish and chips, west of Kings Lock; and Chinese take-away, west of bridge 166) which accompanies it into an increasingly flat and industrialised land-scape, past several salt works and into Middlewich, where a branch of the Shropshire Union leads off westwards towards that canal at Barbridge. The first 100 yards or so of this branch is the Wardle Canal, claimed to be the shortest canal in the country.

● **Wheelock**
Ches. PO, tel, stores, garage, fish and chips. Busy little main road village on the canal.

● **Sandbach**
Ches. MD Thur. PO, tel, stores, garage, bank, station. 1¹/₂ miles north of Wheelock. An old market town that has maintained its charm despite the steady growth of its salt and chemical industries. After walking from the canal you can refresh yourself with a pint of real ale from any of the seven pubs visible from the seat in the market place.

Ancient Crosses In the cobbled market place on a massive base stand two superb Saxon crosses, believed to commemorate the conversion of the area to Christianity in the 7thC. They suffered severely in the 17thC when the Puritans broke them up and scattered the fragments for miles. After years of searching for the parts, George Ormerod succeeded in re-erecting the crosses in 1816, with new stone replacing the missing fragments.

St Mary's Church High Street. A large, 16thC church with a handsome battlemented tower. The most interesting features of the interior are the 17thC carved roof and the fine chancel screen.

The Old Hall Hotel An outstanding example of Elizabethan half-timbered architecture, which was formerly the home of the lord of the manor, but is now used as an hotel.

Boatyards

Ⓑ **Malkins Bank Canal Services** (01270 764595). ⚓ Long-term mooring, slipway, boat building and historic boat restoration, boat repairs. Breakdown service.

Pubs and Restaurants

Nags Head Wheelock (01270 762457). ¹/4 west of bridge 154. A small black and white pub serving Boddingtons and Chester's real ales. Traditional bar food *every lunchtime and weekday evenings.* Garden and aviary. Barbecue *summer Sats.* Children and dogs welcome. Pool and traditional pub games. Chinese take-away opposite.

Commercial Wheelock (01270 760122). Near bridge 154. Set in a Georgian house with an old fashioned and spacious feel this pub serves Boddingtons, Marston's and Thwaites real ale, together with a guest. Also real cider. *Closed lunchtime Mon–Sat. No children.*

Cheshire Cheese Wheelock (01270 760319). Heavily-beamed, canalside pub serving Marston's and Banks's real ale and a wide range of meals and snacks *lunchtimes and evenings.* Vegetarians catered for. Large beer garden.

Market Tavern The Square, Sandbach (01270 762099). Opposite the crosses. Lively, old, traditional town pub serving Robinson's real ales and home-cooked bar food *lunchtimes Wed–Sat.* Children's menu and beer garden. One of the seven real ale pubs in, or close to, the square.

Kinderton Arms (01606 832158). Close to canal 1 mile south of Middlewich, by lock 70. Ignore its dour appearance and walk in to enjoy Tetley's and Boddingtons real ales and a friendly welcome. Excellent pub grub (large portions) served *lunchtimes and evenings, 7 days a week,* at remarkably low prices. Traditional *Sunday* lunches, children and vegetarians catered for, tea and coffee.

Middlewich

The Trent & Mersey skirts the centre of the town, passing lots of moored narrow boats and through three consecutive narrow locks, arriving at a wide (14ft) lock (which has suffered from subsidence) with a pub beside it. This used to represent the beginning of a wide, almost lock-free navigation right through to Preston Brook, Manchester and Wigan (very convenient for the salt industry when it shipped most of its goods by boat), but Croxton Aqueduct had to be replaced many years ago, and is now a steel structure only 8ft 2in wide. The aqueduct crosses the River Dane, which flows alongside the navigation as both water courses leave industrial Middlewich and move out into fine open country. Initially, this is a stretch of canal as beautiful as any in the country. Often over-hung by trees, the navigation winds along the side of a hill as it follows the delightful valley of the River Dane. The parkland on the other side of the valley encompasses Bostock Hall, a school for children with learning difficulties. At Whatcroft Hall (privately owned), the canal circles around to the east, passing under a derelict railway before heading for the industrial outskirts of Northwich and shedding its beauty and solitude once again.

NAVIGATIONAL NOTES

There are several privately owned wide 'lagoons' caused by subsidence along this section of the Trent & Mersey, in some of which repose the hulks of abandoned barges and narrow boats, lately being salvaged. Navigators should be wary of straying off the main line, since the offside canal bank is often submerged and invisible just below the water level.

Boatyards

ⓑ **Kings Lock Boatyard** Booth Lane, Middlewich (01606 737564). 🛁 D Gas, overnight mooring, long-term mooring, winter storage, slipway, crane, engine sales and repairs (including outboards), boat repairs, chandlery (including mail order), books, maps, gifts, solid fuel, emergency call-out.

ⓑ **Andersen Boats** Wych House, St Anne's Road, Middlewich (01606 833668). Pump-out, gas, narrow boat hire, boat building, boat fitting out,

DIY facilities, books and maps. Useful DIY shop nearby.

ⓑ **Middlewich Narrowboats** Canal Terrace, Middlewich (01606 832460). 🛁 🛁 ♨ D Pump-out, gas, narrow boat hire, overnight mooring (*not Fri*), long-term mooring, dry dock, groceries, chandlery, books and maps, engine repairs, toilets, laundry service, breakdown service, grit blasting and hull & cabinside painting. *Closed Sun*. Useful tool hire shop next door.

Pubs and Restaurants

Kings Lock Middlewich (01606 833537). Overlooking the lock. Bar food *lunchtimes and evenings. Canalside seating. B & B.*

✕ **Boars Head** Kinderton Street, Middlewich (01606 833191). Large rambling pub offering Robinson's real ale and bar snacks *from 12.00–21.00.* Children's room in hotel next door together with restaurant serving meals *lunchtimes and evenings.* Patio. B & B.

Cheshire Cheese Lewin Street, Middlewich (01606 832097). Basic but welcoming traditional pub offering Cains, John Smith's and Burtonwood real ales (plus 2 guests weekly) together with inexpensive bar snacks *lunchtimes and evenings.* Beer garden. Children welcome.

Newton Brewery Inn Middlewich (01606 833502). ¹/₄ mile south of Big Lock. Marston's real ale served in a small friendly pub with an attractive garden running down to the towpath. Selection of meals and snacks *lunchtimes and evenings (not Sun evening).* Children welcome.

✕ **Big Lock** Middlewich (01606 833489). Canalside. Variously a bottle-making factory and canal-horse stables this pub now serves Ruddles, Courage and Webster's real ales (and guests) together with bar snacks and an à la carte menu. Food available *lunchtimes and evenings, 7 days a week.* Children and vegetarians catered for. Garden area and *weekend music in winter.*

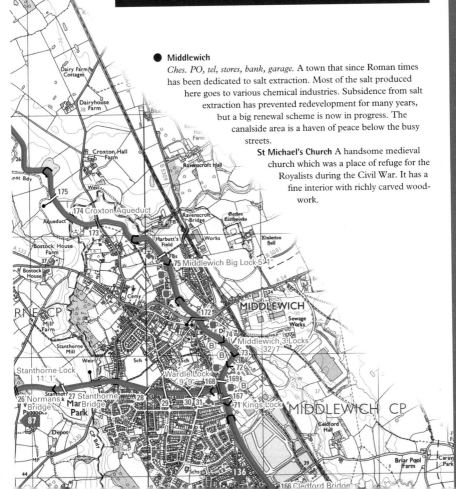

● **Middlewich**
Ches. PO, tel, stores, bank, garage. A town that since Roman times has been dedicated to salt extraction. Most of the salt produced here goes to various chemical industries. Subsidence from salt extraction has prevented redevelopment for many years, but a big renewal scheme is now in progress. The canalside area is a haven of peace below the busy streets.

St Michael's Church A handsome medieval church which was a place of refuge for the Royalists during the Civil War. It has a fine interior with richly carved woodwork.

The outlying canal settlement of Broken Cross acts as a buffer between the beauty and solitude of the Dane Valley and the industrial ravages around Northwich. Beyond is another length in which salt mining has determined the nature of the scenery. Part of it is heavily industrial, with enormous ICI works dominating the scene; much of it is devastated but rural (just), some of it is nondescript, and some of it is superb

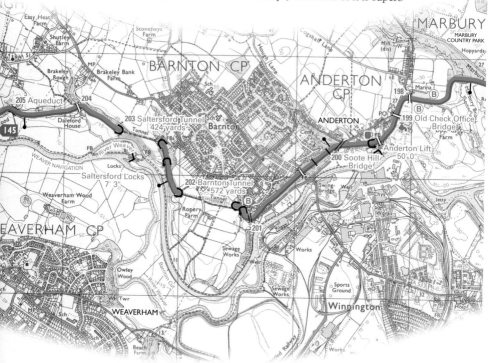

countryside. Donkey engines can still be seen in surrounding fields pumping brine. Leaving the vicinity of Lostock Gralam (*licensed grocer 100 yds east of bridge 189 open every day until 22.00*) and the outskirts of Northwich, one passes Marston (*late opening stores and tel*) and Wincham (*PO, tel, stores*). Just west of the village, one travels along a 1/2-mile stretch of canal that was only cut in 1958, as the old route was about to collapse into – needless to say – underground salt workings. Beyond the woods of Marbury Country Park (attractive short stay moorings) is Anderton (*PO, tel, stores*) – the short entrance canal to the famous boat lift down into the Weaver Navigation is on the left. The main line continues westwards, winding along what is now a steep hill and into Barnton Tunnel. You then emerge onto a hillside overlooking the River Weaver, with a marvellous view straight down the huge Saltersford Locks. Now Saltersford Tunnel is entered: beyond it you are in completely open country again. There are good moorings in the basins to the east of both tunnels.

NAVIGATIONAL NOTES

Saltersford Tunnel is crooked, affording only a brief glimpse of the other end. Two boats cannot pass in this or Barnton Tunnel, so make sure they are clear before proceeding.

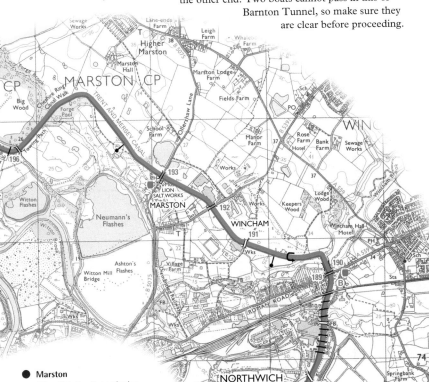

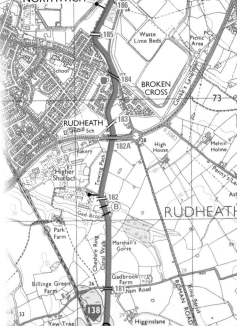

● **Marston**
Ches. Tel. A salt-producing village, suffering badly from its own industry. The numerous gaps in this village are caused by the demolition or collapse of houses affected by subsidence. Waste ground abounds.

The Lion Salt Works Offershaw Lane, Marston (01606 41823). Beside the canal at bridge 193. The Thompson family established an open pan salt works in Marston in 1842, producing fishery salt, bay salt, crystal salt and lump salt. The salt was pumped as wild brine from 45 yds beneath the works and evaporated in a large iron pan. The crystals thus formed were raked into tubs to form blocks, and subsequently dried in brick stove houses, before being exported (with the first part of the journey by canal) to India, Canada and West Africa. The works closed in 1986 but is currently being restored and is well worth visiting. Excellent audio visual and many exhibits. *Open 13.30–16.30.* Charge. Also information on the attractive countryside of Vale Royal and its rich industrial heritage.

Marbury Country Park A 200 acre park occupying the landscaped gardens of the former Marbury Hall and estate, once the home of the Barry and Smith-Barry families. Overlooking Budworth Mere, the house was demolished in 1968 and the much neglected gardens restored to their former glory by Cheshire County Heritage and Recreation service. The Information Centre (1/2 mile north of bridge 196) houses a display of Marbury's wildlife and history, including its use as a POW camp during World War II. Visitor's moorings and picnic area.

● **Anderton Lift**
An amazing and enormous piece of machinery built in 1875 by Leader Williams (later engineer of the Manchester Ship Canal) to connect the Trent & Mersey to the flourishing Weaver Navigation, 50ft below. As built, the lift consisted of two water-filled tanks counterbalancing each other in a vertical slide, resting on massive hydraulic rams. It worked on the very straight-forward principle that making the ascending tank slightly lighter – by pumping a little water out – would assist the hydraulic rams (which were operated by a steam engine and pump) in moving both tanks, with boats in them, up or down their respective slide. In 1908 the lift had to have major

---

BOAT TRIPS
Aquarius operates from the Anderton Lift and provides public trips through Barnton and Saltersford Tunnels; also to the Lion Saltworks and Marbury Country Park. *Sunday lunch and dinner* trips. Refreshments and bar. For further details phone 01606 76204.
Weaver Sovereign offering trips to various destinations along the River Weaver. *All trips leave from Northwich Marine and include a commentary, food and bar.* Weston Docks, Runcorn are also visited. *Sunday lunch and dinner* trips. Boat also available for private charter (maximum 60 people). Details from 01606 76204.

Anderton Lift

Boatyards

ⓑ **Orchard Marina** (01606 42082). Beside bridge 182. 🛏 🚽 🛁 **D** Pump-out, gas, overnight/long-term mooring, slipway, dry dock, boat and engine repairs, boat building, boat fitting out, boat and engine sales, wet dock, DIY facilities, chandlery, books, maps, solid fuel, toilets, showers, laundrette. Emergency call out.

ⓑ **Colliery Narrowboat Co** Wincham Wharf, Lostock Gralam, Northwich (01606 44672). Beside bridge 189. 🛏 🚽 🛁 **D** Pump-out, gas, overnight/long-term mooring, slipway, crane, storage, dry dock, boat building, boat sales, boat and engine repairs, wet dock, DIY facilities, toilets.

ⓑ **Alvechurch Boat Centres** Anderton Marina, Uplands Road, Anderton (01606 79642). Services are on line. 🛏 🚽 🛁 **D E** Pump-out, gas, narrow boat hire, overnight mooring, long-term mooring, slipway, sales, engine repairs, winter storage, boat painting, covered wetdocks for hire, chandlery, restaurant, telephone, toilets.

ⓑ **Barnton Wharf** Barnton Road, Northwich (01606 783320/0410 919009). 🛁 **D** Pump-out, day craft hire, long-term mooring, boat and engine sales, boat and engine repairs, solid fuel. 24hr emergency call-out.

ⓑ **Travelreign** Uplands Road, Anderton (01606 44672). 🛁 Overnight and long term mooring, winter storage, slipway, wet dock.

repairs, so it was modernised at the same time. The troublesome hydraulic rams were done away with; from then on each tank – which contained 250 tons of water – had its own counterweights and was independent of the other tank. Electricity replaced steam as the motive power. One of the most fascinating individual features of the canal system, it draws thousands of sightseers every year. Restoration, to full working order, is now assured following the original 1875 hydraulic design.

- **Northwich**

Ches. MD Fri, Sat. All services. Regular buses from Barnton. A rather attractive town at the junction of the Rivers Weaver and Dane. (The latter brings large quantities of sand down into the Weaver Navigation, necessitating a heavy expenditure on dredging.) As in every other town in this area, salt has for centuries been responsible for the continued prosperity of Northwich. The Weaver Navigation has of course been another very prominent factor in the town's history, and the building and repairing of barges, narrow boats, and small sea-going ships has been carried on here for over 200 years. Nowadays this industry has been almost forced out of business by foreign competition, and the last private shipyard on the river closed down in 1971. (This yard – Isaac Pimblott's – used to be between Hunt's Locks and Hartford Bridge. Their last contract was a tug for Aden.) However, the big BW yard in the town continues to thrive; some very large maintenance craft are built and repaired here. The wharves by Town Bridge are empty, and are an excellent temporary mooring site for anyone wishing to visit the place. The town centre is very close; much of it has been completely rebuilt very recently. There is now an extensive shopping precinct. Although the large number of pubs has been whittled down in the rebuilding process, there are still some pleasant old streets. The Weaver and the big swing bridges across it remain a dominant part of the background.

Tourist Information Centre. This service can be accessed via the local council by ringing 01606 862862.

Dock Road Edwardian Pumping Station Weir Street, Northwich (0161 794 9314). Intriguing listed building housing unique pumps and gas-powered engines fully restored to working order. Building open and engines working *Easter–end Sep on Sat, Sun & B. Hols 14.00–17.00. Charge.*

Salt Museum Weaver Hall, London Road, Northwich (01606 41331). The history of the salt industry from Roman times to the present day, housed in the town's former workhouse. Look out for the remarkable model ship, made from salt of course. *Open all year Tue–Fri 10.00–17.00; Sat & Sun 14.00–17.00; B.Hol Mon 10.00–17.00.* Audio visual introduction. Charge.

Pubs and Restaurants

- **Old Broken Cross** (01606 40431). Canalside, at bridge 184. A very attractive old pub serving well kept Greenalls and guest real ales. A selection of snacks and meals are served *all day, every day.* Vegetarians catered for. Small canalside garden. Chemist, grocer, laundrette and other shops are 1/2 mile past pub, towards Northwich.

- X **Wharf** Wincham Wharf (01606 46099). Canalside by bridge 189. Boddingtons real ale dispensed in a converted warehouse (reputed to be the oldest on the T & M) together with inexpensive bar meals served *every lunchtime and Wed, Thur & Fri evenings.* Pool and large screen TV upstairs.. Children and vegetarians catered for.

- **Salt Barge** Marston (01606 43064). Opposite the Lion Salt Works, beside bridge 193. A deceptively large pub with a friendly atmosphere, neatly divided into cosy areas, and with an inviting family room. Burtonwood and Chester's real ale and good food *lunchtimes and evenings.* Children's menu and *Sunday* lunch. Garden with play area.

- X ♀ **The Moorings** Anderton Marina (01606 79789). Part of the Alvechurch Boat Centres complex. Open for *lunchtime snacks 10.00–16.00 and evenings 18.00–22.00* for full à la carte menu. Children and vegetarians catered for. Canalside seating. Boaters please moor outside the basin.

- **Stanley Arms** (01606 75059). Canalside, right opposite the Anderton Lift (*also PO, stores*). A friendly real ale pub (Tetley's and Greenalls) with a family room, where children are welcome. Bar food is served *lunchtimes and evenings – not Tue evenings* (including regular Indian food nights). Outside seating and children's play area. Vegetarians catered for. The landlord keeps a collection of local Tourist Information. Excellent 'bottom of garden' moorings.

Dutton

This, the northernmost stretch of the
Trent & Mersey, is a very pleasant one
and delightfully rural. Most of the way the
navigation follows the south side of the hills
that overlook the River Weaver. From about
60ft up, one is often rewarded with excellent
views of this splendid valley and the occasional
large vessels that ply up and down it. At one
point one can see the elegant Dutton railway
viaduct in the distance; then the two waterways
diverge as the Trent & Mersey enters the
woods preceding Preston Brook Tunnel.
There is a stop lock south of the tunnel
just beyond a pretty covered dry dock;
there are often fine examples of
restored working boats moored
here. At the north end of the
tunnel a notice announces that
from here onwards one is on the
Bridgewater Canal (see page
23). There are good moorings
north of bridge 213, and to
the south of Dutton
stop lock.

NAVIGATIONAL NOTES

1 Access to Preston Brook Tunnel is restricted to *northbound on the hour to
   10 minutes past the hour; southbound on the 1/2 hour to 20 mins to the hour.*
2 North of Preston Brook Tunnel you are on the Bridgewater Canal, which is
   owned by the Manchester Ship Canal Company, and is described in detail in
   on page 19.
3 A British Waterways licence is valid for seven consecutive days on this canal.

Pubs and Restaurants

■ ✕ **Leigh Arms** (01606 853327). ¹/₄ mile south of bridge 209, overlooking the Weaver and Acton Swing Bridge. Burtonwood and Forshaws real ale in an attractive old coaching inn with stained glass windows in the bar. Good food from an interesting menu available *12.00–21.00, seven days a week.* Vegetarians well catered for. Restaurant and outside seating area. Barbecue *summer weekends.* Children's play area.

■ ✕ **Horns** (01606 852192). 200yds south of bridge 209 on the A49, by Acton Swing Bridge. Friendly, roadside pub serving Greenalls real ale together with bar food *lunchtimes, evenings and all day Sunday.* Cosy bars, large garden and children's play area. Folk night *1st Tue in month.*

■ ✕ **Hollybush** Acton Bridge

(01606 853196). ¹/₄ mile north of bridge 209. One of the oldest farmhouse pubs in the country having a unique charm and character. Four cosy rooms, including traditional tap room, make up the bar area together with the tasteful addition of a new restaurant all set in this listed, timber-framed building. Wide range of interesting, home-cooked food served in the bar and restaurant *L & D, seven days a week.* Children and vegetarians catered for. Tetley's and guest real ales. Traditional pub games. Accommodation.

■ **Talbot Arms** Dutton (01928 718181). Burtonwood and Flowers real ales served in this comfortable pub atop Preston Brook tunnel. Traditional bar food available *lunchtimes 7 days a week and evenings Thur, Fri & Sat.* Outside seating and discos *Fri & Sat.* Quiz nights *Wed.*

Boatyards

Ⓑ **Black Prince Holidays** Bartington Wharf, Acton Bridge, Northwich (01606 852945). 🚻 🚽 ♿ D Pump-out, gas, electric boat recharging, narrow boat hire, day hire craft, long-term mooring, engine repairs, groceries, books and maps, toilets, gifts, laundry, coal, telephone.

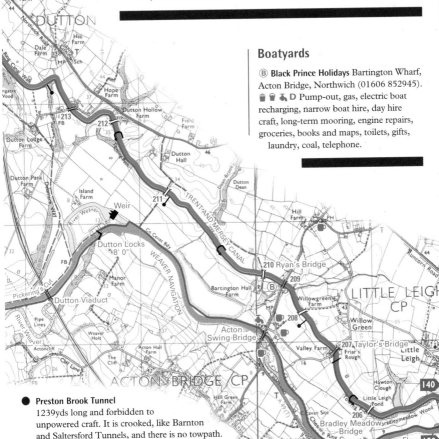

● **Preston Brook Tunnel**
1239yds long and forbidden to unpowered craft. It is crooked, like Barnton and Saltersford Tunnels, and there is no towpath.

● **Dutton**
Ches. Tel, garage. Small settlement on top of Preston Brook Tunnel, at the end of the lane uphill from the south end of the tunnel.

Winsford Bottom Flash, River Weaver (see page 148)

RIVER WEAVER

MAXIMUM DIMENSIONS	MANAGER
Winsford to Winnington	01244 390372
Length: 150' 0"	
Beam: 30' 0"	MILEAGE
Headroom: 29' 0" ★	WINSFORD BRIDGE *to* Northwich: 5¹/₂ miles
Winnington to Weston Point	Anderton Lift (Trent & Mersey Canal): 7 miles
Length: 176' 0"	Acton Bridge: 11 miles
Beam: 30' 0"	Sutton Bridge: 17 miles
Headroom: 56' 0"	WESTON POINT DOCKS (Manchester
	Ship Canal): 20 miles
★Newbridge Swing Bridge is currently fixed and imposes a height restriction on the river above here of 6' 4".	Weston Marsh Lock: 19 miles
	Locks: 5

The river itself, which rises in the Peckforton Hills and proceeds via Wrenbury, Audlem, Nantwich, Church Minshull and Winsford to Northwich and Frodsham, is just over 50 miles long. Originally a shallow and tidal stream, it was long used for carrying salt away from the Cheshire salt area. The mineral was carried down by men and horses to meet the incoming tide. The sailing barges would load at high water, then depart with the ebbing tide.

In the 17thC the expansion of the salt industry around Northwich, Middlewich and Winsford gave rise to an increasing demand for a navigation right up to Winsford. In 1721, three gentlemen of Cheshire obtained an Act of Parliament to make and maintain the river as a navigation from Frodsham to Winsford, 20 miles upstream. By 1732 the Weaver was fully navigable for 40-ton barges up to Winsford.

When in 1765 the Trent & Mersey was planned to pass along the River Weaver the trustees of the Weaver were understandably alarmed; but in the event the new canal provided much traffic for the river, for although the two waterways did not join, they were so close at Anderton that in 1793 chutes were constructed on the Trent & Mersey directly above a specially built dock on the River Weaver, 50ft below. Thereafter salt was transhipped in ever increasing quantities by dropping it down the chutes from canal boats into Weaver flats (barges) on the river. This system continued until 1871, when it was decided to construct the great iron boat lift beside the chutes at Anderton. This remarkable structure (currently undergoing restoration) thus effected a proper junction between the two waterways.

The Weaver Navigation did well throughout the 19thC, mainly because continual and vigorous programmes of modernisation kept it thoroughly attractive to carriers, especially when compared to the rapidly dating narrow canals. Eventually coasters were able to navigate the river right up to Winsford.

In spite of this constant improvement of the navigation, the Weaver's traditional salt trade was affected by 19th-C competition from railways and the new pipelines. However, the chemical industry began to sprout around the Northwich area at the same time. Today, Brunner Mond's chemical works at Winnington supply virtually all the traffic on the river: coasters up to 1000 tonnes deadweight capacity ship cargoes through the Manchester Ship Canal to ports in Scotland on a twice weekly basis.

Winsford

Although Winsford Bridge (fixed at 10ft 8in) is the upper limit of navigation for shipping and the limit of British Waterways jurisdiction, canal boats can easily slip under the bridge and round the bend into the vast, wonderful and deceptively shallow Winsford Bottom Flash. Navigation upstream of the Bottom Flash is unreliable, for the channel is shallow and winding, but can apparently be done by adventurous persons with small craft. The Top Flash is situated just beside and below the Middlewich Branch of the Shropshire Union Canal, but there is no junction between them here. Downstream of Winsford Bridge is a winding stretch of little interest: each bank is piled high with the industrial leftovers of chemical industries. But soon the horizon clears as one arrives at Newbridge, beyond which is the superb stretch known as Vale Royal Cut. The Vale Royal Cut typifies the Weaver at its most attractive. The river flows along a closely-defined flat green valley floor, flanked by mature woods climbing the steep hillsides that enclose the valley. No buildings or roads intrude upon this very pleasant scene. Vale Royal Locks are at the far end of the cut; the remains of the old Vale Royal Abbey (believed to have been founded by Edward I and dissolved by Henry VIII) is just up the hill nearby. Beyond is a tall stone railway viaduct.

NAVIGATIONAL NOTES

1 Newbridge swing bridge no longer opens, imposing a height restriction on the river above here of 6ft 4in.

2 The operating times for locks and bridges are *Mon–Thu 08.00–16.00, Fri 08.00–15.00*. Locks only: Dutton and Saltersford *open weekends from end May (B. Hol)–end Sep.* Other locks *open some weekends in summer.* Telephone (01606) 723900 for further details. All are manned.

3 The Weaver is a river navigation that still carries some commercial traffic – transported not in canal boats or barges, but in small sea-going ships displacing up to 1000 tonnes, which can use the navigation at all times of day or night. The locks are correspondingly large and often paired. The bridges are either very high or are big swing bridges operated by British Waterways staff. With the exception of Town Bridge in Northwich and Newbridge below Winsford (6ft 4in) none of these bridges need to be swung for any boat with a height above water of less than 8ft. Those craft which do require the bridges to be opened should give prior notice to the British Waterways by telephoning (01606) 723900. Unless there has been heavy rain, the current is quite gentle – however, as on any river navigation, an anchor and rope should be carried, and the rules should be adhered to. There are few facilities for pleasure craft.

4 Short-term licence holders must pay a lockage charge – currently £20.00 – for use of Marsh Lock.

● **Winsford**

Ches. MD Sat. All services. A busy salt-mining town astride the Weaver. The centre of town used to be very close to the river, but now a huge new shopping precinct has shifted the heart of the town well away from it. Up the hill, east of the river, there is a pub, take-away and stores (straight on at the roundabout). Turn left at the roundabout for a large supermarket and garage. To the south west of Winsford Bridge there is a cycle shop and another garage. Up the High street, west of the bridge, there are shops and the Golden Lion Pub.

● **Winsford Bottom Flash**

This very large expanse of water, in an attractive setting among wooded slopes, was created by subsidence following salt extraction in the vicinity. It is a unique asset for the town, whose citizens obviously appreciate it to the full. Three caravan sites and a sailing club are based along its banks and anglers crouch in the waterside bushes. It is, however, quite shallow in places – those in canal craft *beware!*

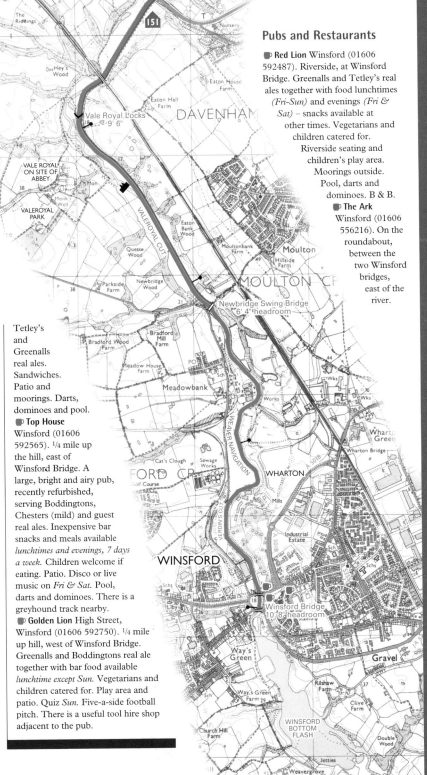

Pubs and Restaurants

🍺 **Red Lion** Winsford (01606 592487). Riverside, at Winsford Bridge. Greenalls and Tetley's real ales together with food lunchtimes *(Fri-Sun)* and evenings *(Fri & Sat)* – snacks available at other times. Vegetarians and children catered for. Riverside seating and children's play area. Moorings outside. Pool, darts and dominoes. B & B.

🍺 **The Ark** Winsford (01606 556216). On the roundabout, between the two Winsford bridges, east of the river.

Tetley's and Greenalls real ales. Sandwiches. Patio and moorings. Darts, dominoes and pool.

🍺 **Top House** Winsford (01606 592565). ¼ mile up the hill, east of Winsford Bridge. A large, bright and airy pub, recently refurbished, serving Boddingtons, Chesters (mild) and guest real ales. Inexpensive bar snacks and meals available *lunchtimes and evenings, 7 days a week.* Children welcome if eating. Patio. Disco or live music on *Fri & Sat.* Pool, darts and dominoes. There is a greyhound track nearby.

🍺 **Golden Lion** High Street, Winsford (01606 592750). ¼ mile up hill, west of Winsford Bridge. Greenalls and Boddingtons real ale together with bar food available *lunchtime except Sun.* Vegetarians and children catered for. Play area and patio. Quiz *Sun.* Five-a-side football pitch. There is a useful tool hire shop adjacent to the pub.

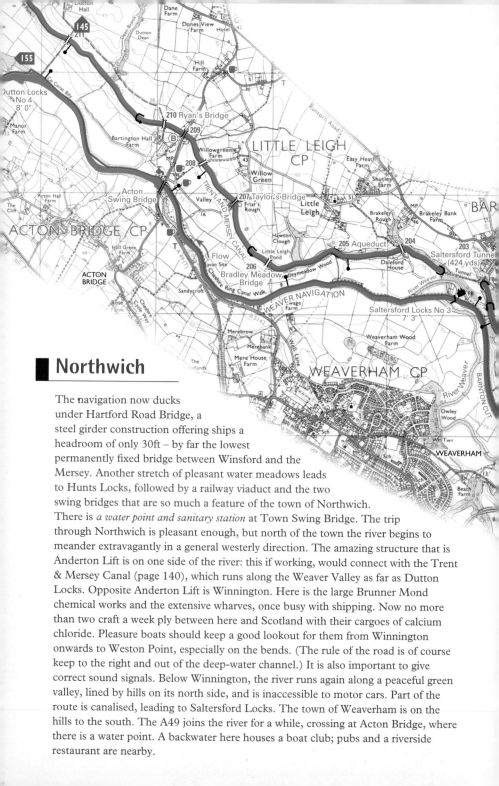

Northwich

The navigation now ducks
under Hartford Road Bridge, a
steel girder construction offering ships a
headroom of only 30ft – by far the lowest
permanently fixed bridge between Winsford and the
Mersey. Another stretch of pleasant water meadows leads
to Hunts Locks, followed by a railway viaduct and the two
swing bridges that are so much a feature of the town of Northwich.
There is *a water point and sanitary station* at Town Swing Bridge. The trip
through Northwich is pleasant enough, but north of the town the river begins to
meander extravagantly in a general westerly direction. The amazing structure that is
Anderton Lift is on one side of the river: this if working, would connect with the Trent
& Mersey Canal (page 140), which runs along the Weaver Valley as far as Dutton
Locks. Opposite Anderton Lift is Winnington. Here is the large Brunner Mond
chemical works and the extensive wharves, once busy with shipping. Now no more
than two craft a week ply between here and Scotland with their cargoes of calcium
chloride. Pleasure boats should keep a good lookout for them from Winnington
onwards to Weston Point, especially on the bends. (The rule of the road is of course
keep to the right and out of the deep-water channel.) It is also important to give
correct sound signals. Below Winnington, the river runs again along a peaceful green
valley, lined by hills on its north side, and is inaccessible to motor cars. Part of the
route is canalised, leading to Saltersford Locks. The town of Weaverham is on the
hills to the south. The A49 joins the river for a while, crossing at Acton Bridge, where
there is a water point. A backwater here houses a boat club; pubs and a riverside
restaurant are nearby.

BOAT TRIPS

Northwich Marine Hayhurst Boatyard, Chester Way, Northwich (01606 47299). Rowing and motor boats for hire on the river.

Sovereign Cruises offer public trips - departing Northwich Marine – *Easter-Dec (including Sunday lunch trips)* on different days dependent upon the month of operation. *All day* public trips, with lunch, to the Manchester Ship Canal and Weston Point on *some Saturdays.* Extensive choice of charter programmes, commentary, wide choice of food, bar, toilets and central heating all on an elegant, traditional Dutch Barge.

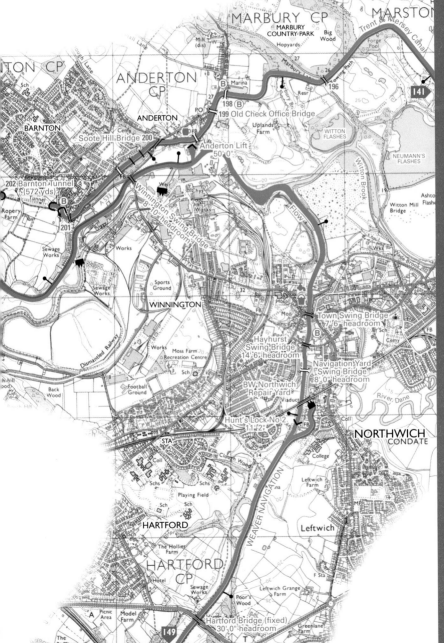

ANDERTON LIFT

An amazing and enormous piece of machinery built in 1875 by Leader Williams (later engineer of the Manchester Ship Canal) to connect the Trent & Mersey to the flourishing Weaver Navigation, 50ft below. As built, the lift consisted of two water-filled tanks counterbalancing each other in a vertical slide, resting on massive hydraulic rams. It worked on the very straightforward principle that making the ascending tank slightly lighter – by pumping a little water out – would assist the hydraulic rams (which were operated by a steam engine and pump) in moving both tanks, with boats in them, up or down their respective slide. In 1908 the lift had to have major repairs, so it was modernised at the same time. The troublesome hydraulic rams were done away with; from then on each tank – which contained 250 tons of water – had its own counterweights and was independent of the other tank. Electricity replaced steam as the motive power. One of the most fascinating individual features of the canal system, it draws thousands of sightseers every year. Funding is now in place to completely restore the lift to working order, and to the original hydraulic design, using oil as the motive force rather than the chemically contaminated water that was the cause of the 1908 failure. It is likely that the more recent counter balance weights, together with their ungainly support structure, will be retained to demonstrate the engineering development of the lift.

Boatyards

British Waterways North West Region Offices and Repair Yard (01606 74321). Alongside the extensive workshops is the N.W. Region office – formerly the Weaver Navigation Trustee's offices. As usual, this yard contains many mellow 18thC buildings. There is also an elegant clock tower on the office block that has recently been completely refurbished.

Ⓑ **Jalsea Marine** Weaver Shipyard, off Darwin Street, Northwich (01606 77870). 🛉 🛠 D Overnight and long-term mooring, winter storage, undercover storage & workshops, slip-way, crane (15 tons), boat sales, engine sales and repairs, specialist refits and repairs on older wooden boats, boat building, DIY facilities, chandlery, books, maps, gifts, telephone, toilets, showers. Will make arrangements for transit passage to the sea via the Manchester Ship Canal including mandatory certificate of seaworthiness. Special package available for Anderton Lift users.

Ⓑ **Northwich Marine** Hayhurst Boatyard, Chester Way, Northwich (01606 47299). 🛉 🛉 🛠 D

Pump out, gas, overnight and long-term mooring, winter storage, covered slipway, side slip, crane (3 tons), boat sales and repairs, engine sales and repairs including outboards, chandlery, boat fitting-out, DIY facilities, toilets.

The following are on the Trent & Mersey Canal.

Ⓑ **Alvechurch Boat Centres** Anderton Marina, Uplands Road, Anderton (01606 79642). Services are on line – do not enter the marina unnecessarily. 🛉 🛉 🛠 D E Pump-out, gas, narrow boat hire, overnight mooring, long-term mooring, slipway, boat sales, engine repairs, winter storage, boat painting, covered wetdocks for hire, chandlery, books and maps.

Ⓑ **Barnton Wharf** Barnton Road, Northwich (01606 783320/07710 919009). 🛠 D Pump-out, day craft hire, long-term mooring, boat and engine sales, boat and engine repairs, solid fuel. 24hr emergency call-out.

Ⓑ **Travelreign** Uplands Road, Anderton (01606 44672). 🛠 Overnight and long term mooring, winter storage, slipway, wet dock.

● **Northwich**
Ches. MD Fri, Sat. All services. A rather attractive town at the junction of the Rivers Weaver and Dane. (The latter brings large quantities of sand down into the Weaver Navigation, necessitating a heavy expenditure on dredging.) As in every town in this area, salt has for centuries been responsible for the continued prosperity of Northwich. The town's motto is *Sal est Vita*, Salt is Life, and there

is a salt museum in London Road. The Brine Baths at Moss Farm Sports Complex are still open throughout the year for the benefit of salt-water enthusiasts. The Weaver Navigation has of course been another very prominent factor in the town's history, and the building and repairing of barges, narrowboats, and small seagoing ships has been carried on here for over 200 years. Nowadays this industry has been almost forced out of business by foreign competition, and the last private shipyard on the river closed down in 1971. The wharves by Town Bridge are empty, and are an excellent temporary mooring site for anyone wishing to visit the place. The town centre is very close; much of it has been completely rebuilt, with an extensive shopping precinct. Although the large number of pubs has been whittled down in the rebuilding process, there are still some pleasant old streets. The Weaver and the big swing bridges across it remain a dominant part of the background.

Dock Road Edwardian Pumping Station Weir Street, Northwich (0161 794 9314). Intriguing listed building housing unique pumps and gas-powered engines fully restored to working order. Building open and engines working *Easter–end Sep, Sat, Sun & B. Hols 14.00–17.00.* Charge.

Salt Museum Weaver Hall, London Road, Northwich (01606 41331). The history of the salt industry from Roman times to the present day, housed in the town's former workhouse. Look out for the remarkable model ship, made from salt of course. *Open all year Tue–Fri 10.00–17.00, Sat & Sun 14.00–17.00, B. Hol Mon 10.00–17.00.* Audio visual introduction. Charge.

Tourist Information Centre This service can be accessed via the local council by telephoning (01606) 862862.

● **Weaverham**
Ches. PO, tel, stores, garage. The heart of this town contains many old timbered houses and thatched cottages – but these are now heavily outnumbered by council housing estates. The church of St Mary is an imposing Norman building containing several items of interest.

● **Acton Swing Bridge**
An impressive structure weighing 650 tonnes, which uses a very small amount of electricity to open it; 560 tonnes of its weight is borne by a floating pontoon. It was built in 1933, and extensively refurbished in 1999.

Pubs and Restaurants

There are plenty of pubs in Northwich.
● ✕ **Quality Hotel** Northwich (01606 44443). Close to Northwich Marine at the junction of the Rivers Dane and Weaver. A floating hotel complex launched about twelve years ago and built locally. Family establishment serving bar snacks and à la carte and carvery restaurant food, *L & D, 7 days a week (except Sat L).* Children and vegetarians catered for. Riverside veranda and own moorings. Sauna, gym and fitness centre (with showers) available to non-residents. Cabin B & B.
● **Stanley Arms** (01606 75059). Canalside, right opposite the Anderton Lift *(also PO, stores).* A friendly real ale pub (Tetley's and Greenalls) with a family room, where children are welcome. Bar food is served *lunchtimes and evenings – not Tue evenings* (including regular Indian food nights). Outside seating and children's play area. Vegetarians catered for. The landlord keeps a collection of local Tourist Information. Excellent 'bottom of garden' moorings.
✕ ♀ **The Moorings** Anderton Marina (01606 79789). Part of the Alvechurch Boat Centres complex. Open for *lunchtime snacks 10.00–16.00 and evenings 18.00–22.00* for full à la carte menu. Children and vegetarians catered for. Canalside seating. *Boaters please moor outside the basin.*
● **Riverside Inn** Acton Bridge(01606 852310). Riverside on the south side of the river. *Open all day, every day,* serving food and Marston's and a guest real ale. Children and vegetarians catered for. Conservatory and riverside terrace. Own moorings outside.
● ✕ **Horns** (01606 852192). 300yds north of Acton Swing Bridge on the A49. Friendly, roadside pub serving Greenalls real ale together with bar food *lunchtimes, evenings and all day Sunday.* Cosy bars, large garden and children's play area. Folk night *1st Tue in month.*
● ✕ **Leigh Arms** (01606 853327). Overlooking the Weaver and Acton Swing Bridge. Burtonwood and Forshaws real ale in an attractive old coaching inn with stained glass windows in the bar. Good food from an interesting menu available *12.00–21.00, 7 days a week.* Vegetarians well catered for. Restaurant and outside seating area. Barbecue *summer weekends.* Children's play area.
● ✕ **Hollybush** Acton Bridge (01606 853196). ¹/₂ north of Acton Swing Bridge. One of the oldest farmhouse pubs in the country having a unique charm and character. Four cosy rooms, including traditional tap room, make up the bar area together with the tasteful addition of a new restaurant all set in this listed, timber-framed building. Wide range of interesting, home-cooked food served in the bar and restaurant *L & D, 7 days a week.* Children and vegetarians catered for. Tetley's and guest real ales. Traditional pub games. B & B.

Frodsham

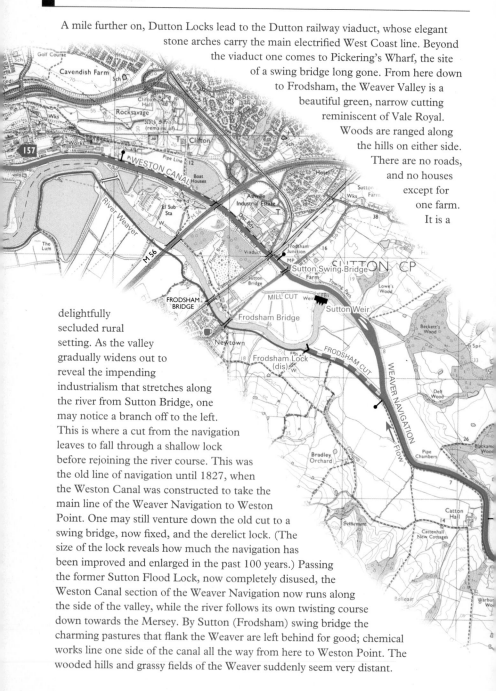

A mile further on, Dutton Locks lead to the Dutton railway viaduct, whose elegant stone arches carry the main electrified West Coast line. Beyond the viaduct one comes to Pickering's Wharf, the site of a swing bridge long gone. From here down to Frodsham, the Weaver Valley is a beautiful green, narrow cutting reminiscent of Vale Royal. Woods are ranged along the hills on either side. There are no roads, and no houses except for one farm. It is a delightfully secluded rural setting. As the valley gradually widens out to reveal the impending industrialism that stretches along the river from Sutton Bridge, one may notice a branch off to the left. This is where a cut from the navigation leaves to fall through a shallow lock before rejoining the river course. This was the old line of navigation until 1827, when the Weston Canal was constructed to take the main line of the Weaver Navigation to Weston Point. One may still venture down the old cut to a swing bridge, now fixed, and the derelict lock. (The size of the lock reveals how much the navigation has been improved and enlarged in the past 100 years.) Passing the former Sutton Flood Lock, now completely disused, the Weston Canal section of the Weaver Navigation now runs along the side of the valley, while the river follows its own twisting course down towards the Mersey. By Sutton (Frodsham) swing bridge the charming pastures that flank the Weaver are left behind for good; chemical works line one side of the canal all the way from here to Weston Point. The wooded hills and grassy fields of the Weaver suddenly seem very distant.

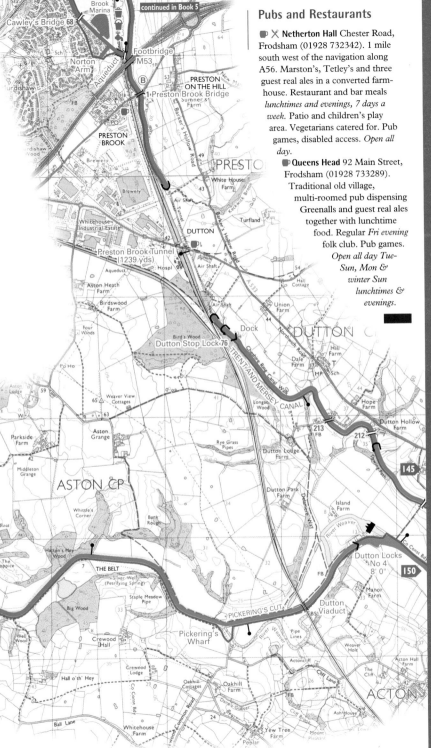

Pubs and Restaurants

Netherton Hall Chester Road, Frodsham (01928 732342). 1 mile south west of the navigation along A56. Marston's, Tetley's and three guest real ales in a converted farmhouse. Restaurant and bar meals *lunchtimes and evenings, 7 days a week.* Patio and children's play area. Vegetarians catered for. Pub games, disabled access. *Open all day.*

Queens Head 92 Main Street, Frodsham (01928 733289). Traditional old village, multi-roomed pub dispensing Greenalls and guest real ales together with lunchtime food. Regular *Fri evening* folk club. Pub games. *Open all day Tue-Sun, Mon & winter Sun lunchtimes & evenings.*

Weston Point

At Weston Marsh there is a lock down into the Manchester Ship Canal (see navigational note below). Beyond here the navigation goes right alongside the Ship Canal from which it is separated by a tall bank. Eventually, after passing the entrance lock up into the abandoned Runcorn & Weston Canal, one arrives at a low (about 5ft) swing bridge. Beyond it are the Weston Point Docks and another lock into the Ship Canal. There are *shops, fish & chips* and *pubs* at Weston Point, through the dock gates.

NAVIGATIONAL NOTES

Those wishing to pass through Weston Marsh Lock should give British Waterways (01606 723900) advance notice and obtain clearance from the Manchester Ship Canal Company (0151 327 1461). For full details, including entry into the Shropshire Union Canal, see page 96.

● **Weston Point Docks**
The docks, at the junction of the Weaver Navigation's Weston Canal and the Manchester Ship Canal, are an industrial centre. The docks have been modernised and their facilities expanded to handle ships up to 2500 tonnes. However there is currently no one using this facility. *Northern Star* runs regular calcium chloride cargoes from ICI Runcorn's plant, on Weston Canal, to Ireland via Weston Marsh Lock and the Ship Canal.
Christ Church Situated between Weston Point Docks and the Manchester Ship Canal, this church was built by the Weaver Navigation Commissioners. Known as the island church, its tall spire is a distinctive landmark.

● **Runcorn**
Ches. MD Tue, Thu, Sat. All services. Runcorn's industrial growth began with the completion of the Bridgewater Canal in the latter part of the 18thC. The old town is to be found down by the docks, where the elegant curved 1092-ft single span of the steel road bridge (built 1961), with the railway beside, leaps over the Ship Canal and the Mersey. West of the bridge, by the Ship Canal, is Bridgewater House, built by the Duke as a temporary home to enable him to supervise the construction of the Runcorn end of the canal. The massive flight of ten double locks which connected the canal to the Mersey was finally abandoned in 1966, and filled in, much to the dismay of thousands of industrial archaeologists and canal enthusiasts. Since 1964 Runcorn has been a new town, its rapid growth being carefully planned. It is interesting to note that Runcorn, following local government reorganisation, is now part of Halton (which includes Widnes on the north bank of the Mersey), an echo of the time following the Norman Conquest when it was a dependent manor of the Barony of Halton.
Tourist Information Centre 57–61 Church Street, Runcorn (01928 576776).

Norton Priory Tudor Way, Manor Park, Runcorn (01928 569895). The undercroft was the only part of this 11th-C priory to survive the reformation: now the abbots' lodgings above have been converted into a viewing area from which you can see, with the aid of a recorded commentary, other points of interest. After 1545 the remains of the priory were sold to Sir Richard Brooke for 1s 9p, and he used the stones to build his Tudor manor house. This was demolished around 1750, and a new Georgian house was built. This was finally knocked down in the 1920s, following years of neglect. Enjoy the walled garden and modern sculptures, together with the restored 18th-C summer-house by James Wyatt. Also museum, priory remains, woodland gardens, picnic area, family events, croquet area. There are temporary exhibitions, gift and produce shops. Coffee shop. *Open Apr–Oct, weekdays 12.00–17.00, weekends & B. Hols 12.00-18.00; Nov–Mar daily 12.00–16.00. Closed 24–26 Dec & 1 Jan.* Charge for over fives. Inexpensive family day tickets. Regular bus service.

Catalyst Mersey Road, Widnes (0151 420 1121). Unique, award-winning museum of the chemical industry. Interactive exhibits and hands-on displays unravel the mysteries of how chemicals are made and used in every day products. 'Industry in view' is a computer and video based exhibition 100ft above the Mersey, embracing spectacular river views. Reconstructions and original film footage trace the development of the industry from ancient times to the present day. Elements café with riverside views; shop selling educational toys, etc and activity guide for home-based experiments! *Open Tue-Fri & B. Hol Mondays 10.00-17.00, Sat & Sun 11.00-17.00. Closed 24 & 26 Dec & 1 Jan.* Charge for over fives. Inexpensive family tickets. Any Widnes bus will drop you close to the museum.

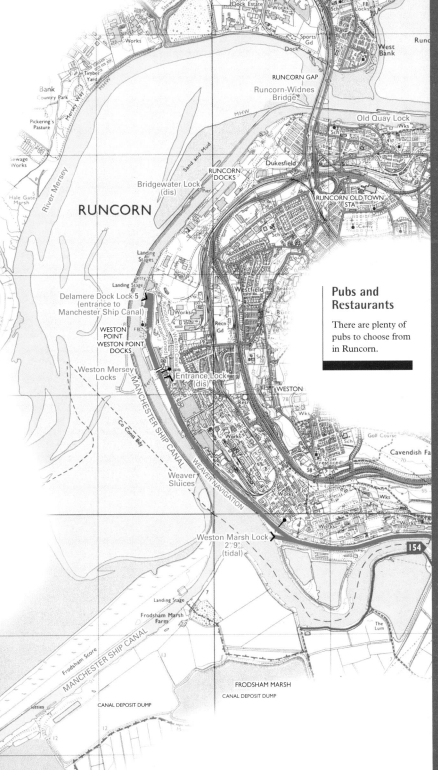

West-Bank Dock Estate

FB

West Bank

RUNCORN GAP
Runcorn-Widnes Bridge

Old Quay Lock

Bank
Country Park

Dukesfield

RUNCORN DOCKS

Bridgewater Lock (dis)

RUNCORN OLD TOWN STA

RUNCORN

River Mersey

Hale Gate Marsh

Sewage Works

Pickering's Pasture

Landing Stages

Landing Stage

Delamere Dock Lock 5
(entrance to
Manchester Ship Canal)

WESTON POINT
WESTON POINT DOCKS

Weston Mersey Locks

Entrance Lock (dis)

WESTON

Pubs and Restaurants

There are plenty of pubs to choose from in Runcorn.

MANCHESTER SHIP CANAL

Go Coast Bay

Weaver Sluices

WEAVER NAVIGATION

Golf Course

Cavendish Fa

154

Weston Marsh Lock
2"9"
(tidal)

Frodsham Score

Landing Stage

Frodsham Marsh Farm

The Lum

MANCHESTER SHIP CANAL

FRODSHAM MARSH
CANAL DEPOSIT DUMP

Jetties

CANAL DEPOSIT DUMP

INDEX